HESI A2 Study Guide 2021-2022

New Outline + 652 Questions and Detailed Answer Explanations for the HESI Admission Assessment Exam (Includes 2 Full-Length Practice Tests)

Table of Contents

Background Information

Health Education Systems Incorporated (HESI)—also known as the Evolve Reach A2, Evolve Reach and Evolve Reach HESI—is a test each prospective nursing student must pass before being admitted to nursing school. The A2 stands for Admission Assessment, an indication of the exact purpose the test serves.

The HESI A2 was developed by Dutch company Elsevier, specializing in technical, scientific and medical information and content. Elsevier Student Life designed the HESI exams as an effective screening tool for applicants who are looking to pursue a career in allied health-care programs, including nursing.

The HESI A2 is multiple-choice and computer-based. The test is administered online and the total time varies depending on your location. It can be anywhere from 4 hours to 5.25 hours (315 minutes). However, some exam locations do not impose a time limit.

A good way to ensure that you prepare adequately for the test is to study this guide diligently. Go over the question and answer sections carefully, where you will find useful information to improve your exam performance.

General Section

If you are preparing for the nursing entrance examination, this section gives you insight into what is expected of you. It covers the test format, simple rules, important tips that will help you to pass the test and other pieces of information that will contribute to enhancing your overall performance.

You will also learn about what to take to the exam center, the dos and don'ts, as well as the actual testing process.

Test Format

The HESI A2 exam is a multiple-choice test that is divided into eight sections. Each section covers knowledge of a specific subject. The entrance examination will test your knowledge in the following areas:

1. Math

The math section will focus on the mathematical skills you need as a medical practitioner. The test will cover basic subtraction, fractions, addition, percentage, algebra, multiplication and decimals. You should also be able to perform simple calculations and basic measurements and understand Roman numerals and conversion.

Prospective candidates must especially be able to solve word problems. This knowledge will come in handy when calculating solutions and drug dosages.

The math subtest contains 50 multiple-choice questions.

2. Reading

The entrance examination will test your ability to identify the main idea in a reading passage, your reading comprehension, ability to understand the contextual meanings of words, as well as your ability to make logical inferences.

In this section, you will learn some practical tips that can assist you in improving your reading and comprehension skills. There are 47 multiple-choice questions in this section.

3. Vocabulary and General Knowledge

The focus of this test section is on common vocabulary in the nursing and health-care field. The vocabulary section will cover both general and medical fields. There will be terminology that you will be expected to know the meaning of. This section has 50 multiple-choice questions.

4. Grammar

The entrance examination will test your knowledge of each part of speech and its appropriate use. It will also test your knowledge of common grammatical errors. To ace this section, you must understand nouns, pronouns, verbs, adjectives and other parts of speech. This section has 50 multiple-choice questions.

5. Biology

Photosynthesis, metabolism and basic biological processes are some of the areas in which you will be tested. Be prepared to answer questions on cellular respiration, matter and biological molecules such as lipids, proteins, carbohydrates and nucleic acids. This section has 25 multiple-choice questions.

6. Chemistry

Some areas of chemistry you must be familiar with when preparing for the exam include atoms and atomic structures, the periodic table, elements, matter and chemical reactions, nuclear chemistry and chemical bonds. This section has 25 multiple-choice questions.

7. Anatomy and Physiology

The anatomy and physiology subtest assesses how well you understand the human body. To pass this test, you must know the location of different body parts as well as their individual functions. Each candidate is expected to have a deep knowledge of the circulatory system, the skeletal system, nervous system, muscular tissue and the other systems and organs that form the human body. This section has 25 multiple-choice questions.

8. Physics

Some topics in physics you must understand fully before taking the exam include projectile motion, average speed, rotation, gravitation and optics. Other topics include Newton's Laws of Motion, uniform circular motion, friction, light, speed and acceleration, as well as waves and sound. This section has 25 multiple-choice questions.

Test Rules

There are some basic rules you must follow in order to avoid being disqualified from taking the test.

- Arrive at the test center at least 30 minutes before your appointment. This allows the examiner to follow check-in procedures before the exam commences. Arriving early also gives you a chance to sign appropriate forms, find parking and settle down for the exam before taking it. This puts you in a better frame of mind than when you rush into the exam center. Late arrival at the center automatically disqualifies you and you will forfeit your exam fee.
- Although you need a calculator for the test, applicants are forbidden from bringing their own calculators. The exam center will provide that.

Most schools and Prometric test sites allow four hours for HESI A2 tests. The same rule applies in some postsecondary institutions. However, some institutions extend the exam time to five hours, and in some special cases, certain schools don't impose time limits. Hence, it's important that you are familiar with the time limit allowed by the school you are applying to. You can find such information on a school's official website or other public sources of information.

During the admission period, you may take the exam either between August 1 and January 15 or between January 16 and August 1.

How to Register for the Test

Registration for the exam can be done online. Visit the website of your desired exam center and apply for the exam.

Some of the approved payment methods include MasterCard, Visa and American Express.

Applicants are advised to submit their application a couple of days before the examination day because it makes the application process go more smoothly.

When registering for the test, ensure that there is no disparity between your personal information during the registration and the information on your ID or you will not be allowed into the exam center.

Cost of the Test

The cost varies from location to location. The test fee ranges from $40 to $65. Some schools charge more. Especially if you are taking the exam at another school where you are not seeking admission, you may be required to pay some extra fees. Therefore, make sure you double-check how much your school of choice charges.

Where to Take the Test

Applicants are encouraged to take the test in the nursing school of their choice. You have a long list of available options to choose from. Each examination center has a list of subjects that applicants are tested upon, and this differs from one examination center to another. Thus, making the right choice is crucial to your success in that it helps you understand what to study for and how best to prepare.

You can also take the test in any Prometric testing site at different locations across the United States. Check the list of available Prometric sites and choose the nearest or the most convenient for you to write the test.

Regardless of your choice of examination center, it is advisable that you know the registration process. This enables you to register without delay and avoid mistakes that may disqualify you from taking the exam.

Basic Advice

Generally, when taking any entrance examination, applicants are expected to:

- Understand the basic requirements for the examination
- Prepare in advance for the examination
- Understand the rules and regulations and abide by them
- Arrive at the examination center early

What to Bring to the Test Center

To be admitted to the exam center, you must bring personal identification with a photograph. Acceptable documents include a valid and government-issued ID such as a passport or driver's license. Sometimes, you may be required to provide at least two photo IDs for identity verification, so make sure you take at least two with you.

What *Not* to Bring to the Test Center

Don't bring cell phones, your own calculator, pens, notes or anything else personal into the exam center. You must lock personal items in a locker during the test for security purposes. Thus, it is advisable that you travel light and only take along with you what you really need for the test.

What is the Passing Grade?

Eighty percent is the minimum passing score. However, when your scores are very high, you have better chances of securing admission to your nursing school of choice. Thus, you should aim to score well above the minimum required score in order to be competitive with your peers.

Can I Retake the Exam?

The decision to allow students to retake the exam or not is at the discretion of the nursing school. Most nursing schools give applicants with low scores a second chance to take the exam.

However, schools that allow a second attempt have some requirements you must meet before your retake request is considered. This includes a waiting period in between retakes.

Since not all schools allow retakes, it is wise to check whether or not your school of choice does, before submitting your application.

Cancel/Reschedule Policy

If you wish to cancel or reschedule your exam, you must do so at least five days before your appointment. Failure to do so may cause you to forfeit your exam fee.

Note that different exam centers don't share the same cancel/reschedule policy, so make sure you check the rules for the specific center you will be testing at.

How Long is an HESI A3 Exam Score Valid?

If you pass the exam, your scores are valid for two years. If you're not admitted to a school before your scores expire, you must take another exam if you still hope to pursue nursing career.

Introduction

The HESI A2 tests are mandatory for individuals that wish to pursue nursing or other health sciences programs in colleges and universities. This includes radiologic technology, medical sonography or surgical technology, among other health-related careers.

This preparation book is designed to assist individuals who wish to prepare well for the test. The book covers all the subjects that will be tested in the entrance examination.

Each subject is followed by a set of questions to test your knowledge of the subject. A subsequent section answers the questions to enable you to identify the questions you answer incorrectly. A short explanation is given for each answer to enable you to understand why that is the right answer.

Your performance in the questions section is a reflection of how adequately prepared for the examination you are. If you are not satisfied with your initial performance, don't give up. Go over each section until you are familiar with the subject.

Tips to Help You Pass the Test

Here are some tested and proven practical tips that will assist you to pass the test with ease:

1. Be time-conscious when taking the test. You must understand the most effective way to optimize your time. For instance, if you have just 60 minutes to attempt 60 questions, you will be wasting precious time if you spend more than a minute on a question. The longer you spend on a question, the shorter the time you have to attempt other questions. If you get stuck on a question, skip it and come back when you are done with the other questions in a section, if time allows. Don't answer some questions at the expense of the others. That may be counterproductive.

2. Be positive. If you approach the test with a negative mindset, you are likely to fail it. Prepare carefully, have confidence in yourself and you will do far better on the exam.

3. Carefully read the questions and answers before choosing an answer. Remember that some options may seem identical except for slightly different wording. Remember that, so long as time allows, you can come back to a question once you finish a section.

4. Devote enough time to preparing for the exam and practicing as many questions as you can.

5. Obey the rules of the test. They're there to help you, but if you don't follow them they will most assuredly work against you.

6. Create a study schedule that allows you to prepare well for the exam. Waiting until the last minute to start your preparations can be counterproductive. After selecting your test date, get to work immediately. Create a practical study schedule that is both convenient and easy to follow.

7. While preparing for the exam, don't overlook the importance of a good night's sleep, especially the night before the test. Your efforts will be fruitless if you spend the entire night before the exam cramming.

8. Find out the important tests to take. Most nursing schools make it mandatory for applicants to attempt all the sections in the HESI A2 exam. Some schools, however, don't require students to complete all the sections. You must check the nursing school of your choice to know the specific sections you are required to complete.

9. Attempt the easiest section first. You are not required to take the test in a predefined order. Rather, go through the sections and attempt the questions you are more comfortable with. Move from the easiest questions to the most difficult.

10. Double-check your answers before you log out of the computer. This is especially important in mathematics and other calculation-based aspects of the test. Remember, you can't change your answers after you submit the exam.

Chapter One: Mathematics

Mathematics is one of the subjects you may be required to attempt in the entrance examination. The math section is a test of your knowledge of the following topics.

Decimals

A decimal number is a number expressed with a decimal point. The decimal point separates the whole number from the fraction. For instance, in 7.9, the whole part of the expression is 7, while 9 is the fractional part.

As the fractional part, 9 is not a whole number. Rather, it is 0.9, nine parts of 10.

You can perform basic operation such as addition, subtraction, division and multiplication on decimal numbers as you would on regular numbers.

Percentage

Percentage is another subset of math you must master before the exam. You will find percentages very useful when calculating certain values in nursing school.

A percentage is simply expressing the part of a whole number with respect to 100. It is usually represented by the symbol '%' or the word "percent." The term "percent" is derived from the Latin words "per centum," meaning "for 100" or "through 100."

To convert a number into a percentage:

Step 1: Convert the number into a fraction.

Step 2: Find the fractional value.

Step 3: Multiply the fractional value by 100. That's your answer.

Example 1: What percentage of 50 is 37?

Following the rules above:

First convert the numbers into a fraction with the fractional part on top (numerator) and the whole part at the bottom (denominator).

That gives you 37/50. With the division method, 37/50 = 0.74.

Then, multiply the value by 100 and add the percent sign. Hence, 0.74 * 100 = 74%.

Therefore, 37 is 74% of 50.

Example 2: Out of 20 balls, 4 are red while the rest are blue. What percentage of balls are blue?

Let's break it down.

- Number of balls (denominator) = 20.
- Number of red balls = 4
- Number of blue balls = Number of whole balls – number of red balls
- Number of blue balls = 20 – 4 = 16.
- Thus, percentage of blue balls = 16/20 = 0.8
- Multiply by 100 = 0.8 * 100
- Thus, percentage of blue balls = 80%.

Roman Numerals

Roman numerals represent numbers via a combination of letters derived from Latin alphabets.

Some common Roman numerals are:

1. I
2. II
3. III
4. IV
5. V
6. VI
7. VII
8. IX
9. X
10. XI
11. XII
12. XIII
13. XIV
14. XV
15. XVI
16. XVII
17. XVIII
18. XIX
19. XX
30. XXX
40. XL
50. L

60. LX
70. LXX
80. LXXX
90. XC
100. C
200. CC
300. CCC
400. CD
500. D
600. DC
700. DCC
800. DCCC
900. CM
1,000. M

Addition of Roman Numerals

1. Add XL and XV and give the answer in Roman numerals.

Solution:

Write the question in Arabic numerals.

XL = 40

XV = 15

Therefore, XL + VX = 40 + 15

40 + 15 = 55

Therefore, XL + XV = LV

2. Add L, XV and XX and give the answer in Roman numerals.

Solution:

Write the question in Arabic numerals.

L = 50

XV = 15

XX = 20

Therefore, L + XV + XX = 50 + 15 + 20

50 + 15 + 20 = 85

Thus, L + XV + XX = LXXXV.

Subtraction of Roman numerals

1. Subtract LXX from C.

Write the answer in Roman numerals.

LXX = 70

C = 100

Solution:

Write out the equation:

C – LXX = 100 – 70.

100 – 70 = 30

Thus, C – LXX = XXX.

2. Subtract XX from the sum of XV and CX.

Solution:

Write the answer in Roman numerals.

XX = 20

XV = 15

LX = 60

The addition should be performed before the subtraction based on how the question is worded.

Thus, add XV and CX = 15 + 60.

15 + 60 = 75.

75 = LXXV.

Then, subtract XX from the addition.

LXXV – XX = 75 – 20

$75 - 20 = 55$

Thus, LXXV − XX = LV.

From the examples above, it is obvious that it is easier to perform calculations on Roman numerals once you express the information in Arabic numerals. Once you are done with your calculations, convert your final answer into Roman numerals again.

Algebra

Algebra is an interesting branch of mathematics that deals with symbols. The symbols in question represent a wide range of variables or quantities without fixed values. The relationship between such variables is described with equations.

Some examples of algebraic expressions are:

- $5y$
- $3y + 5x$
- $ab_2 + 2x_2$

These are simple algebraic expressions. Note that some of the alphabetical expressions are prefixed by numbers. For instance, in the first example, 5 prefixes y. while 3 and 5 prefix y and x in the second example. Such numbers are called coefficients. Thus, the coefficient of y in example 2 is 3, while x has a coefficient of 5 in the same example.

There are also like and unlike terms in algebra. Two terms are said to be similar when they have the same variables while an expression with different variables is said to be composed of unlike terms.

These two examples show what like and unlike terms are:

- $3a + 5a$
- $3b + 5y$

In the first expression, both values are a, while b and y are the values in equation 2. Thus, while example 1 deals with like terms, example 2 shows unlike terms.

Addition and Subtraction Operations in Algebra

Note that you can only add or subtract like terms. Basically, if two terms have the same variable (the letter), they can be added or subtracted together.

Consider the following examples:

1. Add 3y + 4y + 2z + 8 z

In this example, there are two like terms, represented by y and z variables.

Add the like terms together.

Thus, the equation 3y + 4y + 2z + 8 z becomes 7y + 10z.

Note that we didn't add variables y and z. Can you guess the reason? That's right. They are unlike terms. Remember, such terms can't be added or subtracted from each other.

2. Solve the algebraic equation below:

7a + 6b − 2a + 3b.

There are two variables here, a and b. Arrange the equation by bringing like terms together.

7a + 6b − 2a + 3b = 7a - 2a + 6b + 3b.

Thus, the final result is 5a + 9b.

Let's consider some other operations you can perform in algebra.

Multiplication of Algebraic Expressions

You are not limited to simple addition and subtraction in algebra. You can perform multiplication as well. Some multiplication operations in algebra are shown below:

1. Multiply (a + 2) (a+3)

You can solve this problem by expanding the equation. Break the first part of the equation into two and use the number and figure to multiply the second part of the equation thus:

(a + 2) (a+3) = a(a + 3) +2(a + 3)

= a^2 + 3a + 2a + 6

= a^2 + 5a + 6

Hence, (a + 2) (a + 3) = a^2 + 5a + 6.

2. Multiply the equation

(a + 5) (a - 6)

Expand the equation as above and rearrange it where possible.

Thus, $(a + 5)(a - 6) = a(a - 6) + 5(a - 6)$

$= a^2 - 6a + 5a - 30.$

$= a^2 - a - 30.$

Note, $-6a + 5a = -a$. If that's unclear, learn as much as you can about adding negative numbers. In the meantime, consider this analogy. If you owe someone \$6 but can only pay \$5 at the moment, you still owe the creditor \$1. That's indicated by the negative sign beside a.

Division of Algebraic Expressions

You can perform division operations in algebra as well.

1. Simplify $3ab(2a^2 4b^3)/ 2ab^2$

Solution:

First, multiply the numerator out. This gives $6a^3 12b^4$

Then, write the equation out in full. Hence, $6a^3 12b^4 / 2ab^2$

$= 18 \, a^3 12b^4 / 2ab^2 =$

$= (18 * aaa * bbbb) / (2 * a * bb)$

Thus, the division results in $9ab^2$

Solving Algebraic Equations

1. Solve the equation $y - 2 = 6$.

Solution:

A look at the equation reveals that there are two like terms and a single unlike term. As usual, rearrange the equation.
Hence, $y - 2 = 6$ can be arranged as $y = 6 + 2$
Therefore, $y - 2 = 6$ gives $y = 8$ as the final answer.

Note that during the rearrangement, the -2 was moved to 6 since both are figures. The negative sign associated with 2 changes to a positive sign after the rearrangement.

These are general rules involving negative and positive numbers. The sign changes once the figure is placed on the other side of the equal sign. Always remember that.

Conversion of Numbers

A nurse may have to do some metric conversions from time to time. Thus, the entrance examination tests your ability to convert from one metric to another. Some common conversions you may have to do include:

1. Length

Know the following length values by heart:

- 1 inch = 2.540 centimeters
- 1 centimeter = 0.3937 inches
- 1 foot = 30.4878 centimeters
- 1 mile = 1.6093 kilometer
- 1 kilometer = 0.6214 miles.

2. Mass

When doing mass conversion, know these:

- 1 pound = 0.4536 kilograms
- 1 kilogram = 2.2046 pounds
- 1 ounce = 28.3495 grams.

3. Volume

These are some basic volume values you must know:

- 1 teaspoon = 5 milliliters
- 1 tablespoon = 15 milliliters
- 1 cup = 0.23658 liters
- 1 pint = 0.4732 liters
- 1 gallon = 3.7853 liters
- 1 fluid ounce = 30 milliliters.

Let's consider some conversion examples.

1. Convert 5 miles to kilometers.

Solution:

1 mile = 1.6093 kilometer

Hence, 5 miles = 5 * 1.6093

Thus, 5 miles = 8. 0465 kilometers.

2. How many centimeters are in 12 feet?

Solution:

1 foot = 30.4878 centimeters.

Therefore, 12 feet = 12 * 30.4878.

Thus, 12 feet = 365.8536 centimeters.

3. A man filled his reservoir with 15 gallons of water. How many liters is that?

Solution:

1 gallon = 3.7853 liters.

Thus, 15 gallons = 15 * 3.7853

Therefore, 15 gallons of water = 56.7795 liters of water.

4. Convert 100 kilometers to miles.

Solution:

1 mile = 1.6093 kilometers.

Thus, 1 kilometer = 1/1.6093

1 kilometer = 0.6214 miles.

100 kilometers = 0.6214 * 100.

Thus, 100 kilometers = 62.14 miles.

5. A man weighs 400 pounds. What's his weight in kilograms?

Solution:

1 pound = 0.4536 kilograms.

Thus, 400 pounds = 400 * 0.4536

Therefore, 400 pounds = 181.44 kg.

Knowing the conversion rates by heart will make your work a lot easier.

Temperature Conversion

Temperature can be measured in degrees Fahrenheit or degrees Celsius. Occasionally, converting from one unit of measurement to another may be necessary.

You can easily convert from one unit to the other by using the following conversion formulas:

From Fahrenheit to Celsius

Step 1: Subtract 32 from Fahrenheit.

Step 2: Multiply the result by 5/9 or 0.5555.

For example, convert 212°F to °C.

Step 1: Subtract 32 from Fahrenheit = 212 − 32 = 180.

Step 2: Multiply the result by 0.5555 = 180 * 0.5555.

180 * 0.5555 = 99.99. This is approximately 100°C.

From Celsius to Fahrenheit

Converting from Celsius to Fahrenheit is done the opposite way.

Step 1: Multiply the Celsius value by 9/5 or 1.8.

Step 2: Add 32 to the result.

For example, convert 100°C to °F.

Step 1: Multiply 100 by 1. 8 = 100 * 1.8 = 180.

Step 2: Add 32 to the result = 180 + 32 = 212

Hence, 100°C = 212°F.

Word Problems

Mathematical equations can also be expressed in word problems.

Solving math problems is a two-step process. The steps are:

- Translate a word problem into a numeric equation. This may involve breaking the problem down into simpler expressions.
- Solve the simplified problem.

Some helpful suggestions to make the simplification a lot easier are:

- Read the entire word problem carefully.
- Identify important variables and information. If there are variables, attach their units such as miles, centimeters, meters and so on. If you don't figure out what you need before attempting to solve the problem, you are more likely to arrive at the wrong answer.
- Keep your calculations well organized. This is crucial to getting your answers right.

1. In a government hospital, there are 6,780 employees. 2,345 employees come in for the first shift and 1,380 for the second shift. How many employees come in for the third shift if there are no employees on leave?

Solution:

Number of employees: 6,780

First shift: 2,345

Second shift: 1,380

Third shift: ?

Note that you can only get the number of employees in the third shift if you know the number of workers who come in for the first and second shifts.

Thus, number of employees for first and second shifts = 2,345 + 1,380

= 3,725

Therefore, number of third shift = total number of employees − (first and second shift)

= 6,780 − 3,725

= 3,055.

2. After spending $50 on groceries and $35 on gas, how much do you have left from $200?

Solution:

Groceries: $50

Gas: $35

Total money: $200

Total spent = Gas + groceries

= $50 + $35

= $85.

Total left = Total amount − total spent

= $200 - $85

= $115.

Fraction and Percentage Word Problems

The following examples will help you to understand the best way to handle word problems involving fraction and percentage.

1. What fraction and percentage of 20 is 16?

Solution:

To find the percentage, you must first convert the figures into fraction.

Note that the smaller number is the numerator while the bigger number is the denominator.

Hence, you have 16/20.

Since both figures are multiples of 2, you can break them down into the simplest forms by dividing them by 2 repeatedly until you reach the final stage.

Then, 16/20 becomes 4/5.

To find the percentage, multiply 4/5 by 100.

= (4/5)/ 100

= 0.80 * 100

= 80%

Hence, 16/20 = 80%.

2. In a small clinic with 25 staff members, 18 are nurses while the rest are doctors. What percentage of the staff are doctors?

Solution:

Number of staff: 25

Number of nurses: 18

Number of doctors: ?

Number of doctors = number of staff – number of nurses

= 25 – 18

Therefore, number of doctors = 7

Percentage of doctors = (number of doctors / number of staff) * 100

= (7/25) * 100

= 0.28 * 100 = 28

Therefore, the percentage of doctors is 28%.

Note that the expression (number of doctors/number of staff) is a fractional representation of the number of doctors with respect to the number of staff. That is necessary before the percentage can be calculated.

Chapter Two: Reading

Extensive reading will be a part of your responsibilities as a trainee nurse. Thus, this subsection of the nursing school entrance examination will test your comprehension of short passages. The test will also cover your ability to understand word meanings, main ideas in a sentence, contextual meanings and logical inferences. Hence, your comprehension skills should be sound enough to enable you to read between the lines.

Reading comprehension is not restricted to knowing the words used in a passage and their meanings; you should be able to make meaningful inferences from the passage and form correct opinions as well.

Imagine trying to draw a conclusion from a conversation with someone whose speech you don't really understand. That can be quite challenging. This is why it's important for a nurse to have excellent reading comprehension, to be able to translate medical orders, read paperwork, etc.

Signs of Poor Reading Comprehension

How do you know whether you are a fluent reader with great comprehension skills? Consider the following signs of reading difficulties:

• *Inability to answer questions correctly about a passage you just read:* This can be traced to a lack of understanding of the passage, a problem that may be caused by a wide range of factors that include, but are not limited to, poor vocabulary, lack of attention, etc.
• *Inability to retell a story you just read:* You can't pinpoint the main idea because you are lost while reading the story. This is an indication that your comprehension level is too low to understand the particular passage.
• *Inability to identify the meaning of individual expressions and words:* If you don't understand the basic vocabulary and verbiage in a text, you won't be able to understand the passage as a whole.
• *Inability to connect concepts:* If you can't connect the various pieces of a passage, whether it's a theme carried across several passages, an underlying message, orders given, etc., and arrive at a cohesive final conclusion, that's an indication of a reading comprehension issue.

If you have noticed you struggle with any of the above, work on your reading skills before taking the exam.

Barriers to Reading Comprehension

Many students find reading and comprehension very challenging. This can be attributed to several factors that include:

- *Lack of motivation:* Lack of motivation to read may be caused by a wide range of factors that may include boring material or lack of previous knowledge of the text. Regardless of the cause, lack of motivation may prevent you from understanding a given material.
- *Lack of linguistic and grammatical competence:* Grammatical and linguistic gaps can cause comprehension problems. If you don't understand the rules of grammar and other relevant information about linguistics, reading can be tough and comprehension may be tougher.
- *Lack of concentration:* Social media, your mobile device, Netflix and a wide range of other things may serve as distraction when reading. If your mind is constantly drifting to other things while reading, your comprehension will undoubtedly be affected. You must be able to focus on the passage.
- *Difficulty identifying and isolating sounds:* If you can't differentiate between one sound and another, you may not easily associate the right meanings with some words. That will interfere with your comprehension too.
- *No previous knowledge of the content:* When you don't have previous knowledge of certain reading material, your understanding will be impaired. For instance, as a nursing student, if you stumble on a passage that discusses a non-medical topic, you may struggle to understand it.
- *A learning disability:* If you are suffering from a learning disability, your comprehension skills may suffer. For example, dyslexia increases reading difficulty. In the same vein, ADHD makes concentration challenging.
- *Limited vocabulary:* Limited vocabulary is a major problem among people with poor comprehension skills. You can't understand a given text if your vocabulary doesn't match the reading level of the text.

You need some basic skills for efficient reading and comprehension. Some of these fundamental skills are:

- Know the meanings of words, their antonyms and synonyms. This knowledge will not only help you to easily identify words and know their meanings, it will also enable you to find the right substitute for a word, or its opposite.
- Ability to discern the contextual meaning of words is useful to increase your comprehension.

- Ability to follow the organization of the content of a passage. The way a passage is structured, and understanding the reason for that structure, is vital to comprehension.
- Ability to identify a passage's main idea. Once you understand the overall message of the passage or text you are reading, you will be better prepared to understand the passage.

Your comprehension is influenced by your reading and information processing skills. If recognizing words and their meanings is a chore, you will spend an unnecessarily long period of time processing the words. This may interfere with your comprehension because by the time you move on to the next part of the passage, you'll have forgotten what you just read.

Good reading comprehension is dependent on four language skills. These are:

Syntax

Syntax refers to the rules that govern joining words, sentences, paragraphs, etc. into coherent reading passages. Syntax also includes understanding word order.

A link between reading comprehension and syntax skills has been established for decades. Thus, as a student, you must pay special attention to grammar, parts of speech, word order, special word usage and other things that can improve your overall comprehension.

Phonology

Phonology is a branch of linguistics that deals with the study of sound patterns in a language. Consider words like 'full' and 'pull.' It has been established that your ability to read and understand the text depends on your phonological awareness. In essence, if you don't have a good grasp of phonology, you may struggle with reading and comprehension.

Word-learning activities such as the following require good phonological awareness:

- Identifying unfamiliar words. If you can't identify unfamiliar words, it is nearly impossible to understand them.
- Making comparisons between familiar and unfamiliar words. Such comparisons will deepen your vocabulary. As you do this regularly, you become able to easily identify familiar words and their meanings.

- Repeating words and pronouncing them correctly. While pronunciation may not have a direct impact on your reading skills, it impacts your general understanding. If you can't pronounce a word correctly, you are less likely to understand such words when communicating with people who pronounce them correctly.
- Remembering words accurately to enable you to use such words when necessary. Learning new words on a daily basis and using them in sentences is an important part of progressively building your vocabulary, a necessary tool for improved reading and better understanding.
- Differentiating similar-sounding words to enable you to contrast their meanings. Keep on increasing your knowledge of homophones and related words.

Semantics

Semantics is the study of meaning in a language. Semantics involves understanding the relationship between words, signs, phrases, symbols and other signifiers. It also focuses on the actual meanings of such signifiers, which is their denotation.

Semantic knowledge is important to reading and comprehension. Your understanding of the meaning of words will determine how much you comprehend when reading. People with a poor vocabulary find it more difficult to understand a passage. They may also struggle with reading comprehension if their limited understanding of words and meanings hinders them from making logical inferences when answers to certain questions aren't written explicitly in a passage.

As you grow older, you will come across more complex reading passages. As you progress in your nursing studies, you will need to expand your medical vocabulary to be able to draw from it when necessary to understand the many texts you'll need to read to carry out your daily responsibilities.

Here are some practical reading strategies you can employ both before and during reading to increase your comprehension and retention:

Pre-Reading Tips

- Know the purpose. Before reading any passage, consider: why do you want to read the text? Is it for pleasure or for academic purposes? Are you required to discuss the passage with your friends or you are expected to answer questions about it?
For instance, your approach to reading an academic text may be quite different from your approach to pleasure reading. The kinds of details you pay attention to will depend on why you are reading a given text. If you're reading for fun, you may concentrate on the overall big picture, for example. But if you're reading for academic purposes, you'll

need to pay careful attention to details such as definitions, keywords, specific examples, dates and concepts.

- Do a preview of the text. Don't jump straight into the reading.
If there are diagrams, pictures or tables in the text, glance through them first. Do the same for headings, subheadings, bolded words, key questions and summaries. All of this will give you important information which will improve your comprehension when you read the main text.
- Identify any prior knowledge you have about the topic. You may come across a familiar text, so leverage that knowledge. Take a moment to determine how much you know about the material and how you can use that to your advantage.
- Break the reading into smaller chunks. Rather than go through the entire passage at once, especially if there are several paragraphs to cover, you may break the reading into smaller chunks for better understanding. Read and understand a paragraph before you move to the next one. Take your time to ensure you don't skip a paragraph or jump to another one without understanding the current one.

Effective Reading Tips

Once you have applied pre-reading strategies, consider the following to help you while reading the passage:

- *Self-monitor:* Make sure you are focusing on the passage in front of you. Don't let your mind drift away. Be self-aware of where your thoughts are, and keep them engaged in the text at hand.
- *Note-take and summarize*: Note-taking is vital to reading comprehension, as is briefly summarizing what you've read. Both techniques greatly improve your overall retention of material read.
Use context clues: Words can have multiple meanings depending on the context in which they are used. Use the context around words—textual structure, text themes, visual aids, paragraphs above and below, etc.—to help you determine the real meaning of what you're reading.

PQ4R System

If you come across some unfamiliar words or concepts, use the PQ4R system to help you better understand what you're reading:

o Preview: Scan the text first. This gives you a general overview of the content.

o Question: While previewing the material, develop a few questions you want to answer when reading.
o Read: Read the text with the questions in mind.
o Reflect: When you are done with the text, briefly reflect on what you read and see if your questions were answered.
o Recite: Mentally recite the major points of the text as you remember them.
o Review: Finally, go through the answer section and see how much you have learned based on the number of questions you can answer correctly.

Annotate: While highlighting the main points in a passage is helpful, annotation is more productive. This involves writing key points or important information you identify during the reading in the margins to improve your understanding of the entire text. Develop an effective way to note major points, keywords, unfamiliar words and important information.

Some practical annotation tips are:
➢ Identify key concepts and ideas
➢ Briefly summarize key points in your own words
➢ Jot down any questions you have or short comments you want to address later
➢ Develop a system of *consistent* symbols and abbreviations that you always know refer to specific topics and which can make your note-taking faster and more efficient. Consistency is important or you'll never know what these symbols/abbreviations mean, and so their use will be moot.

As a student, reading should be an integral part of your daily life. The more you practice, the better your comprehension will get.

Reading Fluency and its Importance

Reading fluency is another important tool for improved comprehension skills. There are several components of fluency in reading. These are:

Speed

Fluent reading requires that you read at the appropriate speed for your academic level. When reading aloud, you should be able to effortlessly scan a minimum of three words ahead. Your visual tracking of each line should be smooth. This makes reading easier and less stressful.

Remember that the entrance test will test your knowledge of a wide range of subjects. You'll have a specific amount of time to answer all the questions, so you need to be able to read quickly but accurately.

Accuracy

Accuracy is another skill you should develop. As a fluent reader, you shouldn't have to waste your precious time trying to recognize a specific word. You should already have that covered as you build up your accuracy.
Poor word recognition and skipping words are hallmarks of dysfluent readers. They are also notorious for substituting similar-sounding or appearing words and skipping words at will. Fluent readers don't do that and therefore have better overall comprehension, which means they score better on exams (as well as have an easier time reading any job-related materials!)

Once you master fluent reading and combine that with other skills discussed in this book, your comprehension skills will improve drastically. That will make a difference in your overall performance in the entrance examination.

Chapter Three: Vocabulary

Effective communication skills are necessary to become a competent nurse. Starting from your undergraduate days, the importance of understanding the general vocabulary used in the medical field can't be overemphasized.

Your communication skills will increase if you are familiar with common medical terms, whether in the operating theater or when dealing with your colleagues and patients. Of course, you must be familiar with general day-to-day vocabulary as well.

The importance of a great vocabulary is highlighted by the variety of topics you must read about as a nursing student. Without a strong vocabulary, you may struggle through your studies.

The test will cover two areas of vocabulary: general and medical. Thus, your understanding of general vocabulary used in daily conversations and some of the industry-specific medical terms will boost your understanding and performance.

While it is impossible to know every single vocabulary word, understanding the general terms will go a long way in helping you to communicate effectively when necessary. This chapter will familiarize you with some root words, prefixes and suffixes that will make it easier to understand unfamiliar words and expressions you may come across from time to time. You may have to memorize these learning aids to help you determine the meaning of unfamiliar words, especially medical terminologies.

Understanding Medical Terms

The medical field is vast. Thus, understanding the common terms requires a lot of work. However, the huge benefits you may derive from knowing the medical terms will justify whatever effort you invested in it.

Thus, you must be passionate about reading many medical journals, textbooks, articles and reports. If you do this frequently, you will understand the terminologies and their usage.

While individual words may have some general meanings, understanding their meanings within specific contexts will help you immensely as well. Placement and context are very important factors in medical terminology.

Here are some medical terms you should include in your vocabulary:

Pathology: The names for diseases and disorders. Your knowledge of pathology must be top notch as a medical or nursing student.

Surgery: A medical operation procedure.

Urology: Problems associated with the kidneys and bladder. Most kidney and bladder-related health problems are corrected with medications, and in some cases, with surgical operations.

Hematology: The treatment of malignancies and blood diseases.

Neonatal: Special care for newborn babies who have special needs. It is the first line of medical assistance to ensure that such a child overcomes the health challenges without having a huge or permanent impact on him/her.

Psychiatry: The study of mental disorders and their treatments. Psychiatry is a medical field for professionals who are interested in helping people with mental illnesses to overcome them.

Microbiology: Related to viral infections and bacterial infections. If you are interested in helping the world understand the causes of viral and bacterial infections, microbiology is the best fit for you.

Remission: The disappearance of the symptoms and signs of a disease, mostly noticed in recuperating patients in response to treatment by a medical team.

Syndrome: A disease or a condition's set of symptoms. A disease's syndrome gives a clue into its nature and helps medical professionals find a solution to the problem.

Intractable: A disease or ailment that is difficult to alleviate or cure. HIV/AIDS is an example of an intractable disease.

Phlebitis: Vein inflammation that commonly occurs in the legs. The veins become inflamed and block blood flow, leading to marked swelling. Phlebitis is caused by many factors that may include smoking cigarettes, obesity, leg injury, a sedentary lifestyle, varicose veins, pregnancy, blood disorders and cancer.

Myocardial infarction: Otherwise known as a heart attack, this ailment affects the coronary arteries. When plaque blocks the arteries that supply blood to the heart muscles, there is a gradual reduction in the amount of blood transported to the heart. As a result, the heart is damaged as the heart muscles die.

Cardiac arrest: This occurs when the heart stops its primary function of supplying the body with blood. While this is similar to a heart attack, someone may suffer cardiac arrest without an apparent cause.

Coronary heart disease: When plaque deposits on the wall of the blood-carrying coronary arteries, they are narrowed, preventing the heart from receiving sufficient oxygen to function properly.

Hypotension: Low blood pressure. This occurs when the blood pressure reads below 90/60. Note that low blood pressure can lead to inadequate blood flow to some important body parts such as the brain, heart and other vital body organs.

Hypertension: High blood pressure. Someone whose blood pressure reads 140/90 and above is said to suffer from high blood pressure. Uncontrolled high blood pressure can cause health challenges such as blocked arteries, kidney damage and failure, as well as chest pain, otherwise known as angina.

Heart/pulse rate: The number of times the heart beats each minute. The normal heart rate isn't same from person to person. However, for an adult, a normal range is between 60 and 100 beats per minute.

Epistaxis: Acute hemorrhaging (blood discharge) from the nasal cavity, nostril or nasopharynx. It is usually caused by trauma, or sometimes, may be triggered by increased blood pressure.

Common Medical Suffixes

Medical suffixes function similarly to general suffixes. They are attached to the end of root words and clarify them.

In the medical world, suffixes are used in reference to a procedure or an operation. Hence, knowing them helps you get a clearer image of the procedure or information.

Consider the following suffixes and their meanings:

-algia: Indicates pain in a specific part of the body. Some examples include myalgia (muscle pain), mastalgia (breast pain), arthralgia (joint pain) and neuralgia (nerve pain), among others.

-ectomy: The surgical removal of a part of the body. For instance, the removal of the appendix is known as an appendectomy while that of a lump is referred to as a lumpectomy.

-ectasis: The dilation or expansion of a hollow organ in the body. Several medical conditions suffixed with -ectasis include esophagectasis (dilation of the esophagus), bronchiectasis (the dilation or expansion of the lung's bronchi), pyopyelectasis (dilation of the renal pelvis) and a host of others.

-pepsia: A recurrent or persistent discomfort or pain in the upper abdomen, caused by issues with the digestive tract or indigestion. Otherwise known as dyspepsia, indigestion may be triggered by another health problem such as ulcers, gastroesophageal reflux or gallbladder disease.

-lysis: The separation or destruction of the membrane or cell wall. This is usually caused by osmotic or viral mechanisms.

-iatry: Medical field or medical treatment. It is derived from the Greek word "iatreia" which means healing or treatment, when its other source "iatros" is considered.

-tensive: Causing tension or pressure. Some examples are hypertensive and hypotensive.

-plasty: Reconstruction or repair; the term is used extensively to form compound words such as galvanoplasty, angioplasty, heteroplasty, etc.

-gnosis: Knowledge picture, record, or graph. This includes prognosis, barognosis, topagnosis, autognosis and lalognosis.

-plexy: A seizure or stroke. Apoplexy and cataplexy are two of the medical terms with the suffix.

-itis: A medical condition that is characterized by inflammation. Examples are arthritis, appendicitis and bronchitis.

-rrhagia: Rapid or excessive blood flow. Some words ending with rrhagia are metrorrhagia, rhinorrhagia, haemorrhagie, colporrhagia and rectorrhagia.

-centesis: A process that involves the puncturing of a body organ or cavity with a hollow needle with the aim of drawing out fluid.

-cyte: Denotes 'cell.' Some examples are chondrocyte, granulocyte, gangliocyte, electrocyte, thrombocyte and spongiocyte.

-aemia (or -emia): A blood condition or a certain substance in the blood. For instance, hypoglycemia refers to the presence of little glucose or sugar in the blood. Other examples include hypervolemia and anemia, referring to excess volume of blood and lack of blood respectively.

-ismus: Denotes a contraction or spasm. Vaginismus, psellismus, mycetismus and myocrismus are some examples of words with this suffix.

-abdominocentesis: A cosmetic surgery performed on the abdomen for the removal of wrinkles and the tightening of the skin covering the stomach.

-tendon: A band of tissue connecting the muscles and the bones.

-adenitis: Inflammation of a lymph node or a gland. In this category are words such as lymphadenitis.

-amenia: The suppression or absence of normal menstrual flow. This is otherwise known as amenorrhea.

Medical Prefixes and their Meanings

Your knowledge of common medical prefixes should be extensive. Just like in regular English usage, prefixes change the meanings of root words, giving them new meanings.

Some common medical prefixes and their meanings are:

Bi-: Double or twice. Some examples are bicuspid, two cusps or flaps; biceps, two-headed muscle; or bisexual. Others are binary vision, bifocal, bi-articulate and bifurcation.

Ferri-: Iron.

Arthro-: Bone joint.

Mast-: Breast

Hist-: Tissue.

Osseo-: Bone.

Lacto-: Milk.

Melan-: Black.

Kerat-: Cornea.

Pan-: Entire or all.

Ante-: In front of, before, forward.

Extro-, **extra-**: Outside of, beyond, outward.

Micro-: Small or tiny.

Ultra-: Beyond, excessive.

Intra-: Within or inside.

Medical Abbreviations and Meanings

Some common medical abbreviations you should be familiar with include:

HPS: Hantavirus Pulmonary Syndrome. This is a contagious and infectious disease transmitted by rats.

IDDM: Insulin-Dependent Diabetes Mellitus. This is generally known as Type 1 diabetes. This form of virus is more difficult to treat and maintain than the Type-2 variant of the ailment.

IBS: Irritable Bowel Syndrome. This medical disease affects the gastrointestinal tract.

ACL: Anterior Cruciate Ligament. This is a common knee injury. It occurs when the ACL is completely torn or sprained.

CPR: Cardiopulmonary Resuscitation. This is an emergency health procedure that involves using artificial ventilation and chest compressions to maintain brain function until a better procedure is available.

At lib: This simply means "at liberty." It is the expression used when a patient is allowed to move around freely.

ANED: The abbreviation means "alive, no evidence of disease." This expression is used when a patient is brought to a hospital alive and reportedly has no evidence of disease.

Anuric: Not producing urine. This is a critical health condition where dialysis may be urgently required.

ARDS: Acute Respiratory Distress Syndrome refers to a respiratory failure with a wide range of symptoms that include rapid breathing, shortness of breath and skin discoloration.

ASCVD: Atherosclerotic Cardiovascular Disease. ASCVD is a form of heart disease that is triggered by the buildup of plaque in the arterial walls. ASCVD refers to health conditions such as coronary heart disease, peripheral artery disease and cerebrovascular disease such as carotid artery stenosis and ischemic stroke. Aortic atherosclerotic diseases such as descending thoracic aneurysms and abdominal aortic aneurysms are also examples of ASCVD.

B.I.D.: This means the medicine should be taken twice daily.

Bibasilar: Refers to a health problem that affects the bases of both lungs.

BSO: Bilateral Salpingo-Oophorectomy: This medical term refers to the removal of the two ovaries and the fallopian tubes. This procedure is performed during a total abdominal hysterectomy.

PE: Pulmonary Embolism. This is a blood clot condition that affects the lungs.

CABG: Coronary Artery Bypass Graft. This is a form of surgery performed on the heart.

CVA: Cerebrovascular Accident. A health condition that is commonly referred to as a stroke.

DOE: Dyspnea on exertion. This refers to activity-triggered shortness of breath.

DVT: Deep Venous Thrombosis. DVT is a form of blood clot that affects the large vein.

ETOH: ETOH is the medical term for alcohol.

H&P: This is the medical term for a patient history and physical examination.

IBD: Inflammatory Bowel Disease. A health condition associated with the gastrointestinal tract. Ulcerative colitis and Crohn's disease are both refer to as IBD.

ICU: Intensive Care Unit. A unit within the medical facility where patients with critical health problems can receive special medical attention.

LCIS: Lobular Carcinoma in Situ. A type of breast cancer.

PRN: As needed. This refers to a procedure that is done only when it is absolutely necessary.

Medical Terms and Their Meanings

1. **Neurofibroma**: Tumor of the fibrous that covers the peripheral nerve. The ailment can develop in any minor or major nerve in any part of the body.

2. **Bradycardia**: Extremely slow or abnormal heartbeat. This condition is determined by the patient's age and physical condition. Elderly people are more prone to the ailment. Thus, what is considered a slow heartbeat in an adult is different from what constitutes the same in young people.

3. **Bronchospasm**: Spasm that occurs in the bronchi. It makes exhalation extremely noisy and difficult. This problem is usually associated with the bronchi and asthma.

4. **Cardiology**: Medical field that specializes in the heart and heart-related diseases. A cardiologist is a medical expert that treats such ailments. Don't confuse this with a cardiac surgeon, who performs surgical operations on internal organs.

5. **Chemotherapy**: Treating ailments with powerful chemicals. This treatment method is mostly used for treating cancer and other fast-growing cells.

6. **Diagnosis**: Conducting medical tests or a patient examination to identify the nature of an ailment.

7. **Cystitis**: Inflammation of the ureters and the urinary bladder.

8. **First aid**: Medical assistance given to someone in dire need of urgent medical attention. The primary objective of administering first aid is to prevent the patient's condition from worsening.

A first aid kit must include the following items: Band-Aids, disposable sterile gloves, triangular bandages, sterile eye dressings, safety pins, tweezers and a host of other items that make it easier to render the needed assistance without delay.

9. **Sprain**: Occurs when ligaments are stretched or torn. The ligaments are fibrous tissues in the joints for connecting two bones together. Sprains mostly occur in the ankle or wrist.

10. **Rupture**: Refers to a tear or break in any soft tissue, like the Achilles tendons, or any organ, such as the spleen.

11. **Strain**: A chronic or acute injury to the tendon, muscle or both muscle and tendon.

12. **Amnesia**: A temporary or permanent memory deficit or loss caused by a disease or an injury. The excessive use of hypnotic drugs or sedatives can trigger this health condition. Other nonmedical causes include stress, aging or lack of sufficient sleep.

13. **Atrophy**: Condition characterized by the wasting away or the decrease in size of a tissue or body part. The ailment is usually caused by the degeneration of the patient's cells. Some forms of atrophy include muscle atrophy and vaginal atrophy.

14. **MTBI**: Mild Traumatic Brain Injury, or a concussion, in simpler terms. This may be caused by a violent shaking or a blow to the body or head. Symptoms include fatigue, headaches, anxiety, impaired cognitive function, depression and irritability.

General Vocabulary

In addition to medical terminology, your vocabulary test will cover general vocabulary used in daily conversations, not restricted to medical terms.

Some general words that can equally be used in the medical field and some examples of their usages are:

1. **Complications**: An undesirable health problem that is triggered by another problem. *To avoid* <u>*complications*</u>, *the surgeon has postponed the surgical operation until the patient improves considerably.*

2. **Contraindication**: A reason why an action isn't advisable. *The doctor gave a plausible* <u>*contraindication*</u> *for her decision to suggest chemotherapy for treating the cancer patient.*

3. **Deficit**: A lack or deficiency of something. *Vitamin A* <u>*deficiency*</u> *is listed among several reasons for a pregnant woman's complications.*

4. **Deteriorating**: Not improving, worsening. *Despite the medical team's best efforts, the patient's condition is* <u>*deteriorating*</u> *at an alarming rate.*

5. **Dilute**: To reduce the concentration of a liquid. *She was told to* <u>*dilute*</u> *her medication with two liters of clean and boiled water.*

6. **Exogenous**: Produced externally to the body. *The doctor determined that the patient's ailment was caused by some* <u>*exogenous*</u> *factors such as weather changes.*

7. **Endogenous**: Produced internally. *Depression is more often triggered by* <u>*endogenous*</u> *factors.*

8. **Impaired**: Lacking some level or quality. *After the accident, the driver became visually* <u>*impaired*</u>.

9. **Impending**: Very close or likely to happen in the near future. *The increasingly warm weather indicates that summer is* <u>*impending*</u>.

10. **Hydrated**: Ensuring that the body has sufficient water. *It is advisable that people stay* <u>*hydrated*</u> *in dry weather to stay alive.*

11. **Fatigue**: Exhaustion or extreme tiredness. <u>*Fatigue*</u> *may set in after working for hours on end without taking a break.*

12. **Gender**: An individual's sex, male, female, etc. *Some chromosomes in the body determine a newborn baby's* <u>*gender.*</u>

13. **Hygiene**: Good health or a measure that contributes to cleanliness. *Proper* <u>*hygiene*</u> *is a prerequisite to healthy living.*

14. **Latent**: Invisible and inactive but existing. *The HIV is* <u>*latent*</u> *in its victims before it becomes full-blown with visible symptoms.*

15. **Labile**: Changing often at a rapid rate. *Technology is* <u>*labile*</u>*; keeping up with it may be difficult.*

16. **Inflamed**: Swollen, reddened, and warm. *The boxer was treated for an* <u>*inflamed*</u> *face after his last bout with an opponent who battered him.*

17. **Prognosis**: The expected or anticipated outcome of an event. *The prognosis tallied with the symptoms of the disease.*

18. **Precaution**: Preventive measures. *To curb the spread of a deadly disease, people must take some precautions as recommended by doctors.*

19. **Predispose**: To make more likely to occur. *A cough and catarrh predispose a person to cold and other related ailments.*

20. **Supplement**: To complement or in addition to something. *She was given some drugs to supplement the treatments she was given earlier.*

21. **Rationale**: The underlying reason behind something. *The rationale behind the doctor's decision to perform surgery on the pregnant woman was best known to him.*

22. **Symptom**: The indication or signs of a problem. *Most ailments are identified with some common symptoms.*

23. **Exaggerate**: To present something in a better, worse or greater manner than it actually is. *The patient sees no reason why she should exaggerate the ailment—it's painful enough already.*

24. **Endure**: To suffer through a difficult or painful experience. *Pain is a difficult thing for patients to endure.*

25. **Abrupt**: Sudden. *There was an abrupt change in her condition after trying the new drug regimen.*

26. **Adhere**: To stick together or hold fast. *It is important that the surgical tape adhere to the area.*

27. **Adverse**: Harmful, undesired. *Self-medication may have a serious adverse effect on people.*

28. **Apply**: Put on, to place, to spread something. *Apply pressure on the swollen leg to reduce the swelling.*

29. **Consistency**: How thin or thick a fluid is; the degree of its viscosity. *The consistency of a fluid and several other factors may determine its usefulness.*

30. **Distended**: Expanded or enlarged from pressure. *The area was distended from blood and needed immediate attention.*

The words listed above are a guide. You will come across many other words and expressions that are not covered in this book.

Vocabulary-Improving Tips

Your vocabulary can make or break both your chances of communicating effectively with patients or passing the entrance examination. Limited vocabulary makes it quite challenging to speak to people, as well as read and understand study materials. On the other hand, an extensive vocabulary will not only boost your communication skills, it will also enable you to read and pass any examination with ease.

A surefire way to improve your vocabulary is extensive reading. Cultivate the habit of reading a wide range of materials. Academic journals, magazine articles and novels are some materials that will build your vocabulary over time. While reading, you will come across new words and expressions you can include in your vocabulary list.

Chapter Four: Grammar

Understanding grammar is key to comprehension. Everything you will do in nursing school requires a good understanding of the English language. Hence, in this chapter, we will take a look at some grammar components and their usage.

Parts of Speech

There are eight parts of speech. These parts of speech, and their regular usage, are discussed below:

Noun

Nouns are words used to represent people, things and places. They can also be used to express ideas, feelings and a wide range of other things.

For instance, your name is a noun. You live in a city, a noun. You are reading this guide on your tablet or any other mobile device. Those are other nouns. Practically everything around us is a noun. Hence, nouns are an important part of speech.

Types of Nouns

Nouns can be classified into six groups. These are:

1. Common Nouns

A common noun is a word that is used for naming a general item or a group of similar objects or items. Some examples of common nouns are:

➤ People: Man, woman, mother, sister, father, daughter, son, etc.
➤ Places: Park, gym, home, school, office, etc.
➤ Things: Chair, table, pen, computer, phone, television, etc.
➤ Ideas: Respect, love, pride, hate, etc.

Some official titles or names can be common nouns as well. Examples include police officer, delivery person, clerk, cousin, teacher and a host of others. Since they don't refer to an individual but are used to represent a group of people or an unspecified person, they are common nouns.

Example: Frank is the best deliveryman ever.

In this case, "deliveryman" is a generalization (common noun).

2. Proper Nouns

A proper noun is a noun that is used to identify specific nouns. Note the distinction between a proper and a common noun. A common noun refers to any noun that has no name. A proper noun *names* a noun.

In the example above, Frank is the name of a specific deliveryman. Thus, "Frank" is a proper noun.

Example: Mr. Benson is my favorite teacher.

"Teacher" is a collective noun while "Mr. Benson," which *names* the teacher, is a proper noun.

Proper nouns begin with capital letters, while common nouns are written in lowercase until they start a sentence.

Other examples of proper nouns include:

➢ People: John, Helen, Karen, Smith, Troy
➢ Places: New York, Walmart, McDonald's, Disneyland
➢ Special occasions or holidays: Halloween, Thanksgiving, Christmas, Diwali

Note that nouns that have a specific name are proper nouns. For example "festival" is a common noun, but "Caribana Festival" is the name of a *specific* festival and therefore a proper noun.

3. Abstract Nouns

Just as the name implies, abstract nouns don't refer to physical or visible nouns. Rather, they are used for intangible ideas that can be experienced but can't be seen. Thus, you can't touch, smell, see or hear abstract nouns. Some examples include social concepts, emotions, traits, events, qualities, concepts, feelings and political theories.

Other examples of abstract nouns include:

➢ Love, hate, intelligence, knowledge, freedom, liberty, charity and anger

We are aware of the existence of these concepts but we can neither touch nor see them.

Abstract nouns are the opposite of another noun type: concrete noun.

4. Concrete Nouns

Concrete nouns refer to substances and objects we can feel with our senses. Thus, any type of noun you can smell, feel, hear, touch or taste belongs to this group.

The largest percentage of nouns fall into this group. People and animals are typical examples, as well as objects. When we visit a museum, we take in the antiquities and objects of historical values. The objects in these places that we can see and touch are examples of concrete nouns.

Other examples of concrete nouns include:

➢ Flowers, animals, rain, sunset, clouds

Concrete nouns can be classified into countable and uncountable concrete nouns. Countable nouns are objects we can pluralize.

Examples of countable nouns include:

➢ Bricks, books, horses, cars, houses

Uncountable nouns consist of concrete nouns that can't be pluralized because they don't have a plural form, nor can they be counted. For instance, you can count grains of rice or sugar.

Other examples of uncountable nouns include:

➢ Milk, water, electricity and air

5. Collective Nouns

Collective nouns refer to a collection of nouns. In other words, they are used for groups of objects.

Some collective nouns are:

➢ Crowd, flock, group, committee, team

Here is a common use of collective nouns:

➢ A choir of singers
➢ A band of musicians
➢ An army of ants
➢ A board of directors
➢ A team of players
➢ A litter of puppies

- ➤ A flock of birds
- ➤ A hive of bees
- ➤ A panel of experts
- ➤ A class of students
- ➤ A troupe of dancers
- ➤ A gang of thieves
- ➤ A crowd of people
- ➤ A galaxy of stars
- ➤ A bouquet of flowers
- ➤ A pair of shoes
- ➤ A fleet of ships
- ➤ A bunch of flowers
- ➤ A forest of trees

Whenever a word is used to represent a group of items, it is a collective noun.

6. Possessive Nouns

Possessive nouns show possession. The possession is usually indicated with the use of an apostrophe (') and the addition of an "s" after the apostrophe. However, if the noun is possessive and already has an "s" to indicate its plural form, the apostrophe comes immediately after the word. Examples are:

- ➤ The boy's books.
- ➤ The boys' books.

In example 1, the noun is singular. Hence, the "s" comes after the apostrophe to indicate possession. However, in the second example, "boys" is plural. Hence, the apostrophe will come after the "s."

Pronoun

A pronoun is a word or phrase that is used as a replacement for a noun phrase or a noun in a sentence.

As substitutes for nouns, pronouns can perform the functions of a noun. They can act as direct objects, subjects, objects of prepositions or indirect objects. They can replace an animal, person, thing or place in sentences.

Pronouns allow us to avoid needless and boring noun repetition in writing and in speech. Examples of pronouns are *it, her, she, he, they, we, their* and so on.

Pronouns are divided into several classes. These are:

49

➢ Indefinite pronouns

Indefinite pronouns reference nouns without directing attention to anything specific. Examples include *everyone, few, some, nobody, everybody, anything* and *all.*

➢ Personal pronouns

People's names can be replaced with personal pronouns. These pronouns can either act as the object of a sentence or its subject. Hence, they are classified into subjective and objective personal pronouns.

Some examples are: *you, I, it, he, we, she, they, him, them, her, us* and *it.*

➢ Possessive pronouns

These pronouns are used to denote possession or ownership.

Some examples are: *your, my, his, hers, their, our* and *its.*

Mine, yours, hers, theirs, ours, and *his* are the other class of possessive pronouns referred to as independent possessive pronouns. As independent pronouns, no noun follows them as they stand alone.

➢ Relative pronouns

Relative pronouns connect a phrase or a clause to a pronoun or a noun. They are more often used for adding more information to the pronoun or noun.

Some common relative pronouns are *who, which, whichever, whom, that* and *whomever.*

➢ Intensive pronouns

Emphasizing pronouns and nouns requires using intensive pronouns. They mostly end in -selves or -self and are found immediately after the specific noun or pronoun they are emphasizing.

Some examples of intensive pronouns are *themselves, myself, yourself, herself, himself,* and *itself.* While these pronouns on their own are referred to as reflexive pronouns, when they are used with the noun they are replacing, they become intensive.

> I *myself* felt that the shot was too painful.

> He *himself* said he wasn't feeling well.

➤ Demonstrative pronouns

Demonstrative pronouns replace nouns in sentences. They are used to indicate a noun. Demonstrative pronouns include *this, that, these, those, none, neither, or* and *such*.

➤ Interrogative pronouns

As the name implies, these are pronouns that are primarily for questioning. Notable examples are *what, who* and *whose*.

Verbs

A verb is a word or a combination of words that describes the action being performed by the subject of a sentence. It ranks alongside nouns as the most important element of a sentence.

The absence of a verb in a sentence will make the sentence incomplete because you will have zero idea of what action(s) the subject performs.

Types of Verbs

There are different types of verbs. These are:

1. Finite Verbs

Finite verbs are types of verbs performed by the subjects. They can only serve as a reference to the subject.

Finite verbs can exist in different forms and their status is determined by the number of people or the subject.

2. Action Verbs

Action verbs specifically provide information about what the subject actually does. They can give readers insight into a subject and bring its action to life, stirring up emotions in the process.

Action verbs are classified into transitive and intransitive. The former are verbs with a direct object. They demand a recipient for the action.

Example: I'm playing soccer game.

Here, "playing" is a transitive verb and needs something to act upon, "soccer game."

On the other hand, the intransitive form requires nothing to act upon. These verbs may be followed by a wide range of parts of speech such as adverbs, adjectives, prepositions and a host of others.

Some examples are:

- I danced.
- She is sitting.

In both cases, the intransitive verbs act independently of a recipient of the actions.

3. Auxiliary Verbs

An auxiliary verb is a form of verb that makes its clause more meaningful. Thus, it can express a wide range of concepts such as aspect, tense, emphasis and modality. Another name for this class of verbs is helping verbs. These verbs show the tense and time of the verb and can be used both in perfect or continuous tenses.

Some auxiliary verbs include *has, have, had, do,* and the different forms of the "be" verb such as *are, am, were, is, been, was,* and *being.* Others auxiliary verbs are *need, may, should, can,* and *will.*

4. Modal Verbs

A modal verb is another form of auxiliary verb. It sheds light on the main verb's attributes. Modal verbs are *may, might, can, could, shall, will, ought to, should* and *would.*

Consider some examples. What type of verbs are used in these sentences?

- Fred is preparing for his entrance exam.
- I have seen her play before.
- Please come home immediately after your lectures.

Adjectives

Adjectives are words used for describing or modifying a noun. When modifying a noun, an adjective highlights the attributes of the noun.

Adjectives can be used to describe touch, taste, size, color, sound, shape and appearance. They are also used for describing situations, personality, amounts and time.

Some adjectives are:

- Long
- Short
- Tall
- Beautiful
- Blue
- Expensive
- New
- Old
- Two-year-old
- Annual
- Daily
- Triangular
- Melodious
- Thundering

Types of Adjectives

Adjectives can be classified into different types. These are:

- **Articles**: Adjectives used for discussing non-specific people and things. There are three articles: *the, a* and *an.*
Articles can be definite or indefinite. "The" is an example of a definite article while "a" and "an" are indefinite articles. Definite articles are used for indicating specific things or people, while indefinite articles don't refer to a specific person or thing.
- **Numbers:** Numbers are mostly used as adjectives in sentences. When a number in a sentence provides answers to the question "How many?", it is an adjective.
Example: There are six boys in the class. "Six" is a number adjective.
- **Indefinite adjectives**: When discussing non-specific things, indefinite adjectives are used. These adjectives are pretty easy to spot because they are similar to indefinite pronouns and are actually derived from such pronouns. *None, any, few, many* and *several* are common examples of such adjectives.
- **Attributive adjectives**: These are adjectives that are used for specific qualities, traits or features of an object. They are used to modify shapes, size, age, color, material and quality. In this class are *qualifier adjectives* that give specific information about a noun; *material adjectives* showing the material something is made of; *age adjectives*, origin adjectives showing the source of a thing; and *observation adjectives* that express value.

Adverb

Adverbs are words that are used to describe or modify another adverb, adjective, verb or a group of words. They are also expressions that are used for modifying a clause, determiner, sentence or preposition. Adverbs provide more information about the object's manner, time, circumstance, place, degree and manner. They also express frequency, level of certainty, place and to what extent something happens.

Types of Adverbs

There are five types of adverbs. These are:

- **Adverbs of time:** Adverbs of time provide more information about the specific time that an action takes place. You can find such adverbs at the end or beginning of a sentence. However, if the time of the occurrence of an event is of paramount importance, the adverb will be put at the beginning of the sentence.
Some examples of adverbs of time are *always, during, never, usually, sometimes, recently, soon, so far* and *yet*.
- **Adverbs of place:** You can usually find adverbs of place after the main object or verb. They are sometimes used to end a sentence. Notable examples include *everywhere, here, outside, nowhere, below, out, there, outside* and *above*.
- **Adverbs of manner**: These are arguably the most common adverbs and are easily identifiable. Most of these adverbs are identified with the "-ly" suffix. Examples are *slowly, kindly, neatly, loudly*, etc.
- **Adverbs of degree**: The intensity of the level of an adjective or another adverb is explained with adverbs of degree. Such adverbs include *enough, almost, so, quite* and *more*.
- **Adverbs of frequency**: The frequency of the occurrence of a verb is the focus of this adverb type. You can identify adverbs of frequency since they are usually written before a sentence's main verb. Examples are *always, normally, seldom, rarely, again* and *sometimes*.

Prepositions

A preposition is a word used within a sentence to connect phrases, pronouns or nouns to other words in the sentence.

As a connecting word, a preposition can connect objects, people, locations or the time of a sentence. They are usually found before a noun or in some special cases, they prefix gerund verbs.

Types of Prepositions

Prepositions are classified into the following classes:

- Prepositions of Time

This class of preposition indicates the time when something occurs, occurred or will occur.

An example is:

➢ We arrived home late in the *evening*.

- Prepositions of Place

This class of preposition is used to address relation to places. Examples are *on, in* and *at*. These prepositions are guided by some rules.

"In" is a preposition used when a place with a virtual or physical boundary is mentioned in a sentence.

Examples are:

➢ In a school
➢ In the USA
➢ In a room

"On" is the preposition specifically used for the surfaces of things. Examples include:

➢ On the table
➢ On the roof
➢ On the TV set

"At" is the preposition use when specific places are in question. Some examples include:

➢ At the entrance
➢ At home

- Prepositions of Direction

Some prepositions that are used to indicate direction fall in this group. Some examples include:

➢ They are going *towards* the bus stop.

➢ The boy threw the bottle *into* the river.

- Prepositions of Instruments

These are prepositions that are used to express different instruments, devices, machines or other related nouns to other words in a given sentence. Examples include:

➢ He comes to school *by* bus.
➢ He chopped the wood *with* a sharp ax.

Note that a preposition is followed by a noun, not a verb.

- Prepositions of Agency

When expressing a casual relationship between a doer or noun and an action or verb, prepositions of agency are used. Examples include:

➢ The bestseller was written *by* Arnold Green.
➢ The young girl is playing *with* her doll.

Conjunctions

Conjunctions are words that are used to connect two or more words, clauses or phrases together. They are also coordinators in a clause.

Types of Conjunctions

Conjunctions are classified into four types. These are:

- Subordinating conjunctions

Subordinating conjunctions are used for connecting two clauses with different grammatical values. They are ideal for connecting independent clauses and dependent clauses.

The most common subordinating conjunctions are *since, as though, after, though, whether, before, unless, because* and *while*. Some others *are although, as if, after, until, when, since, than, how* and *so that*.

Consider some examples:

➤ The couple tidied up their home *before* going to work.
➤ *Until* you pay off your debt, you can't have access to another loan.
➤ *After* passing her exams, she got a good job.

- Coordinating conjunctions

Coordinating conjunctions are used to connect sentence elements of the same grammatical type. Thus, they are used for connecting phrases with phrases, words with words, sentences with sentences and clauses with clauses.

Seven common conjunctions are in this group, often referred to as the FANBOYS: *For, and, nor, but, or, yet, so.*

- Adverbial conjunctions

Adverbial conjunctions are otherwise called conjunctive adverbs. They are used for connecting independent clauses. Common examples are *meanwhile, consequently, however, accordingly, otherwise, indeed* and *however*. Other examples are *therefore, in contrast, meanwhile, finally, likewise, in contrast, on the other hand* and *then*.

In a sentence, a semicolon precedes a conjunctive adverb and a comma follows. Consider these examples:

➤ They have been married for years; nevertheless, they can't do without each other.
➤ They went on picnic on Sunday; however, they didn't have much as they expected.

- Correlative conjunctions

Correlative conjunctions are used for showing contrasting or comparative relationship between ideas or words by connecting pairs.

Some examples are:

➤ The guy is both tall and handsome.
➤ The driver had neither the experience nor the license to drive such a vehicle.
➤ The dog not only killed its prey but also ate it.

Interjections

Interjections are used for expressing sudden emotions or showing strong feelings. They serve as exclamations in sentences to convey an emotional emphasis.

Interjections are often included at the start of a sentence to express a wide range of strong feelings or emotions that include excitement, surprise, enthusiasm, happiness or disgust.

Common examples of interjections are *Alas, Oh, Ouch* and *Wow*. Note that an interjection is a separate idea. It has no correlation to other parts of the sentence.

Some examples of interjections include:

- Oh! What a mistake!
- What lovely attire!
- Hey! Put out the fire.
- Congrats! You have won the contract.
- Ugh! I'm completely lost.
- No! That's a complete waste of time.

Other words used as interjections include *indeed, really, yes* and *no*. Note that interjections are mostly followed by an exclamation mark as seen in the examples above.

Glossary of Common Grammatical Terms

Here are some grammatical terms you should understand to improve your knowledge of the English language.

1. **Grammar**: Includes the rules guiding both spoken and written forms of English.
2. **Object**: The person or thing that receives the action performed by the subject in the sentence.
3. **Passive voice**: Verb usage that suggests the verb's action is received by the subject.
4. **Active voice**: Verb usage that suggests the subject performs the verb action.
5. **Prefix**: Word attached to the beginning of another word to alter its meaning. Examples are *re-, counter-, en-, ex-, de, dis-, un-, im-*, etc. For instance, the word, "happy," can take on a new and even negative meaning with the addition of the "un-" prefix. Then, happy becomes unhappy, a negative state. The same applies to the word "possible." The "im-" prefix changes the meaning entirely.
6. **Clause**: Group of words with a subject and a verb, or predicate. Some typical examples are: "you are reading" or "she laughs uncontrollably."
7. **Suffix**: While a prefix is attached to the beginning of another word, a suffix is attached to the end of the word. Examples include *–ful, -er, -ity, -ment, -ness*, and *-or*.
8. **Phrase**: Group of words without a predicate and a subject.
9. **Clause**: Group of words with a subject and a predicate. While a phrase may be incomplete and sometimes meaningless, a clause is complete and meaningful.

10. **Independent clause**: Clause that can stand on its own and is meaningful.

11. **Subordinate clause**: Otherwise known as a dependent clause, a subordinate clause can't stand on its own and is meaningless without an independent clause.

12. **Gerund**: Verb that is converted to a nominal with the addition of -ing. Examples include *reading, dancing, sleeping, working*.

13. **Synonyms**: Two words that are similar in meaning. Ex: *happy* and *joyful*.

14. **Antonyms**: Two words that are opposite in meaning. Ex: *happy* and *sad*.

15. **Homophones**: Two words with similar sounds but different spellings and meanings. Ex: *sun* and *son*.

16. **Idiom**: Expression with a different meaning than the individual words' literal meanings. An example is *shedding crocodile tears*. This simply means insincere sympathy.

17. **Irregular verbs**: Verbs that take exceptions to the general rules of verb formation. Verbs without the -ed suffix in their past forms are parts of irregular verbs.

18. **Present tense**: Present-tense verb expresses present action. They are also used for expressing general truths or habitual actions.

19. **Subject**: The place, person or object that the statement is about. For instance, in the statement, *Bill Gates is a philanthropist*; the person the sentence is about is Bill Gates. Hence, Bill Gates is the subject.

Common Grammatical Errors

The common causes of grammatical errors are discussed below:

1. **Wrong use of apostrophes**: Some people are confused when using apostrophes. They end up using them wrongly in sentences.
Example: This is the boys' house.
This is an incorrect use of an apostrophe if you are talking about one boy.
Correction: This is the boy's house.

2. **Subject/verb agreement**: This is another common source of grammatical errors. The rule states that a singular subject (without an "s") should go with a singular verb (with an "s") while plural subjects (with an "s") should go with a plural verb (without an "s").
Example: "He go to school daily" is wrong.
Correction: He goes to school daily.

3. **Wrong word usage**: This occurs when words are used incorrectly, especially with homophones.
Example: The whether is insanely hot.
The homophones *whether* and *weather* are mistaken for each other in this sentence.

Correction: The weather is insanely hot.

4. **Double negatives:** This involves using two negatives within a sentence to indicate you mean the exact opposite of what you are writing or saying.
Example: I am not going to make no friends.
Correction: I am not going to make any friends.

5. **Missing comma**: An introductory phrase, word or clause should be followed immediately by a comma. This makes the sentence clearer and enables readers to avoid unnecessary confusion.
Example: If you are not ready to participate in the picnic you can sit at home and watch your favorite TV program.
Correction: If you are not ready to participate in the picnic, you can sit at home and watch your favorite TV program.

6. *It's and its*: "Its" is a possessive pronoun, indicating possession. On the other hand, "it's" is a contraction of "it is."
Example: "It's a lovely day" versus "The dog carried its toy around."

7. **Vague pronoun reference**: Pronouns replace nouns. Whatever the pronoun replaces should be its antecedent. This can be a place, person or thing. However, in a vague pronounce reference, the reference is ambiguous, leaving readers confused about what you are actually referring to.
Example: She beat her daughter because she is drunk.
Who is drunk? The mother? The daughter? This is an example of a vague reference.
Correction: Because the woman is drunk, she beat her daughter.
This removes the ambiguity by clearly indicating the subject of the sentence.

8. **Unnecessary Commas**: It is imperative that you understand when and where to use commas and where you can do better without them.
An example is: I can drive a car, and ride a bike.
In the sentence above, the comma is unnecessary because the subject is the same.
Correction: I can drive a car and ride a bike.

9. **Run-On Sentence**: This is a common error that occurs when two main clauses are connected together without the appropriate punctuation.
Example: I prepared the meal I couldn't eat it.
The appropriate punctuation marks are missing.
Correction: I prepared the meal but I couldn't eat it.

10. **Compound sentence missing a comma**: When two or more independent clauses are separated by a conjunction in a sentence, they should be separated with a comma.
Example: The driver filled up his tank and he hit the road.
This is an incorrect sentence. "And" is a conjunction separating two independent clauses. Thus, a comma should separate them.
Correction: The driver filled up his tank, and he hit the road.

This is an inexhaustive list of some common grammatical errors. Identifying and avoiding such errors will contribute immensely to your mastery of the language.

If you are running out of time, concentrate on the discipline of your interest. For instance, you are preparing for nursing entrance examination. Thus, if you don't have enough time to embark on comprehensive vocabulary building, concentrate on building your medical vocabulary.

Let's also compare some commonly mixed-up words.

1. Effect vs affect

Affect means to have an impact on something or someone. On the other hand, *effect* means the impact that something or someone has on another thing or person.

- His father's death will affect his performance.
- The effect was so huge he couldn't concentrate on anything else.

2. Between and among

Between is used for expressing the relationship between two things or people while *among* expresses relationship between more than two things or people.

- Share the money between Tony and Sharon.
- The books are to be shared among the 20 students.

3. Further and farther

Further and *farther* mean metaphorical and physical distance respectively. For instance, "You can move *farther* than that" and "He is *further* away from getting home."

4. Less and fewer

Fewer is the ideal word when the subject is countable. On the other hand, use *less* when discussing singular mass nouns.

- There are *fewer* people in attendance than we actually expected.
- She loves him *less* than he loves her.

5. All together and altogether

Altogether is an adverb. It means "entirely" or "completely." *All together* is a phrase and means "in a group."

- That is an *altogether* false conclusion.
- *All together*, we climbed the mountain.

6. Illusion and allusion

An *illusion* creates a false impression of reality to deceive the senses or mind while an *allusion* is a direct or implied reference to someone or something.

- She is under the *illusion* that she is a daughter of a billionaire.
- The *allusion* to Mike Tyson as a great sports icon is spot on.

7. Already and all ready

All ready means "completely prepared." It is a phrase. On the other hand, *Already* is an adverb for describing things that happened before a specific time.

- By the time I went inside, he was *all ready* for the outing.
- I have *already* decided against going for the walk.

8. Their and there

There means "that place" as an adverb. It can also be used to introduce a sentence or a clause, in which case it acts as a pronoun. However, *their* is a possessive pronoun. In that capacity, it is used to express ownership or possession of a concept or a thing.

- *Their* house is beyond the airport.
- When you get *there*, don't forget to give me a call.

9. Lose and loose

Lose is a verb that means not to win or to misplace. Conversely, *loose* is an adjective. It means not tight.

- Without adequate preparation, you will *lose* the match.

- His *loose* clothing tangled in his feet and he fell facedown.

10.   Stationary and stationery

Stationary means standing still, while *stationery* means a writing paper or other writing material.

- The vehicle has been *stationary* for days.
- You can purchase the *stationery* across the street.

11. Eminent and imminent

Eminent means popular, influential and wealthy. *Imminent*, on the other hand, means close at hand or nearby. It also means approaching.

- The professor is an *eminent* scholar.
- As the old dog started gasping for breath, it was obvious a trip to the hospital was *imminent*.

12.   Complement and compliment

A *complement* makes something else complete while a *compliment* is a positive remark about something or someone.

- This white shoe *complements* your outfit.
- It is a well-deserved *compliment*.

13.   Flout and flaunt

Flaunt means showing off, while *flout* means scornful defying.

- He *flouted* the traffic light while *flaunting* his new Ferrari.

14.   Principle and principal

A *principal* can mean the head of an organization or a school when used as a noun. It also refers to the most important thing when used as an adjective. On the other hand, a *principle* refers to a firmly held ideal or belief, in which case it is always a noun.

- Mr. Johnson is the *principal* of the school.
- The *principal* reason for this guide is to assist students to pass the nursing school entrance examination.

- As a matter of *principle*, vegans don't eat meat.

15.   Toward and towards

Both are correct. However, Americans prefer *toward* while *towards* is preferred in British English.

16.   Infer and imply

Imply is an indirect reference to something while *infer* refers to what you gather from subtext.

- Failing to pass *implies* that he has automatically lost his scholarship.
- I can *infer* from her silence that she is not interested in the business.

17.   Immigrate and emigrate

Emigrate refers to moving away from a country or city to live elsewhere, while *immigrate* means moving into a country or city from somewhere else.

- The family is contemplating *emigrating* to Europe from America.
- He *immigrated* to the US from Africa.

18.   Breathe and breath

Breathe is a verb that means to inhale or exhale while the noun *breath* refers to the air we inhale or exhale.

Chapter Five: Biology

Biology is derived from two Greek words. These are "bios," which means "life," and "logos," which means "study." Hence, biology can be defined as the study or science of life.

Biology is a very wide subject that covers nine different fields and each field has subfields. The major branches of biology are:

1. **Cellular biology**: The study of the basic units of all living things.
2. **Genetics**: The study of heredity.
3. **Botany**: The study of plants and agriculture.
4. **Molecular biology**: The study of biological molecules.
5. **Ecology**: The study of organisms' interactions with their environment.
6. **Physiology**: The study of the organisms and their different parts.
7. **Evolutionary biology**: The study of the origin of life.
8. **Zoology**: The study of animals and their behavior.
9. **Biochemistry**: The study of the components of living things.

These are the different fields of biology, but the entrance exam will assess your general understanding of biology, focusing on topics such as:

Cells

"Cell" is derived from the Latin word *cella*, which means "small room." It is the basic structural unit of any living organism—the smallest unit of life.

Robert Hooke discovered cells in 1665. However, it was Theodor Schwann and Matthias Jakob Schleiden who developed cell theory in 1839. The theory covers some fundamental facts that describe what a cell actually is.

Cell theory states that all organisms are made up of one or more cells. Cells are the fundamental unit of all living organisms. The theory adds that cells are created from preexisting cells.

A single cell is a complete organism in some cases. Typical examples are yeast and bacterium. In other animals and humans, the cells work together with specialized cells to form the building blocks of life.

Cells are usually studied separately as cellular biology, cell biology or cytology.

Cell Composition

Cells are made up of a cytoplasm, encased in a membrane. It contains nucleic acids and proteins, alongside other biomolecules. Cells are invisible and can only be seen with the aid of a microscope.

Organisms are classified as either unicellular or multicellular. In the former, such organisms have only one cell. A bacterium is an example of a unicellular organism. Most unicellular organisms are further classified as microorganisms. In the latter, the organisms have more than one cell. Animals and plants are multicellular organisms.

Characteristics of Cells

As the basic units of life, cells have the following essential characteristics:

- Each cell has a nucleus in the cytoplasm. Membrane-bound organelles are housed there too.
- The nucleus of a cell holds all the genetic information necessary for cell growth and reproduction.
- In the cell, the lysosomes are responsible for digesting unwanted materials.
- Energy transaction is handled by the mitochondria, a double membrane-bound organelle that ensures that the cell has the energy needed for survival.
- The interior of the cell is organized into organelles. A distinct membrane surrounds them.
- The endoplasmic reticulum synthesizes some molecules. It also processes them into the right locations.

Cell Types

Cells are classified into two groups. These are:

1. Prokaryotic cells
Prokaryotic cells are otherwise known as prokaryotes. They include archaea and bacteria that make up two-thirds of the domains of life.
Prokaryotic cells laid the foundation for other forms of life on earth. They are smaller and simpler than the other cell type: eukaryotic cells. More so, they don't have a nucleus and membrane-dependent organelles.

These cells have three regions:

Cell envelope. The envelope encloses the cell. It consists of a plasma membrane that is fully protected by a cell wall that covers it. In some bacteria, it is further covered with a capsule, a third layer.

The cytoplasmic region. This region exists inside the cell. It contains ribosomes, DNA and some other components. The cytoplasm hosts the genetic material in the cell.

Pili and flagella. These structures are found on the outside of the cell and consist primarily of proteins. They aid communication between cells and facilitate movement.

2. Eukaryotic cells
Eukaryotic cells are common in slime molds, plants, algae, fungi and protozoa. The cells are 15 times wider and 1000 times more voluminous than an average prokaryote.
The following are some features of eukaryotic cells:

- They have a true nucleus
- They engage in both sexual and asexual reproduction
- The cells range in sizes and diameter
- The plant and animal members of the group have distinct features. For instance, while the plant cells contain central vacuoles, chloroplasts and some plastids, these are absent in animal cells.

Organelles

Both prokaryotic and eukaryotic cells contain organelles. These cell parts perform vital functions similar to those performed by the lungs, hearts, kidneys and other human bodily organs. However, prokaryotic cells have simpler organelles that are not bonded to the membrane.

The organelles are classified into many groups. Some, such as the Golgi apparatus and nucleus, are alone, while others such as chloroplasts, mitochondria, lysosomes and peroxisomes exist in groups of hundreds or thousands.

Some common cell organelles and their functions are described below:

1. Nucleolus
This is where ribosome synthesis takes place. It also controls cellular reproduction and other cellular activities.

2. Chromosomes
Chromosomes, found inside the nucleus, carry the DNA of the cell, and are replicated when the cell divides to reproduce.

3. Nuclear membrane

The nuclear membrane acts as a protective barrier for the nucleus.

4. Vacuoles
Vacuoles are the storage organs. They store water, food and a wide range of other waste materials.

5. Chloroplasts
Chloroplasts are important organelles. They contain the chlorophyll pigment necessary for photosynthesis.

6. Lysosomes
The lysosomes engulf foreign invaders entering the cell. They also ensure cell renewal occurs. No wonder they are referred to as "the cell's suicide bags."

7. Golgi bodies
These are known as the cell's post office, considering their involvement in the transportation of different materials from one part of the cell to another.

8. Endoplasmic reticulum
This part of the organelle helps with transporting substances from one part of the cell to another. It also plays a crucial role in other activities such as carbohydrates' metabolism and the synthesis of steroids, lipids and proteins.

9. Cell walls

A cell wall is a structural layer that surrounds some cells, mainly plant cells. The cell wall is flexible, tough and sometimes, rigid. In addition to protecting the cell, it provides structural support. Cell walls can be found in fungi, algae, some prokaryotes and in eukaryotes such as plants.

Cell walls' composition vary from one species to another. The composition is dependent on several factors such as the cell's developmental stage and type.

A plant's primary cell wall is composed of hemicelluloses, cellulose and pectin. Aside from these polysaccharides, other polymers make up the cell wall including suberin, lignin and cunin.

Algae's cell walls contain polysaccharides such as agar and carrageenan, components that other plants don't have. They contain some glycoproteins too.

A bacterium's cell wall is made up entirely of peptidoglycan while archaea's cell walls are composed of a wide range of substances such as pseudopeptidoglycan and glycoprotein

S-layers. Chitin, an N-acetylglucosamine polymer, is the major component of fungi's cell wall.

Functions of a Cell

A cell performs major functions in living organisms.

1. It provides structure
The cell membrane and the cell wall are the major components of a cell. They give each organism a structure. For instance, cells make up an organism's skin.

2. It helps transport substances
During a cell's chemical process, waste is produced. The waste products are eliminated from the cell through both passive and active transport. Additionally, nutrients must be transported.

3. It aids energy production
Without energy, cells can't perform the chemical processes they are associated with. Cells produce energy for living organisms either through photosynthesis or respiration.

4. They aid growth
The multiplication of cells, known as mitosis, results in tissue growth and reproduction in complex organisms. The parent cell forms two identical daughter cells by dividing.

5. It aids reproduction
Cells aid reproduction through two major processes: meiosis and mitosis.

Mitosis

Mitosis is the duplication of the genetic material or DNA in a cell. DNA is divided between two cells equally. Then, the dividing cells undergo the cell cycle.

To trigger the cell cycle, some growth factors are needed to indicate the need for the production of new cells. Sometimes, some signals may suffice to trigger the cycle.

Somatic cells in the human body replicate through mitosis. Some examples of such cells are blood cells, fat cells, skin cells and other non-sex cells.

As a beneficial process, mitosis helps with the replacement of damaged or dead cells. It also replaces cells with short life spans.

Meiosis

Meiosis is a process that leads to the generation of gametes or sex cells in sexually reproducing organisms. Gametes are produced in both female and male gonads. After meiosis, there are only half of the number of chromosomes remaining in the original cell.

Thus, while mitosis produces genetically identical cells, meiosis produces four genetically different cells.

A breakdown of the differences between mitosis and meiosis is shown below:

- Although both are the products of cell division, mitosis leads to the division of body cells while sex cells are divided in meiosis.
- Cell division occurs once in mitosis and twice in meiosis.
- Mitosis produces two genetically identical daughter cells while meiosis produces four non-identical daughter cells.
- Mitosis' daughter cells are diploid while meiosis' daughter cells are haploid.
- Tetrad formation doesn't occur in mitosis but does in meiosis.

Photosynthesis

Photosynthesis is the complex process through which plants and some organisms, such as algae, and some bacteria convert light into chemical energy. During the process, the captured light is used for the conversion of carbon dioxide, water and minerals into energy-rich chemical and oxygen.

Photosynthesis is a three-stage process.

Stage 1: Radiant Energy Harvest

The entire process starts in the chloroplasts. Photosynthesis begins with the harvesting of radiant energy from the sun by a green, leafy plant. A pigment in the plant cell, chlorophyll, absorbs light photons from the plant cells' chloroplasts.

Stage 2: Radiant Energy Conversion

The plant can't use the sunlight in its raw form. Thus, the plant will convert the light energy into chemical energy, a form of energy that can be used to fuel its cells.

Stage 3: Radiant Energy Storage

This is the last stage, known as the Calvin-Benson cycle. At this stage, the plant uses water from the soil and atmospheric carbon dioxide for the conversion of NADPH and adenosine triphosphate (ATP). The latter is an important component in the relationship between living things and energy. This is why it is called the "energy currency for all life."

During the Calvin-Benson cycle, the energy produced by the light reactions is used for the production of carbohydrate needed by the plants. NADPH is also produced during the reaction. NADPH is a special form of NADP with hydrogen and electron ion, as well as adenosine triphosphate.

During the cycle, the plant uses both ATP and NADPH to fix the carbon dioxide while carbon from atmospheric carbon dioxide is used for the production of carbohydrates. Another product of the cycle is $C_6H_{12}O_6$, commonly known as glucose.

Both ATP and NADPH have a short shelf life. Thus, plants must convert and store them for use. A cell needs energy from both molecules to use atmospheric carbon dioxide. This will result in the production of fatty acids, sugars and glycerol during the last stage of photosynthesis. Needed energy is used immediately while the unused energy will be stored for future use.

Note that photosynthesis can happen at any hour of the day because it is light-independent.

Importance of Photosynthesis

Aside from being the source of energy for plants and some organisms, photosynthesis offers several other benefits for plants, animals and humans. Some of these benefits are:

- It is the primary source of oxygen for both animals and humans
- It is the primary source of energy for animals and plants
- It plays a significant role in the carbon cycle between the oceans, earth, animals and plants
- The symbiotic relationship between animals and humans is impossible without photosynthesis.

It is noteworthy that not all plants depend on photosynthesis for energy production, although the majority do. Most plants that don't depend on photosynthesis as a source of food and energy are parasitic. Some plants, such as Indian pipe (Monotropa uniflora), and beechdrops (Epifagus americana) are known for stealing nutrients from other host organisms.

Some other plants, such as molds, mushrooms, yeasts and other members of the fungi kingdom are not parasitic, although they are photosynthesis-independent. These plants obtain their food from their environment.

Metabolism

Metabolism refers to the chemical reactions that occur within a living organism to maintain the organism and its cells. Simply put, it is the process by which the body converts food into useful energy.

Each individual has a resting metabolic rate (RMR). This refers to the amount of calories necessary for organs to function properly. A whopping 75% of the calories each person burns daily is due to RMR.

Metabolism serves three main purposes. These are:

1. Convert food to energy that is needed for running cellular processes
2. Convert fuel and food to building blocks for several essential elements such as nucleic acids, proteins, some carbohydrates and lipids
3. Eliminate nitrogenous wastes

Metabolism can be classified into two types:

Anabolism/anabolic metabolism: The synthesis of all the compounds the cells need. This process uses simple molecules to build complex molecules. Energy is needed for this reaction to occur. A typical example is the synthesis of compounds such as carbohydrates, nucleic acids, proteins and lipids. Protein synthesis from amino acids is another example. It also includes the DNA strands' synthesis from nucleotides or nucleic acid building blocks. The biosynthetic processes take place constantly, reflecting their importance to the life of a living cell. They use energy provided by ATP and from other energy-storing molecules.

Catabolism/catabolic metabolism: Catabolism is the breakdown of complex molecules into simpler ones for the singular purpose of obtaining energy. Thus, catabolic metabolism releases energy, unlike anabolic metabolism that requires energy. During the reaction, energy stored in the bonds of glucose, fats and other complex molecules is released. Such energy is then harvested in a useful form that the cell can use for its activities.

In a nutshell, while anabolism consumes energy, catabolism releases it. More so, metabolism is not an automatic reaction. Each step of the chemical reaction requires the presence of an enzyme to facilitate the reaction.

Metabolism can't occur in the absence of the necessary nutrients. The body needs the energy for the synthesis of new proteins such as ribonucleic acid (RNA) and deoxyribonucleic acid (DNA).

The human body needs a wide range of essential nutrients such as oxygen, carbon, sulfur, hydrogen, phosphorus, nitrogen and some 20 inorganic elements. These elements are supplied through lipids, carbohydrates, protein, minerals, vitamins and water.

The different classes of food perform a wide range of functions in the body after undergoing metabolism.

Fats in Metabolism

For instance, fat supplies the body with twice the amount of energy that either protein or carbohydrates will produce by weight.

Some of the functions of fats are:

- Protecting the vital organs by forming protective insulation around them
- Helping with the absorption of fat-soluble vitamins
- Reserving energy for future use.

Some essential fatty acids that the human body can't do without include unsaturated fatty acids such as linolenic, linoleic and arachidonic acids.

Vitamins and Minerals in Metabolism

Vitamins and minerals play a vital role as body regulators in addition to making meaningful contributions to the body's metabolic pathways.

Some examples of important minerals are sodium, fluorine, calcium, iodine, potassium and iron. Others are phosphorus, fluorine, zinc, cobalt, chloride ions, manganese, cobalt and copper.

Metabolism requires the following important vitamins:

- Nicotinic acid or niacin
- Vitamin A
- Pantothenic Acid
- B2 (riboflavin).

Carbohydrates in Metabolism

Foods provide humans with carbohydrates in three different forms: sugar, starch or cellulose, otherwise known as fiber. Sugars and starches are the major sources of human energy.

All body tissues derive energy for performing their activities from glucose. When carbohydrates and sugars are consumed, they undergo metabolism or digestion to produce glucose.

The equation for glucose combustion to release energy is:

$C_6H_{12}O_6 + 6O_2 \longrightarrow 6CO_2 + 6\ H_2O + energy$

The majority of people consume about 50% of their carbohydrate needs through their diet. Some good sources of carbohydrates are pasta, wheat, rice, potatoes, bread and macaroni.

Proteins in Metabolism

Proteins are found in every human cell and are responsible for tissue building. They assist with hemoglobin formation for oxygen transportation and support the enzymes for vital reactions as well as assist cell functions and structure. Proteins also supply the needed nitrogen for both RNA and DNA as well as energy production.

Proteins are made up of essential amino acids that the human body can't synthesize on its own. Their amino acid composition makes protein very necessary for nutrition. Although the body contains about 20 amino acids, the body can only synthesize 12.

Common essential amino acids are methionine, lysine, leucine, phenylalanine, tryptophan, isoleucine, threonine and valine.

Some good sources of protein in food include milk, eggs, vegetables, soybeans, grains and meats.

Metabolism, Nutrition and Energy

Importance of Metabolism

Metabolism is crucial to human existence. It is equally of great importance to animals and plants.

Without energy, living organisms can't grow. It is also important for reproduction.

The chemical reactions that are involved in metabolism are grouped together and organized into metabolic pathways. The pathways refer to the linking of the series of chemical reactions that occur within a cell. This usually involves the transformation of one chemical into another through a series of processes. Each step involved in the transformation receives a major boost through a specific enzyme that facilitates the reaction.

Cellular Respiration

Cellular respiration refers to a set of metabolic processes and reactions that take place in organisms' cells with a view to converting biochemical energy received from food nutrients into ATP.

During the process, CO_2 is produced. The waste product forms carbonic acid when it binds with water. The acid helps with maintaining the blood's pH. However, if too much CO2 is removed from the body, it can be dangerous. This calls for a balance during cellular respiration

Stages of Cellular Respiration

Cellular respiration is a three-stage process. The three stages are:

1. **Glycolysis**: Glycolysis means "glucose splitting." This is the first stage and takes place in the cell's cytoplasm. In this stage, enzymes break a glucose molecule into two smaller molecules, otherwise known as pyruvate.
During the process, two molecules of ATP are gained. It also produces some energy-storing molecules as well.
When glucose and other organic fuel molecules from fats, carbohydrates and proteins are broken down during glycolysis, the released energy is stored in ATP. The pyruvate molecules that are produced during glycolysis move into the mitochondria, where they are converted into acetyl coenzyme A.
Note that some sources treat pyruvate conversion into acetyl coenzyme A as a separate test called pyruvate oxidation.
2. **The Krebs Cycle**: The molecules produced during the glycolysis stage enter a mitochondrion's matrix where the second stage takes place. During this stage, two ATP molecules and some energy-storing molecules are produced. Oxygen is an important element here. The oxygen combines with carbon with the pyruvate molecules to form carbon dioxide as a waste product.
3. **Electron Transport**: This is the final stage. The energy stored from the previous two stages is used for the production of more ATP molecules. In all, 34 ATP molecules are produced in this stage.

Oxygen is also required for electron transport. Thus, this is another aerobic stage. The oxygen combines with the hydrogen from the molecules storing energy to form water as a waste product.

There are two types of cellular respiration. These are:

1. **Aerobic (using oxygen)**: This respiration process involves a reaction between oxygen and glucose to produce a large amount of energy. The result is ATP. Water and carbon dioxide are produced as waste products.

2. **Anaerobic (without oxygen)**: In the absence of oxygen, anaerobic respiration is not as efficient as aerobic respiration because it produces a smaller amount of energy. Lactic acid, alcohol and some other compounds are the waste products. The type of active cells determine the waste product.

In summary, aerobic respiration comes in handy for long-term energy needs while anaerobic respiration takes care of short-term energy needs.

During aerobic respiration, 38 glucose molecules of energy are produced while anaerobic respiration produces just two glucose molecules.

Another important difference between the two forms of cellular respiration is combustion status. Complete combustion occurs in aerobic respiration while anaerobic respiration results in incomplete combustion.

The Role of Mitochondria in Cellular Respiration

One of the primary objectives of food degradation is the conversion of energy in chemical bonds into ATP. ATP sources energy from chemical energy obtained during the breakdown of food molecules. It releases the captured energy to serve as the source of energy for other cellular processes.

In eukaryotic cells, the enzymes that speed up the rate of each stage of the reaction are located in the mitochondria. On the other hand, the enzymes exist as the cell membrane's component in microorganisms.

Biological Molecules

Biological molecules, also known as biomolecules, refer to any substance produced by either living organisms or cells. They come in an array of structures and sizes and perform different functions too.

There are four types of biomolecules: lipids, proteins, carbohydrates and nucleic acids.

Carbohydrates

As a product of photosynthesis, carbohydrates are the sources of energy for most living organisms.

There are three classes of carbohydrates. These are:

1. **Starch**: Starch is a complex carbohydrate. Starchy foods provide some key nutrients such as calcium, iron and B-complex vitamins. They are found in grains, vegetables and beans.
2. **Sugar**: Sugar is a colorless, sweet and water-soluble compound found in vegetables, fruits, and milk. Carbohydrates with the "-ose" suffix are sugar. Some common examples of sugar are sucrose or table sugar, fructose from fruit and milk-based lactose.
3. **Fiber**: Fiber is another member of the complex carbohydrate class. Fiber is not digested and keeps humans feeling full after eating.
As healthy carbs, fiber is present in whole grains, fruits, beans and vegetables.

Carbohydrates are sometimes classified according to their chemical structure. Hence, you can have simple and complex carbohydrates.

- **Simple Carbs**: Simple carbs contain one or two molecules of sugar. The body breaks them down quickly as a source of energy. They are commonly found in foods such as milk, fruits and milk products.
You can also find simple carbs in refined sugar, candy, soft drinks and syrups. Some common examples of simple carbohydrates are sucrose, glucose, lactose and fructose.
- **Complex Carbs**: Although this class of carbs contains sugar molecules as well, the molecules are present as long chains. Complex carbs are considered "good" and include major foods such as peas, beans, fiber-rich vegetables, whole grains and fiber-rich fruits. In addition, nutrients such as vitamins, fiber and minerals are present in complex carbs.

Carbohydrates perform several functions in the human body. Some of these functions are:

- Stimulating insulin production
- Increasing blood sugar
- Producing energy
- Aiding digestion.

Proteins

Proteins perform the following functions in the body:

- Aid growth
- Cause biochemical reactions, thanks to enzymes such as sucrose and lactase. Blood clotting, digestion, muscle contraction and energy production are some bodily functions that can't happen without these enzyme.
- Some proteins, such as hormones, serve as chemical messengers. They aid communication between tissues, cells and organs.
- They regulate acids and bases' concentrations in the blood. The pH range is between 1 and 14. The most acidic is 0 while 14 is the most alkaline. Seven is neutral.
- Proteins bolster immune health through the formation of immunoglobulin or antibodies that fight infections in the body.
- Proteins transport and store nutrients such as minerals, cholesterol, blood sugar and oxygen.

Nucleic Acids

Nucleic acids are naturally occurring chemical compounds. They are a member of the macromolecules found in viruses and cells. When they break down, nucleic acids produce sugars, phosphoric acid and some organic bases as a mixture.

These acids are responsible for directing protein synthesis and carry information within a cell.

Nucleic acids are classified into RNA and DNA.

DNA makes up the genetic material in most viruses and all living organisms, making it life's master blueprint. On the other hand, RNA is the master blueprint for some viruses although they are present in all living cells. Its contributions include protein formation.

Nucleic acids perform several functions that are determined by how genetic information is expressed and stored.

DNA is the storage cellular molecule for the information cells need to function. It is present in the nucleus of human cells and where it is organized into chromosomes. It stores the "programmatic instructions" without which cellular activities are impossible.

The major components of DNA are four nitrogenous bases and a phosphate-deoxyribose sugar. The bases are guanine (G), thymine (T), adenine (A) and cytosine (C). Deoxyribose is a five-carbon sugar with a double-stranded structure.

On the other hand, RNA supports protein synthesis. The genetic code contains some pieces of information that are passed to the RNA from the DNA, and eventually to the protein.

RNA components include the four nitrogenous bases Guanine (G), Uracil (U), Adenine (A) and Cytosine (C). Ribose is RNA's five-carbon sugar and has a single-stranded structure.

Lipids

Lipids are organic compounds with carbon, hydrogen and oxygen atoms as the major components. They are nonpolar molecules and are insoluble in water, but soluble in nonpolar solvents such as benzene, carbon tetrachloride, hexane, diethyl ether, gasoline and methylene chloride.

Lipids are generally found in whole milk, oil, fried foods, butter, cheese and some red meats.

Types of Lipids

Lipids are classified into simple lipids and complex lipids.

Simple lipids are primarily various alcohols and esters, members of the fatty acids group. Oils are liquid fats.

Complex lipids are esters with a fatty acid and alcohol. Some notable examples are carbohydrates, amino lipids and sulfolipids.

Steroid hormone, a well-known lipid, passes chemicals between tissues, cells and organs.

Genetics

Genetics is a branch of biology that deals with the study of genes. It also focuses on heredity in organisms and genetic variation.

Genes are responsible for the transfer of traits from parents down to their offspring. The study of genetics' primary objective is identifying these inherited traits and how they are passed down from one generation to another.

For instance, some traits such as height, eye color and hair color can be transferred from parents to children. Others traits include resistance to diseases and blood types.

Organisms read the information contained in genes through their genetic code. It is noteworthy that a gene may carry non-identical information between an organism and another. Thus, when a gene is copied, the result may be different from the copied information or instructions.

When a gene is copied, each unique form is known as an allele. An allele determines how each instruction is processed. Thus, different alleles from a single gene may produce different results. This may explain why a woman with black hair may give birth to a daughter with a different hair color.

How Do Genes Work?

Within your genes are pieces of information that determine your appearance and your entire being. Whether you are short or tall, slim or chubby, you inherited these traits from your parents, thanks to the genes.

Each of the genes is saddled with a special responsibility. DNA spells out instructions for protein-making in the cell. The instructions are used by the proteins to build everything in your body. Your hair, bones, teeth, blood and muscles are made up of proteins. Each of your genes contains a recipe for making a specific protein.

The importance of protein in your body is highlighted by the fact the human body is made of proteins. A dry cell is made up of 50% of one form of protein or another. From circulation to digestion, communication between cells to immunity, proteins are responsible for them. Your body can perform these functions and more, thanks to the over 100,000 different forms of protein present in your body.

According to scientists, humans have some 25,000 different genes. There are genes for controlling eye color, genes that support protein metabolism and a wide range of genes for various functions in the body.

Each gene comes in pairs and each parent has two copies of their respective genes. Each parent contributes a copy of their genes to make up yours. Thus, you may inherit some traits from each of your parents.

This isn't unique to humans. All animals also have genes they inherit from their parents.

Genetic Disorders

Genetics are not all about transferring traits from parents to children. Some disorders can also be transferred from parents to their children through the genes. Some of these genetic disorders are:

Albinism

Albinism is a genetic condition that is characterized by little or no melanin pigment in a person's hair, skin and eyes. It is a common genetic disorder that cuts across all races and ethnic groups.

Although the parents who have these genes may not experience the impact of the genetic disorder, they may pass it to their offspring.

Albinism is classified into two groups:

- **Oculocutaneous albinism**: This type of albinism affects a person's skin, hair and eyes.
- **Ocular albinism**: In this type of albinism, only the eyes are affected while the person's skin and hair color are fairly normal.

Cystic Fibrosis

This is a chronic genetic disorder that is associated with the production of thick and sticky mucus. The mucus, by virtue of its thickness, inhibits the digestive, respiratory and reproductive systems.

The disorder can't be passed to children if only one parent carries it. If your family has a history of cystic fibrosis, it is advisable that you contact a gene expert for blood tests to determine whether you carry the cystic fibrosis gene or not.

Down Syndrome

Each individual's cell contains 23 pairs of chromosomes. However, people with Down Syndrome have three pairs of the 21st chromosome. This anomaly triggers this genetic disorder.

People with the genetic disorder display a distinct appearance from other people. Someone with the disorder is at a higher risk of developing other conditions, including sight or hearing impairments. Heart defects, gut defects and hypothyroidism are common in people with Down Syndrome. They also sometimes have learning difficulties.

Research by the Centers for Disease Control and Prevention (CDC) shows that approximately one out of every 700 US babies will have Down Syndrome. A woman's chances of giving birth to a child with Down Syndrome increase with age.

Thalassemia

This hereditary genetic condition hampers an individual's ability to produce hemoglobin naturally. The condition hinders oxygen flow so that the body won't get the sufficient oxygen it needs.

Thalassemia is common among people of Northern African, Chinese, Southeast Asian, Mediterranean and Middle Eastern descent.

This disorder is usually associated with severe anemia. The solution to this disorder may include chelation therapy or blood transfusion.

Sickle Cell Anemia

This is a lifelong genetic condition. It is another genetic disorder that can't be passed to a child by a single parent.

Sickle cell anemia alters the general condition of the red blood cells, first by changing their shape from donut to sickle. The new shape causes the clumping together of the cells, so they become caught in blood vessels. This triggers serious complications and severe pain. It is not uncommon for people with sickle cell anemia to develop serious health issues such as organ damage, infections and acute respiratory syndrome.

Although sickle cell anemia mortality rate used to be very high, medical advances have improved patients' life span. People now have access to a variety of treatment options and vaccines that can prolong their lives.

Chapter Six: Chemistry

This chapter covers some chemistry topics that will be tested in the entrance examination. Some of these topics are:

Atoms and Molecules

Atoms are the simplest form of any non-living matter. (As discussed in the previous section, the basic building block of living matter is referred to as a cell.) They are the basic building block on which other things are built. Everything around you, from your mobile device to your personal computer, your bed and TV, is made up of atoms.

Atoms are made up of three *sub-atomic particles*. These are called protons, neutrons and electrons. Protons are positively charged while electrons are negatively charged. Neutrons have no charge.

Both neutrons and protons reside inside an atom's nucleus while electrons revolve around it. Hence, the nucleus of an atom is positively charged due to the presence of the positively charged protons.

Each element has an atomic number which denotes the number of protons in the element's nucleus. The atomic number is represented by Z.

A single atom is made up of one of the 118 elements in the periodic table, such as gold, carbon, hydrogen, oxygen or iron.

Molecules

When atoms bond together, they form a molecule. A molecule is the smallest unit of a compound, containing all the chemical properties of the specific compound in question. The atoms in a molecule are combined together through chemical bonds formed when atoms share or exchange electrons with each other.

Sometimes, the atoms of some elements such as chlorine and oxygen form molecules by bonding with other atoms. On the other hand, the atoms of some elements such as argon and neon don't bond easily with other atoms.

The differences in molecules are determined by their complexities and sizes. For instance, helium is a simple element with a single atom molecule. Some molecules such as O_2 consist of two atoms of an element in order to be stable, and O_3 (ozone) consists of three oxygen atoms.

Some other familiar molecules are carbon dioxide (CO_2), which consists of two oxygen atoms bonded with one carbon atom, and water (H_2O), which consists of two hydrogen atoms and one oxygen atom. The most commonly found oxygen molecule in the earth's atmosphere is oxygen.

An element consists of only one type of atom that cannot be broken further into simpler matter by either chemical or physical means. Elements can exist as molecules such as nitrogen, or as atoms, such as argon.

Molecules are made up of two or more atoms of different elements or the same element. The atoms are chemically bound together.

Compounds are made up of atoms of different elements that are bound together. Compounds can only be broken into simpler elements by chemical means.

Mixtures are made up of two or more different compounds or elements. However, unlike compounds, mixtures are physically intermingled. Thus, they can easily be separated into their different components. Most often, mixtures exhibit the major properties of their respective components.

Matter

Matter can be defined as *anything that occupies space and has a mass*. Nearly everything around us is part of matter.

The quantity of matter in an object is its mass. Regardless of the location of an object, its mass remains the same. A mole is the basic S.I. unit of mass but mass is measured in kilograms for practical purposes.

Mass is made up of molecules, atoms and ions.

Matter is usually identified by its characteristics or properties. For instance, iron can rust and be magnetized.

The properties of matters are classified into two types:

1. **Physical properties**: The physical properties of matter refer to features that directly impact physical changes. Examples include boiling point, hardness, melting point, crystalline form, density and malleability.
2. **Chemical properties:** Chemical properties are associated with the transformation that matter undergoes to form a new substance. Chemical properties include rusting.

Matter can undergo changes that are either permanent and irreversible (chemical changes) or temporary (physical changes.)

In physical changes, there is no formation of new substances. Physical changes don't involve significant heat changes, barring latent heat changes that are common during fusion, dissolution, vaporization and other changes of state. On the other hand, in chemical changes, new substances are usually formed. Heat change is a common feature of chemical changes.

Examples of chemical changes are the dissolution of limestone or metals in water, slaking of lime, rusting of iron, changes in electrochemical cells, decay or fermentation of substances.

Physical changes include liquefaction of gases, freezing, vaporization, sublimation and demagnetization/magnetization of iron.

Mixtures separated through fractional distillation, evaporation, sublimation, distillation and crystallization are other examples of physical changes.

Elements

An element is a substance that can't be broken down into simpler units by regular chemical processes. There are over 100 elements that can be found in the air, in the earth's crust and in the sea.

Ninety of the 109 elements occur naturally, while the rest are produced artificially. These elements are grouped into the periodic table.

The elements in the periodic table are classified into seven groups:

- **Transition metals**: Transition metals occupy Groups 2 and 3 of the periodic table. These elements display similar attributes. They are all metals and unsurprisingly, display metallic properties such as high melting points and high tensile strength. Some of the transition metals such as nickel and manganese are used as industrial catalysts while copper, iron and silver have commercial value.
- **Reactive metals**: Reactive metals have a very strong oxidization tendency. The periodic table shows different elements and their groups. Towards its bottom left corner are some highly reactive metals. Notable members of the group are sodium, lithium, potassium, cesium, rubidium, francium and barium.
- **Non-metals**: The periodic table also contains some non-metals. These are naturally occurring materials that don't produce electricity or heat. Structurally, they are brittle and thus can't be molded, rolled, pressed or extruded. Some non-metallic members of the periodic table are phosphorus, oxygen, nitrogen, selenium, carbon, sulfur and arsenic. These elements accept electrons to form negative ions and usually have between

four and seven electrons. They also lack all the attributes of a metal. Thus, they are good insulators of electricity and heat. Most non-metals are gasses while a handful are liquid.

- **Lanthanides**: These elements are found in the sixth group of the periodic table. The 15 members of this group include lanthanum, samarium, cerium, erbium, lutetium and others. They are otherwise known as rare-earth elements.

- **Actinides**: The actinides share some similarities with the lanthanides. Occupying the seventh group are the likes of uranium and actinium. It is noteworthy that actinides don't occur naturally but are products of nuclear reactions. Thus, they are known as artificial elements. Due to their artificial nature, such elements can disintegrate easily because they are quite unstable. Typical examples are curium and plutonium.
There are 14 members of this group, starting from atomic number 90 to 103.

- **Pure metals**: Pure metals don't contain atoms of multiple metallic elements. Rather, they contain atoms of a single type of metal.
They have some attractive and useful properties. They are good electricity conductors, although most of them are very malleable and soft.

- **Noble gases**: Noble gases can be found in group 18 of the periodic table. They are made up of chemical elements that exhibit some similar properties under standard conditions. They are usually colorless, odorless and have single atoms.
Noble gases are only active when subjected to some extreme conditions. Their high level of inertness contributes to their usefulness in applications with zero room for reactions because they are the most stable elements in the periodic table.
In nature, there are six noble gases: argon, helium, krypton, neon, radon and xenon. Their interatomic force is pretty low. That is the rationale behind their low boiling and melting points.

Note that the periodic table's horizontal row is called a period while the vertical column is called a group. The table has seven periods and 18 groups.

Elements of the same period share the same energy level at the electron ground state. As you move across a period from left to right, elements gradually shift form metallic to non-metallic properties.

Elements in any of the 18 groups also share similar properties. Within a group, all the elements have the same electron number in their atoms' outermost electron shell. The numbering of a group starts from the left and gradually moves to the right. It starts from 1 and ends with 18.

Due to the similarities in the properties of the lanthanides and actinides, they are set apart from other elements of the table.

In total, there are 118 elements in the periodic table with distinct properties that distinguish one group from another.

Chemical Reactions

A chemical reaction is a process by which one or more substances, known as reactants, are converted into different substances, or products. The substances can be compounds or chemical elements.

Chemical reactions can take different forms such as:

1. **Decomposition:** A decomposition reaction occurs when a single reactant produces two or more products. Thus, the reactant doesn't react with other reactant but undergoes the chemical reaction on its own to produce the products.
Decomposition takes the form AB –> A + B. It is otherwise known as a chemical breakdown or analysis reaction.
A common example of decomposition is water. It can undergo electrolysis separation into oxygen and water, its components. $2H_2O$ –> $2H_2 + O_2$
2. **Synthesis:** In a synthesis reaction, two or more substances combine together to form a single product. Simpler elements, compounds or radicals can undergo synthesis to form a complex compound.
During the reaction, light and heat are released as energy, making synthesis reactions exothermic.
If you reverse the decomposition reaction in the previous example, you get a synthesis reaction because oxygen and hydrogen can undergo synthesis to form water.
3. **Combustion:** This is a redox reaction that involves the combination of an oxidizer and a combustible material. The product is usually oxidized while heat is generated during the reaction.
Combustion reactions are usually between a combustible material and oxygen to produce water and carbon dioxide.
4. **Redox:** A redox (oxidation-reduction) reaction is a chemical reaction where electrons are transferred between the reactants. Thus, an atom, a molecule or an ion will experience a change in oxidation number as they gain or lose an electron during the reaction. When a reactant loses electron, the other reactant gains it to balance the equation. Oxidation refers to electron loss while electron gain is a reduction.
Oxidation and reduction can also be defined in terms of oxygen or hydrogen transfer. Loss of oxygen is oxidation while reduction involves oxygen loss. Similarly, a reactant is oxidized when it loses hydrogen while hydrogen gain is a reduction.
Redox reaction occurs when hydrogen fluoride is formed. The hydrogen loses two electrons to oxidation.
Some typical daily examples of redox reactions are decay, corrosion, combustion, rust, photosynthesis and photography.
Some biological process such as cellular respiration are also redox reactions.
Redox reactions have a wide range of applications that include electroplating, and the production of cleaning products.

5. **Acid-Base:** This chemical reaction occurs between an acid and a base. In the reaction, an acid releases a proton which a base accepts.

Acids are chemical compounds in a water solution and release hydrogen ions. They also donate hydrogen ions or protons while accepting electrons. Some common acids include hydrochloric acid (HCL), sulfuric acid (H_2SO_4) and nitric acid (HNO_3).

Bases are substances that, in an aqueous solution, can neutralize the properties of acids and turn blue litmus paper red. Some typical examples of bases are calcium hydroxide ($CA(OH)_2$) or limewater; magnesium hydroxide ($Mg(OH)_2$) or milk of magnesia; sodium hydroxide (NaOH) or caustic soda; and ammonium hydroxide (NH_4OH) or ammonia water. Some soaps, bleaches, cleaning agents and toothpastes are common examples of bases. Most hydroxides and oxides of metals fall into this category.

Note that the acid-base reaction is also commonly known as a *neutralization reaction*.

6. **Single Replacement:** A single replacement reaction is said to occur during the replacement of an element with another in a compound. The general equation for a single replacement reaction is A + BC –> B + AC. In most cases, this reaction occurs if B is less reactive than A as this leads to a stable product. While BC is the original compound, A is the more reactive element. This makes it possible for A to replace B and form AC, a compound. In the process, the less reactive B is released.

Some notable examples of single replacement reactions are the reaction between hydrochloric acid and magnesium, with hydrogen and magnesium chloride as a product or the formation of potassium sulfate and hydrogen gas as a result of the reaction between potassium and sulfuric acid.

7. **Double Replacement:** This is a chemical reaction that involves ions exchange between two ionic compounds. The result is usually two new ionic compounds. The general equation is AB + CD –> AD + CB. The two reactant compounds are AB and CD while the reaction produces AD and CB. A simple example of a double replacement reaction is the reaction between sodium chloride and silver fluoride, represented by the equation NaCl + AgF –> NaF + AgCl.

Nuclear Chemistry

The interaction between electrons around the nucleus of an atom triggers traditional chemical reactions. However, Nobel Prize-winning chemist Marie Curie discovered a relationship between radiation and the amount of existing radioactive element. This led to the theory that atoms are the custodians of radiation. This new finding was in opposition to the previous belief that the chemical property of a compound was responsible for radiation.

Nuclear Reactions and Radiation

In 1902, Frederick Soddy discovered that nuclear reactions occur as a result of changes in the particles in the nucleus of an atom. The changes also affect the atom itself.

Nuclear reactions change an element into another element or a different isotope.

Nuclear changes and radiation are classified into three types. These are:

1. Alpha Radiation

Denoted by the alpha sign (α), alpha radiation is the emission of an alpha particle from the nucleus of an atom. This particle contains two neutrons and two protons. When an atom emits an alpha particle, the mass of the atom decreases by four units due to the loss of two neutrons and two protons. Its atomic number loses two units as well.

This is referred to as the transmutation of an element into a smaller element. A typical example is the decay of uranium, resulting in the emission of an alpha particle. The final result is the element thorium (Th).

Some common properties of alpha radiation are:

- It travels a short distance in the air
- Inhaling or swallowing alpha-emitting materials is hazardous to human health
- The radiation isn't penetrating and instruments can't detect it through dust, a thin layer of water or any other material
- Alpha radiation typically can't penetrate human skin

Radon, radium, thorium and uranium are examples of substances that emit alpha radiation.

2. Beta Radiation

Denoted by the β symbol, in this radiation type, a neutron is transmuted into an electron and a proton, leading to the emission of the electron residing in the nucleus of the atom.

An atom won't experience a change in mass after emitting a β particle, thanks to the zero changes in the number of nuclear particles. Nevertheless, a unit will be added to the atomic number due to the transmutation of the neutron into an extra proton. Carbon-14 decay is an example of beta radiation, leading to the formation of nitrogen.

Beta radiation has the following characteristics:

- If consumed, contaminants emitting beta radiation are potentially harmful

- This radiation travels more than alpha radiation in the air
- While it is not as penetrating as gamma radiation, beta radiation is more penetrating than alpha radiation
- Beta radiation can penetrate skin and cause injury
- Clothing can serve as a barrier to beta radiation

The following are beta-emitting elements: Tritium, strontium-90, sulfure-35 and carbon-14.

3. Gamma Radiation

This is represented by the γ symbol. Electromagnetic energy is emitted from the nucleus of an atom. Particles are not emitted and thus, gamma radiation isn't responsible for the transmutation of atoms. Nevertheless, this radiation can be emitted during alpha or beta radioactive decay.
A common example of this radiation type is the emission of X-rays when cobalt-60 undergoes beta decay.

Some characteristics of gamma radiation include:

- Also known as penetrating radiation, it can penetrate a wide range of materials
- Gamma radiation includes electromagnetic radiation such as radio waves, visible light and ultraviolet light
- Dense materials, far thicker than clothing, are required to shield against this radiation.

Some notable gamma emitters include cobalt-60, iodine-131, technetium-99m and radium-226.

Nuclear Reactions

Radioactive decay is a natural phenomenon for many elements. Nevertheless, artificial stimulation of nuclear reactions is not unheard of.

Nuclear reactions are divided into two groups. These are:

- **Nuclear fission:** During nuclear fission, the nucleus of an atom splits into two smaller atoms. The fission is the result of a neutron slamming into a larger atom. This forces the atom to spill into two, each smaller than the original atom.
Some neutrons are also released during the splitting. They have the potential to kickstart a chain reaction while releasing a huge amount of energy in the process.

Plutonium and uranium are common materials for fission reactions, thanks to the ease of initiating and controlling the reaction.

During fission, the energy released turns water into steam. The steam produces the power to spin a turbine, a process that results in the production of carbon-free electricity.

- **Nuclear fusion:** Nuclear fusion is the combination of two atoms to form a bigger and heavier atom. A typical example is when two hydrogen atoms slam into each other and form a helium atom.

Nuclear fusion produces a larger amount of energy than fission. The process creates a tremendous amount of energy. Nuclear fusion powers the sun.

Some differences between nuclear fission and nuclear fusion:

- While fission involves the splitting of an atom into smaller ones, fusion involves the fusing together of two lighter atoms into a bigger one
- Fission is not a natural reaction, while fusion is
- Fusion occurs in the sun and other stars
- Highly radioactive particles are the products of fission while fusion produces few radioactive particles
- High-speed neutrons and substantive mass are required for fission while fusion only requires a high-temperature environment and high density
- A fission reaction requires little energy while fusion requires extremely high energy

Chemical Bonds

Atoms are generally arranged in stable patterns that enable them to fill or complete their outermost electron orbits. However, an atom can't form a stable pattern on its own. Rather, it can only achieve that by joining other atoms.

Atoms form bonds in a couple of ways. Consider the following bonding types and their properties.

Ionic Bonds

Electron transfer is the principle behind this bonding type. As one atom loses an electron, another one gains the lost electron. Thus, one of the ions will carry a negative charge (known as an anion) while the other one becomes a positive charge carrier (a cation). The attraction that results from the negative charges on the two atoms results in a form of bonding that enables the atoms to form a molecule.

The most common example of ionic bonding is the bonding between sodium ion and chlorine ions to form NaCl. Others are $CaCl_2$, K_2O, MgO and NaBr.

Covalent Bonding

Unlike in ionic bonding where electron transfer forms the foundation for the bond, covalent bonds are formed through the sharing of outer shell (valence) electrons. These atoms arrange themselves in a manner that supports stability.

A typical example of this bonding is in the hydrogen molecule (H_2) formed by the bonding of two hydrogen atoms. Other examples are ammonia (NH_3), water (H_2O), methane (CH_4), carbon dioxide (CO_2), ethanol (CH_3CH_2OH) and phosphorus trichloride (PCl_3).

Covalent bonds are classified into polar covalent, coordinate covalent and nonpolar covalent.

- **Polar covalent**: This type of covalent bond exists between two nonmetals with different electronegativity. The electron density between them is shared unequally and the majority will go towards the electronegative element, making charge separation possible in the atom.
- **Nonpolar covalent**: If two atoms share similar electronegativities, they will form a nonpolar covalent bond. This enables density sharing between the atoms.
- **Coordinate covalent**: Transition metals form this type of covalent bond. Otherwise known as coordinate bonds or dative bonds, coordinate bonds take electrons from the two atoms. It is a common bonding type between ligands and metal ions, and is commonly referred to as a two-electron, two-center form of covalent bond.

Hydrogen Bonding

Two adjacent water molecules are polarized. Thus, they can combine together to form a hydrogen bond. The hydrogen atom (electronegative) of one of the water molecules becomes attracted electrostatically to the oxygen atom (electropositive) of the adjacent H_2O molecule.

Hydrogen bonds can't boast the same level of strength as a covalent bond. Nevertheless, they are strong enough to affect water structure and are responsible for properties such as specific heat, high surface tension and heat of vaporization, among others.

Biochemistry

Biochemistry is a branch of science that is primarily concerned with the chemistry of life. It is also considered the study of the chemical processes and substances that occur not only in animals, but in plants and microorganisms. The changes that these plants, animals and microorganisms undergo during their life and development are studied in biochemistry.

Biochemistry studies some chemical processes such as:

- Chemical changes in diseases
- Genetics
- Drug action
- Nutrition
- Medicine.

Biochemistry is a subdiscipline of chemistry and biology.

It can be divided into enzymology, structural biology and metabolism. Through these three disciplines, it explains the living processes, helping people with the study of organs, tissues and organism structures.

Biochemistry has a wide range of applications. It can be used for:

- Studying the properties of biological molecules
- Learning about the biological processes taking place in organisms and cells
- Producing useful products such as gene therapy, artificial sweetener and biological machinery
- Understanding the chemical processes in conditions such as hypercholesterolemia, rickets, kidney dysfunction, diabetes and dental fluorosis.

Reaction Rates: Equilibrium and Reversibility

One of the things that determines the result of a reaction is the speed at which the reaction takes place.

Chemical reactions are affected by several factors. These are:

- Temperature

The existing temperature during the reaction will go a long way toward determining the speed of the reaction. The rate of a chemical reaction is directly proportional to temperature. Thus, as the temperature increases, the rate of reaction increases.

The increased temperature causes the molecules of the reactants to collide with each other at a faster rate. This increases the energy generated by the reaction. The two molecules need enough energy to react and increasing the temperature does just that. As the temperature rises, the energy levels of the reactant molecules increase. The molecules move faster and collide more frequently than when the temperature is low.

- Concentration

The concentration of the reactants also has a huge impact on the rate of reaction. As the concentration increases, the two reactants collide with increased frequency of collisions. Higher concentrations increase collision frequency and thus increase the reaction rate.

- Catalysts

Catalysts are generally known for their ability to speed up the rate of a chemical reaction. A catalyst also lowers the activation energy required for a reaction to occur.

In the following examples, some catalysts are needed to increase the reaction rates considerably:

- Decomposition of hydrogen peroxide requires manganese oxide as a catalyst
- Manufacturing ammonia using the Haber Process requires iron as a catalyst
- Hydrogenation of a C=C double bond requires nickel as a catalyst
- Nitration of benzene requires concentrated sulfuric acid as a catalyst
- Conversion of SO_2 into SO_3 for sulfuric acid production during the Contact Process requires vanadium oxide as a catalyst.

Note that while a catalyst provides an alternative route for a reaction to take place at a faster rate, it doesn't lower the activation energy.

- Physical State

The physical state of the reactants is another important factor that affects a chemical reaction. If the molecules of the reactants are a heterogeneous mixture, that is in different phases, the rate of reaction will be adversely affected by the surface areas in contact.

For instance, if solid and gaseous substances are mixed, the reaction will take place between the gaseous substance and the molecules on the surface of the metal because that's the only part that can collide and react with the gas. However, once the surface area of the metal is increased by reducing its size, or pounding it until it becomes flat, the reaction rate will increase considerably.

- Pressure

The molecules or atoms in a gas are not tightly connected but are spread out. Thus, a chemical reaction can't occur. Their atoms or molecules must collide before a reaction can occur. Thus, increasing the pressure between the atoms or molecules will decrease the space between them and squeeze them together. That single act will increase the collision frequency between the molecules and increase the reaction rate.

A very effective way to increase the pressure is to reduce the volume of the vessel used for the reaction.

- Surface area

Surface area is especially important in a reaction between a liquid and a solid. The solid's surface area will have a profound impact on the reaction rate. This is because the reactants can only collide with each other at the interface of the liquid and the gas, which is the solid's surface. Thus, all the solid molecules in the reaction are trapped and can't react. To make them reactive, the surface area of the solid must be increased. The increased surface area will ultimately give more solid molecules access to the liquid, an action that will eventually speed up the reaction rate.

Equilibrium

Some erroneously believe that chemical reactions are irreversible. This not always true. Reversible reactions can reach equilibrium under certain conditions.

When a reversible reaction is taking place in a closed system, that is, a system where no substances are added or lost during the reaction, only the reactants will exist at the beginning of the reaction. However, once the reaction kicks off, the amount of the reactants will gradually but steadily decrease while the amount of the products will increase correspondingly.

If the reaction is non-reversible, the reaction will continue until all the reactants are used up. On the other hand, in a reversible reaction, the product can also take over and start the production of the reactants again.

When the reaction continues for a period of time, a reversible reaction can reach equilibrium, especially in a closed system. Thus, the forward reaction (the reaction of the reactants to produce the products) and the backward reaction (the reaction of the product to produce more reactants) will occur simultaneously. Hence, the amount of the products and the amount of the reactants will remain constant, regardless of the ongoing reactions.

Once equilibrium is reached, the amounts of the products and the reactants may be the same initially. However, the conditions may be adjusted to change the proportions of both the products and the reactants in the equilibrium, going by Le Chatelier's Principle.

The principle states that when the conditions of a reaction at equilibrium are changed, the equilibrium will respond to balance the change. For instance, if the temperature of the equilibrium reaction is increased, the reaction will respond in a way to decrease the temperature.

If the concentration of the reactant is increased, the reaction will respond to decrease the concentration. Thus, a chemical reaction in equilibrium will always respond to counter the effect of changes made to it.

Changes in Pressure

A change in pressure will force the reaction to attempt equilibrium. In the process, the moles of gas created may increase or decrease. For instance, when the pressure of a system is increased or the volume is decreased, this will cause a shift in equilibrium to favor the side that uses fewer moles of gas in the reaction. An increase in the volume of a system or a decrease in the pressure will favor the production of more moles of gas.

Let's consider a reaction involving two gas molecules of the reactant needed to produce one molecule of the product. In this case, increasing the pressure will cause a shift in equilibrium from left to right.

Conversely, a decrease in pressure will cause a shift in equilibrium from right to the left. This will cause an increased production of more gaseous molecules.

Changes in Temperature

In equilibrium reactions, two opposing reactions are involved. If the forward reaction is exothermic, that is, emits heat, the reverse reaction will be endothermic, relying on heat absorption.

Thus, it is imperative that you understand whether you are dealing with an exothermic or an endothermic reaction.

Let's consider an example of an exothermic reaction that is in equilibrium at 200°C. When the temperature of this reaction is increased to 400°C, the backward reaction will be favored because it is an endothermic reaction that thrives on heat absorption.

However, if you decrease the temperature to 1500°C, the equilibrium will face the forward reaction that thrives on heat evolution. This will lead to an increase in production of the product. Thus, more heat will develop as the reaction achieves equilibrium.

Effects of Concentration Changes

Le Chatelier's Principle also indicates that a change in the concentration of the reactants or products will shift the equilibrium in a direction that will reduce the changes introduced into the concentration.

When the concentration is increased by the addition of one of the reactants, the equilibrium will attempt to balance the concentration by shifting from left to right. To achieve the equilibrium, reactant A, whose concentration has been increased, will work with reactant B to ensure the reestablishment of the equilibrium. If the concentration of the product is increased, the equilibrium's shift will naturally be from right to left.

A decrease in concentration can also have a huge impact on the equilibrium. A decrease in the concentration of reactant A will shift the equilibrium from right to left. The goal is to minimize the potential impact of the decrease in concentration. On the other hand, if the concentration of product C is decreased, the equilibrium will shift in the opposite direction: from left to right.

In either case, the reaction will shift the equilibrium in a way to minimize the effect of a change in the concentration. This may favor the reactants or the products, depending on the change introduced into the concentration.

Addition of a Catalyst

A catalyst can be added to a reaction in equilibrium. However, the catalyst will have zero effect on the equilibrium; it won't shift its position. Instead, the catalyst will ensure that the system reaches equilibrium faster than it would ordinarily have achieved without the introduction of the catalyst.

Addition of an Inert Gas

When you add an inert gas such as krypton, neon or argon to a system, the inert gas won't react with the reactants or the products. Thus, the inert gas has zero effect on equilibrium.

In summary, an equilibrium reaction will react to external changes as shown below:

- When the concentration of the reactants is increased, the equilibrium will shift from left to right
- When the concentration of the products is increased, the equilibrium will shift from right to left

- Decreasing the reactants' concentration will cause a shift in equilibrium from right to left
- Decreasing the products' concentration will trigger an equilibrium shift from left to right
- Increasing the pressure will shift the equilibrium to support the formation of fewer gas molecules
- A pressure decrease will shift the equilibrium to favor the formation of gas molecules
- When the number of molecules of the reactants and products is the same, a pressure change won't have any impact on the reaction
- When an inert gas is added to any reaction, it will have zero impact on the equilibrium
- A temperature increase shifts the equilibrium to favor an endothermic reaction
- A temperature decrease shifts the equilibrium to favor an exothermic reaction
- A catalyst won't shift the position of an equilibrium body, although it will speed up the reaction and enable it to achieve equilibrium faster.

Types of Equilibrium

Equilibrium is classified into three types. These are:

Stable

A body is said to have achieved stable equilibrium if it doesn't lose its original position permanently when it is displaced from the position.

A body in stable equilibrium has the lowest center of gravity. When the body is tilted, the center of gravity rises but returns to its stable form when it is set free. Once the center of gravity still acts through the body's base, it will always return to its original position, proof of its stability.

Consider some examples of bodies in stable equilibrium:

1. A book lying on a table
2. A chair lying on the ground
3. A bottle sitting on its base.

Neutral

A system is considered to be in neutral equilibrium if any form of displacement doesn't affect its equilibrium position.

Unstable

A body is said to be in neutral equilibrium if a shift in its position causes it to leave its original position permanently. The slightest tilt may move such a body from its natural position permanently.

When a body is in unstable equilibrium, its center of gravity is said to be at the highest position. When the body is toppled over, there is a change in its center of gravity as it gradually reduces until it gets to its lowest position.

Some examples of bodies in unstable equilibrium are:

1. A pencil standing on its point
2. A stick made to stand vertically.

Conditions for Equilibrium

A body or object must satisfy some conditions before it can be considered to be in equilibrium. The major conditions are:

1. The sum of the resultant force action on the body is zero. In other words, the net force must be equal to zero.

Some examples of bodies that meet this condition are:

a. A book lying on the ground or on a table
b. A picture hanging on a wall.

2. The sum of the moments acting on a body must also be zero. That implies that the net torque must be zero.

Two examples of bodies that meet this condition are:

a. Children using the seesaw
b. The force applied to control the steering of a vehicle.

Characteristics of Chemical Equilibrium

A system in equilibrium has the following characteristics:

1. At equilibrium, the forward and reverse reactions have the same reaction rates
2. At equilibrium, all the reactants and products are present
3. The position of a body at equilibrium is not affected by the presence of a catalyst
4. The concentrations of both the products and the reactants reach constant values that are referred to as equilibrium concentrations.

Chapter Seven: Anatomy and Physiology

Anatomy and physiology are two distinct biology subsets. Anatomy can be defined as the study of animal structure while physiology focuses on animal functions.

This section will focus on the following systems:

- Circulatory System
- Nervous System
- Digestive System
- Muscular System
- Skeletal System
- Respiratory System
- Urinary System
- Immune System

Circulatory System

The circulatory system consists of blood vessels, blood and the heart. Its primary function is to supply the tissues in the body with basic nutrients and oxygen. It also removes waste products as well as transports hormones within the body.

The blood vessels serve as channels for pumping blood throughout the body from the heart. The arteries are responsible for transporting blood into capillaries from the heart. They provide nutrients such as oxygen to cells and tissues.

It takes about a minute for blood to leave the heart, circulate through the body and return to the heart.

Once the oxygen is removed, the blood is transported back to the lungs where it is reoxygenated before its eventual return to the heart through the arteries.

The system is a combination of three systems working together to achieve a common goal. These are the lungs, the heart and the system consisting of the arteries, portal vessels, coronary and veins.

An average adult human has about 4.7 to 5.6 liters, or five to six quarts of blood. Blood's major components are red blood cells, plasma, platelets and white blood cells.

The heart is located behind the breastbone, slightly to the left. The muscular organ pumps blood through veins and arteries through its four chambers.

An important part of the circulatory system is systemic circulation. Here, the arteries, veins and blood vessels form a network that is responsible for transporting oxygenated blood to the heart. Systemic circulation also provides the body's cells with the needed nutrients and oxygen and returns the blood back to the heart after it has been deoxygenated.

Arteries carry only oxygenated blood through the body from the heart. Veins carry deoxygenated blood.

Nervous System

The nervous system is made up of special cells (neurons) and complex nerves for the transmission of signals between the body parts.

The nervous system consists of two components. These are the peripheral nervous system and the central nervous system.

In the central nervous system are the spinal cord, the brain and the nerves. On the other hand, the ganglia, sensory neurons and the nerves are components of the peripheral nervous system. The nerves connect to the central nervous system and to one another.

There are two subdivisions of the nervous system: the autonomic or involuntary and the somatic or voluntary.

The somatic system connects the spinal cord and the brain with the sensory receptors and muscles through the nerves. It also relays responses to the skeletal muscles when necessary. Furthermore, it relays information it gets from the sense organs, skin and muscles to the central nervous system.

On the other hand, the autonomic nervous system regulates body processes such as breathing rate, blood pressure and involuntary bodily responses. When internal organs need information, the autonomic nervous system takes it upon itself to relay such information to them.

Disorders in the nervous system can cause health problems such as:

- Multiple Sclerosis (MS): This occurs when the body's immune system attacks the lining protecting the nerves. The disease affects the spinal cord and the brain. It can also affect sensation, vision, movement, bowel control and bladder control.
- Alzheimer's Disease: A disorder that causes the degeneration of the brain's nerve cells. This gradually leads to dementia, a loss of judgment, memory and ability to function.

- Glaucoma: Glaucoma refers to eye conditions that damage the optic nerve due to excessive pressure in the eye.
- Parkinson's Disease: A brain disorder that causes tremors, usually accompanied with difficulty in coordination and movement.
- Cerebral Palsy: A disorder affecting both the nervous system and brain function. Thus, individuals with this health challenge have difficulty in learning, moving, seeing, learning and thinking.
- Epilepsy: A brain disorder that causes seizures when the electrical discharges in the brain become abnormal.

Digestive System

The digestive system is responsible for breaking down food into smaller components that the body can easily absorb. The system consists of the accessory organs of digestion and the gastrointestinal tract. The accessory organs include the pancreas, tongue, liver, salivary glands and gallbladder.

Digestion is a three-stage process. The stages are:

- **Cephalic phase**: This first stage starts with the secretion of gastric juice; the body's response to the smell, thought or sight of food. The cephalic phase includes the chemical breakdown of food by enzymes or mechanical breakdown that occurs in the mouth by chewing.
Saliva in the mouth promotes the breakdown. It contains lingual lipase and amylase, two digestive enzymes that the serous glands and salivary glands secrete. Other accessory digestive organs that aid digestion are the gall bladder, liver and pancreas. The tongue, mouth, epiglottis, salivary glands and teeth play crucial roles as well.
When you think, smell or see food, the cerebral cortex is stimulated. Through the vagus nerve, the stimulated organ sends messages to the medulla, the hypothalamus and the parasympathetic nervous system. It also sends a similar message through the gastric glands to the stomach.
When food is consumed, the stomach expands and immediately activates the stretch receptors, which in turn send a message to the medulla and through the vagus nerve back to the stomach. More gastric juice is secreted by the gastric glands in response to this stimulation.
This phase accounts for one out of every five gastric secretions associated with food consumption.
- **Gastric phase**: In this second phase, gastric activity is activated in the stomach by the swallowed food. The ingested food stretches the stomach and raises the pH of the stomach's contents to stimulate gastric activity. This triggers a chain of events that eventually cause the parietal cells to release hydrochloric acid. Parietal cells not only

lower the content's pH, but also break apart the food.

Three chemicals stimulate gastric secretion in this stage: histamine, acetylcholine and gastrin. The three trigger the secretion of hydrochloric acid by stimulating the parietal cells.

- **Intestinal phase**: When chyme, a mass of partially digested food, arrives in the duodenum, the intestinal phase is triggered in response to its arrival. This third phase ensures the moderation of gastric activities through nervous reflexes and hormones. Initially, the duodenum boosts gastric secretion, although it inhibits it later. Thus, the duodenum is stretched, leading to the enhancement of vagal reflexes that eventually stimulate the stomach. Then, the amino acids and peptides in the chyme work on the G cells present in the duodenum and stimulate them for increased gastric secretion, another cause of stomach stimulation.

The digestive system is aided and regulated by five main hormones. These are:

- **Secretin**: The duodenum houses secretin, responsible for stimulating bile secretion in the liver. This occurs as a result of sodium bicarbonate secretion in the pancreas.
- **Gastrin**: This hormone resides in the stomach, where it carries out its stimulation activities. It boosts hydrochloric and pepsinogen secretion by stimulating the gastric glands. More gastrin is stimulated when food arrives in the stomach.
- **Cholecystokinin**: CCK also resides in the duodenum, where it specifically carries out the stimulation of the pancreas to release digestive enzymes. It also keeps the gall bladder empty through the removal of the bile in it.
- **Gastric inhibitory peptide:** Another duodenum-based enzyme, it ensures that the stomach is emptied slowly by decreasing stomach churning.
- **Motilin:** This stimulates pepsin production as well as increases the number a gastrointestinal motility component: the migrating myoelectric complex.

Anatomy of the Digestive System

The digestive system is made up of the following organs:

- Mouth

The journey to the digestive system starts from the mouth. The teeth, tongue and salivary glands are the major organs that start the digestive process. Food is chopped into small pieces with the teeth before saliva moistens the pieces. This makes it easier for the tongue to push the chopped and moistened food down into the pharynx.

A tooth is made of dentin, a bone-like substance. A layer of enamel, the body's hardest substance, covers and protects each tooth. There are 32 teeth in the human mouth. These are living organisms whose primary responsibility is cutting food and grinding them into smaller pieces. It is noteworthy that teeth contain nerves and blood vessels in the pulp, like living organisms.

The mouth is surrounded by three sets of salivary glands. They produce saliva that moistens food as a prelude to digestion. Saliva is also used by the body for food lubrication as it makes its journey through the mouth down to the pharynx and the esophagus.

The tongue is a collection of pairs of muscles. These small organs are covered in a skin-like layer. The tongue has taste buds too.

Outside the tongue are papillae. These rough substances make gripping food possible as the muscles in the tongue move the food. The tongue also supports swallowing by pushing food towards the throat.

- Stomach

To the left of the abdominal cavity is this muscular sac. It is as big as two fists. It contains some digestive enzymes and hydrochloric acid. It also stores food to allow the body enough time to properly digest large meals.

- Esophagus

This is a muscular tube in the body about eight inches long. It connects the stomach and pharynx together. It serves as the passageway for swallowed drinks and food to travel from the pharynx to the stomach. To pass food to the stomach, the muscles in the esophagus contract, a process known as peristalsis.

Above the esophagus is the upper esophageal sphincter and the lower esophageal sphincter is underneath, some distance above the stomach. The sphincters relax once food is swallowed to allow the food to enter the stomach. However, when they are not in use, they contract and prevent food and stomach from flowing back to the esophagus.

- Small intestine

The small intestine is about 10 feet long and one inch in diameter. It is tubular and long and an important component of the lower gastrointestinal tract. It occupies the larger part of the abdominal cavity.

Inside the coiled, hose-like tube are many folds and ridges. These folds serve important functions such as maximizing nutrients' absorption and food digestion. Approximately 90% of the nutrients in food are extracted by the small intestine before the food leaves it.

- Large intestine

The large intestine is about five feet long. The thick tube has a diameter of 2.5 inches. It is the home of symbiotic bacteria that are necessary for breaking down waste to make extraction of nutrients from the waste possible. The large intestine also holds feces.

- Pancreas

The pancreas is located posterior to the stomach. The large gland is shaped like a lumpy snake and is about six inches long. Its "tail" points to the left side of the abdominal cavity while the "head" connects to the duodenum.

This part of the digestive system completes the chemical digestion of food by secreting digestive enzymes into the small intestine.

- Liver

The liver is roughly triangular in shape. It is located at the right side of the stomach weighs around three pounds, making it the body's second largest organ.

The liver performs several functions. Primarily, it produces bile and secretes it into the small intestine.

- Gallbladder

This is a small organ close to the liver. This pear-shaped organ is designed for storing and recycling excess bile in the small intestine. The recycling enables the bile to be reused for digestion when the need arises.

- Pharynx

The pharynx is commonly known as the throat. The funnel-shaped tube passes chewed food to the esophagus from the mouth. It also plays a crucial role in the respiratory system during the passage of air through the pharynx from the nasal cavity to the larynx before it eventually finds its way to the lungs.

Due to the dual role played by the pharynx, it contains the epiglottis, a flap of tissue serving as a switch. The epiglottis routes air to the larynx and food to the esophagus.

The Physiology of the Digestive System

For digestion to take place, food must go through the six processes of the digestive system. These are:

Ingestion

Food intake is the digestive system's first function. It takes place in the mouth, where food enters the body. Both the stomach and the mouth handle food storage during its wait for digestion.

Secretion of digestive enzymes and fluids

Seven liters of fluids per day are secreted by the digestive system including mucus, enzymes, saliva, bile and hydrochloric acid.

Mixing and Movement

Foods are mixed and moved during digestion. To ensure proper mixing and movement, the digestive system can choose from three options:

- **Peristalsis**: This muscular wave moves partially digested food down the GI tract. Since it moves food a short distance at a time, the process must be repeated a couple of times before the food reaches the end of the GI tract.
- **Swallowing**: The skeletal muscles in the tongue, mouth and pharynx are used during the swallowing process to push food through the pharynx to the esophagus.
- **Segmentation**: This takes place in the small intestine. A small portion of the intestine contracts, helping to increase the amount of nutrients absorbed by the body. It does this by mixing the food so it comes in contact with the walls of the small intestine several times.

Food digestion

Digestion refers to the process of converting food into component chemicals. During the mechanical digestion process, large pieces of food are broken down, starting in the mouth when they are chewed by the teeth. The process continues in the stomach and intestines where the food is mixed by the muscles.

Bile also contributes to the digestion process by breaking fats in food into smaller globules.

Foods undergo both mechanical and chemical digestion. In the second type of digestion, more complex and larger molecules are broken down to make it easier for the body to absorb them.

Salivary amylase starts the chemical digestion process. It breaks complex carbohydrates down into their simpler forms. In the stomach, the hydrochloric acid and enzymes proceed with the chemical digestion process, although the bulk of it is carried out by the pancreas in the small intestine.

The pancreatic juice can digest a wide range of foods such as carbohydrates, lipids, nucleic acids and proteins. Once a food leaves the duodenum, it has been simplified into amino acids, nucleotides, fatty acids and monosaccharides.

Nutrients Absorption

The next stage of the digestive process is the absorption of nutrients after digestion. This starts in the stomach where alcohol, water and other simple molecules are absorbed into the bloodstream. The larger percentage of absorption occurs in the small intestine's walls. The lymphatic and small blood vessels carry the digested food molecules to the other parts of the body. The large intestine absorbs water and vitamins B and K.

Excretion

Excretion is the final stage of the digestive process. This is otherwise known as defecation, the removal of indigestible substances from the gut. The brain consciously controls the timing of defecation.

A malfunctioning digestive system may trigger a wide range of digestive diseases. These include the following:

- Irritable bowel syndrome
- Cancer
- Cholecystitis
- Gallstones
- Lactose intolerance
- Rectal prolapse
- Hemorrhoids
- Fissures.

Muscular System

The muscular system consists of the smooth, skeletal and cardiac muscles. It allows humans to maintain the right posture, makes movement possible and supports blood circulation throughout the body.

Since the muscular system aids movement, the skeletal system has some 700 muscles attached to it. Each muscle consists of tendons, skeletal muscle tissue, nerves and blood vessels.

You can also find muscle tissue in other parts of the body such as the digestive organs, the heart and the blood vessels. About 40% of a human's total weight is muscles.

Muscle tissues are classified into three groups. These are:

1. **Visceral**: This muscle can be found in the intestines, stomach and blood vessels. It is responsible for contracting organs, so as to transport substances.

This muscle is known as involuntary muscle because it is controlled by the part of the brain known as the unconscious.

The visceral muscle is the weakest of all muscles and is smooth in appearance under a microscope, unlike the skeletal and cardiac muscles, that are banded.

2. **Cardiac**: This muscle pumps blood throughout the body and exists in the heart only. It is another member of the involuntary muscle class and thus can't be controlled consciously.

The cardiac muscle's cells are either Y- or X-shaped and are connected by intercalated disks. The intercalated disks and the branched structure offer resistance to the huge responsibility of pumping blood to the heart as well as resistance to high blood pressure. They also assist with the production of electrochemical signals that make it possible for the heart to beat.

3. **Skeletal**: While the cardiac and visceral muscles are involuntary, skeletal muscles are voluntary. Thus, they can be controlled consciously. When you perform any action such as dancing, singing, walking, or driving you use these muscles. The skeletal muscle supports these actions through contraction. When a skeletal muscle contracts, parts of the body within the vicinity of the bone that a muscle is attached to move.

Some of the muscular system's main functions are:

- **Mobility**: As previously mentioned, the main function of the muscular system is to make movement possible through muscle contraction. It supports running, walking, swimming and other movement. Smaller movements such as speaking, writing and facial expressions also depend on the muscular system.
- **Respiration**: You use the diaphragm muscle for breathing. When it contracts, the chest cavity increases in size and the lungs are filled with air. As the diaphragm contracts, air is pushed out of the lungs, relaxing the diaphragm.

However, deep breathing may also require other muscles such as back muscles, abdomen muscles and neck muscles.
- **Childbirth**: The smooth muscles expand and contract in the uterus during childbirth. The expansion and contraction push the baby out from the womb through the vagina. As the baby comes out head down, it is guided by the pelvic floor muscles.
- **Urination**: Without the muscles, passing urine is impossible. The kidneys, bladder, vagina or penis, ureters, prostate and urethra contain both skeletal and smooth muscles needed for urination.

The nerves and muscles work as a team to achieve a common goal: holding and releasing urine from the bladder when necessary.

- **Organ protection**: Several body organs are protected by the muscular system. Internal organs at the sides of the body or at the back or front are protected by the muscles in the torso. The muscles also absorb shock to protect the body's organs and bones. They equally reduce the friction in body joints as another protective measure. Further protection is offered by the bones of the ribs or the spine.
- **Digestion**: The smooth muscles control digestion. These muscles are present in the gastrointestinal tract and are comprised of the stomach, anus, mouth, small intestines, esophagus, rectum and large intestines. During digestion, food passes through the body. This leads to the expansion and contraction of the smooth muscles. The smooth muscles are also responsible for pushing food out through vomiting or defecation.
- **Posture**: Behind your posture are the skeletal muscles. You must be flexible to maintain proper posture. Imagine your posture if your back muscles are weak or if you have stiff neck muscles. These can adversely affect your alignment and cause joint pain in the spine, shoulders, knees, hips and other joints.

Conditions such as multiple sclerosis, fibromyalgia and Parkinson's disease are triggered by damaged muscles.

Skeletal System

The skeletal system is made up of the joints and bones in the body. Each bone is a distinct and complex organ, comprised of protein fibers, cells and some minerals.

The skeleton provides support and protection for the soft tissues. Without them, movement is impossible because muscles are attached to the skeleton.

There are about 206 bones in the entire skeletal system. These bones are classified into two:

- **Axial skeleton**

The skeleton consists of 80 bones at the midline axis of the body. The axial skeletons are found in the hyoid, ribs, skull, vertebral column, auditory ossicles and sternum. There are between 32 and 34 bones in the vertebral column due to the differences in the number of vertebrae from one person to another, while the skull has 22 bones and seven other associated bones.

There are 12 pairs of ribs. The sternum is located in this region as well. The axial skeleton makes upright posture possible in humans.

- **Appendicular skeleton**

One hundred and twenty-six bones form the appendicular skeleton. These are the bones in the pelvic girdle, upper limbs, pectoral or shoulder girdle and the upper limbs.
The skeleton is divided into six regions that include arms and forearms with six bones; shoulder girdles with four bones; feet and ankles with 52 bones; hands with 54 bones; legs and thighs with eight bones and pelvis with two bones.
While the axial skeleton supports upright posture, the appendicular skeleton supports locomotion. It also protect the organs of excretion, digestion and reproduction.

In the vertebral column, there are 26 vertebrae. There are five vertebrae in the lumbar or lower back region and seven in the cervical or neck region. The sacrum or coccyx regions each have one vertebra apiece while the thoracic region has 12 vertebrae.

The skeletal system performs six functions. These are:

- Support

The body is fully supported by the skeleton. It also helps the human body to maintain its shape and provides rigidity. Without the costal cartilage, rib cage and intercostal muscles, nothing would hold the lungs. They would collapse. The pelvic structure also depends on the pelvis and muscles as well. Thus, the skeletal system is fully designed for support.

- Movement

Between the bones are joints that allow movement. The skeletal muscles play a crucial role here because bones are attached to the skeletal system. Thus, bones, muscles and joints all work together to make movement possible. The nervous system controls them all.

- Blood cell production

The bone marrow produces red blood cells through a process known as hematopoiesis. This takes place in the skeleton. Hematopoiesis (red blood cell production) occurs in the cranium, pelvis, sternum and vertebra of adults and in the tibia and femur of children. In the bone marrow, white blood cells, red blood cells and platelets are produced.

- Protection

Several internal organs are protected by the skeleton. The spinal cord is protected by the vertebrae while the skull serves as the protective shield for the brain. The heart and lungs are protected by the spine, rib cage and sternum. They protect major blood vessels as well.

The ribs and vertebrae protect the heart, spinal cord and lungs by encasing them.

- Endocrine regulation

Osteocalcin, a hormone, is released by the bone cells. This hormone plays a vital part in fat deposition and blood sugar regulation. The hormone boosts insulin secretion and increases the number of cells producing insulin in the body. It also reduces the fat-storing cells.

- Storage

Phosphorus and calcium are two important minerals the body needs for proper functioning. Muscle contraction and other processes use these minerals extensively. Although we find these minerals in our diet, the bones are other sources of these mineral as they are reservoirs for calcium.

Thus, when the body is in need of minerals and can't take them from the blood, the endocrine system goes into action by releasing special hormones. These hormones take calcium from the bones and release it into the bloodstream. This raises the calcium levels needed for physiological processes in the bloodstream. For instance, muscle contractions depend on calcium ions. Nerve impulses can't be transmitted without muscle contractions.

Respiratory System

Respiration means the act of exhaling and inhaling. During respiration, you inhale oxygen and exhale carbon dioxide.

The respiratory system is divided into:

- Upper Respiratory Tract

In this section are the nasal cavity, nose and sinuses.

- Lower Respiratory Tract

Making up the lower respiratory tract are the windpipe or trachea, larynx, lungs, alveoli and airways, comprising the bronchioles and bronchi.

These parts serve different but related functions. The trachea connects the throat to the bronchi. It is divided into two tubes or bronchi, leading to each of the lungs. The bronchi also divide further inside the lungs into smaller bronchi called bronchioles.

The air sacs are tiny sacs also known as pulmonary alveoli. This important part of the respiratory system exchanges carbon dioxide and oxygen molecules to-and-from the bloodstream. Through the air sacs, oxygen enters the blood while carbon dioxide leaves it.

Inhalation is characterized by muscle contractions. The diaphragm muscles contract and as they do, the chest cavity enlarges. The expansion of the chest cavity reduces air pressure to allow enough air into the lungs. As the air passes to the lungs, its pressure status changes from high to low.

The rib muscles also contract, leading to the rise of the ribs. This also results in an increase in the chest volume.

Muscle relaxation occurs during exhalation. Hence, rather than contracting, the muscles are relaxed. The diaphragm is affected too. It first curves and then rises. As a result, the ribs descend, triggering a decrease in the chest volume.

The chest cavity contracts during exhalation. This increases the air pressure and leads to the expulsion of the air in the lungs through the upper respiratory tract. The pressure changes too. As the air passes from the lungs to the upper respiratory tract, the pressure changes from high to low.

The Breathing Process

Breathing is initiated when you inhale air into your mouth or nose. The inhaled air embarks on a journey into your windpipe through the back of your throat. The windpipe is divided into bronchial tubes or air passages.

The airways must always be open, which is crucial for the lungs' optimum performance. If they are inflamed or contain extra mucus, their performance will be drastically hampered.

The bronchial tubes divide into bronchioles. These bronchioles eventually end in alveoli. About 600 million alveoli are in the human body.

These alveoli are surrounded by capillaries, tiny blood cells through which the blood receives oxygen whenever air is inhaled.

The oxygenated blood makes its way into your heart where it is pumped to the cells of the organs and tissues in the body. While using the oxygen, the cells produce carbon dioxide that is eventually passed into the blood. From there, the blood returns carbon dioxide to the lungs, where it exits during exhalation.

During inhalation, the diaphragm pulls down and thus creates a vacuum. This vacuum causes air to rush into the lungs. Upon exhalation, the diaphragm relaxes in the opposite direction. This pushes the lungs so that they deflate, releasing air.

Respiratory System Diseases

When the respiratory system isn't functioning properly, it may trigger the following diseases:

- **Bronchiectasis**: The bronchial walls become thicker due to infection and inflammation.
- **Asthma**: Asthma is a respiratory system disease characterized by narrow airways and excessive mucus secretion.
- **Tuberculosis**: Tuberculosis is usually caused by a dangerous infection that affects the lungs. It may affect the spine, kidneys or the brain.
- **Cystic fibrosis**: This respiratory system disease arises as a result of a problem in the genes. Over time, this condition may worsen and cause stubborn and incurable lung infections.
- **Lung cancer**: Lung cancer is characterized by tumors in the lung, usually triggered by smoking and/or the inhalation of other carcinogenic chemicals.
- **Sarcoidosis**: The formation of inflammatory cells, known as granulomas, develops in the lymph nodes and the lungs to cause this ailment.
- **Pleural effusion**: Your chest and lungs are lined by tissues. When excess fluid builds up between these tissues, it causes flexural effusion.
- **Idiopathic pulmonary fibrosis:** This serious respiratory system disease occurs when the lung tissues are scarred. The scarring interferes with their performance.

Urinary System

The urinary system is also known as the urinary tract or renal system. Its major components are the ureters, kidneys, urethra and bladder.

Some of the notable functions of the urinary system are:

- Regulation of blood, volume and its major compositions such as potassium, sodium and calcium
- Regulation of the blood's pH homeostasis
- Blood pressure regulation
- Supports the kidney in red blood cells production
- Waste product storage
- Waste product disposal
- Helps with the synthesis of calcitriol
- Controls the levels of metabolites and electrolytes in the body.

Let's take a look at how the system functions through the components' array of responsibilities.

Kidneys

The kidneys are the most important organs of the urinary system. They serve a number of purposes that include removal of waste products, blood filtering and most of the other known functions of the urinary system, while the other components are for urine elimination from the body.

In adults, a kidney is about six centimeters wide, three centimeters thick and 12 cm long. Each of the bean-shaped kidneys contains more than a million nephrons through which urine passes into the collecting ducts on its way to being eliminated from the body.

Ureters

The ureters are also important to the urinary system. They are small tubes responsible for transporting urine to the bladder through the renal pelvis. The wall of the 25-cm long tube consists of three layers. There is the outer layer, which consists of connective tissues for supporting the system. In the middle layer, the smooth muscle and the inner circular make up the muscular coat.

The middle layer plays the major role of propelling urine from the body, a process known as peristalsis.

The inner layer is the transitional epithelium. Also known as the mucosa, it is responsible for mucus secretion, protecting the cells' surface.

Urinary bladder

This is where urine is temporarily stored. The bladder is located just below the parietal peritoneum in the pelvic cavity.

The shape and size of the urinary bladder is determined by two factors: the amount of pressure it receives from the organs around it, and the amount of urine in the bladder at a specific point in time.

The kidneys produce urine. From there, urine travels through the ureters to the bladder. The bladder not only stores urine but also supports the control of urine as well as allowing urination as necessary.

While urinating, the muscles in the bladder squeeze while two valves or sphincters open allow for urine flow.

From the bladder, the urine flows into the urethra, where it is passed out of the human body.

As the storage facility for urine, the bladder is susceptible to several conditions that include but are not limited to:

- **Urinary incontinence**: This is characterized by uncontrolled urination. This ailment may be chronic and can be caused by a wide range of factors.
- **Urinary retention**: This is abnormal urine discharge from the bladder. Two major factors that may be responsible for this condition are suppressed bladder muscles and blockage.
- **Hematuria**: This health condition occurs when blood is found in the urine. It may be caused by bladder cancer or an infection. In some cases, hematuria is harmless.
- **Dysuria**: This health condition is generally known as painful urination. It may be triggered by conditions such as irritation, infection, bladder inflammation, inflammation of the external genitals or urethral inflammation.
- **Bladder cancer**: One of the symptoms of this ailment is blood in the urine. This may lead to tumors in the blood. Cigarette smokers and individuals who are exposed to workplace chemicals are more at risk of this condition than others.

Urethra

The urethra is a tube leading from the bladder to the outside of the body. Thus, it transports urine and discharges it.

In females, the urethra can be found above the vaginal opening and is usually shorter than in males. The urethra serves the dual purposes of urine and semen transportation in males.

Immune System

The immune system is one of the most important body systems. It protects the body against all forms of infection.

Many organs and cells form a formidable alliance for protecting the body. Important members of the defensive force are white blood cells, otherwise known as leukocytes. They play a crucial role in the fight against invading forces.

Different types of white blood cells play different roles too. For instance, the lymphocytes keep a record of invaders and destroy them on sight. Phagocytes attack invading organisms and chew them up.

Harmful bacteria in the body are usually attacked by a special type of phagocyte, neutrophils. They are usually among the first line of defense that is summoned when there are invaders. They are very effective at preventing infection by trapping bacteria and thereby preventing it from spreading. They also digest bad cells and ensure the body responds appropriately to potential invaders.

There are two types of lymphocytes serving different functions in the body: T lymphocytes and the B lymphocytes. Both of these types develop from the lymphocytes. The lymphocytes develop in the bone marrow where they may stay and develop into B cells. Alternatively, they may leave the bone marrow and migrate to the thymus gland. In the gland, they can develop into T cells.

B lymphocytes are the first to initiate the chain of events that culminates in the destruction of attackers. Serving as the military intelligence for the body, they identify potential attackers and launch a defense mechanism against them by sending their "soldiers," the T lymphocytes, to destroy enemies. They immediately make antibodies to fight off foreign substances (antigens).

Once the antibodies lock into the antigens, they remain in the individual's body so that if the antigen reenters the body, the immune system already has a potent weapon to fight off the unwanted substance.

In the human body, immunity is classified into three. These are:

1. **Innate**: Innate immunity is inborn. It is a protection we are endowed with from birth, the first form of immunity. Two typical examples of innate immunity are the immune system and the human skin. The former becomes active once dangerous invaders are identified in the body while the latter prevents germs from gaining easy entry into the body.
There are some natural killer cells that provide innate immunity too. These types of white blood cells attack abnormal cells in the body and kill them. When someone is infected by a virus, the natural killer cells take immediate action to prevent the virus from damaging the body.
2. **Adaptive**: Adaptive immunity is also referred to as active immunity. It is the type of immunity individuals develop throughout their life span. When humans receive vaccines against diseases, they develop this type of immunity. They also develop active immunity whenever they are exposed to diseases.
3. **Passive**: Passive immunity is a short-term type of immunity. They are considered "borrowed" from other sources, which is the rationale behind their temporary function. A typical example is breast milk. A baby receives temporary immunity from breast milk to fight off diseases it may be exposed to from the mother.

Organs of the Immune System

The defense system itself is made up of vessels and organs. Individual proteins and cells also play a crucial role in the defense system.

The first preventive mechanisms are the body's outer and inner surfaces, including the mucous membranes and the skin. They work together to form a protective wall for the body. Supporting the skin as the first line of defense is the layer over the cornea, the special tissues lining the bladder, lungs and the digestive system. Unless these tissues are cut or suffer burns, germs can't access your body and infect it.

The protective wall doesn't work alone. It receives support from other body parts such as:

- The bronchi prevent many pathogens from entering the body. Pathogens get stuck in the bronchi's mucus and eventually are removed from the airways by cilia, a hair-like structure.
- The body has antibacterial substances with the ability to render various pathogens inactive before they mature. For instance, the airways and saliva contain an enzyme that renders bacteria inactive by destroying cell walls. The enzyme is also present in tear fluid.
- Hydrochloric acid stops pathogens inadvertently consumed along with food from harming the body.
- Other harmless bacteria that supports the system is normal flora. It protects the body against external invasion too.
- When a person sneezes or coughs, pathogens in the body are removed.

The following immunodeficiency disorders may weaken the immune system and compromise an individual's health:

- **Malnutrition**: This condition is characterized by a poor diet.
- **HIV**: This virus damages the immune system. Thus, the body's weapon for fighting off infections is destroyed.
- **Viral hepatitis**: This disease causes liver inflammation. Such inflammation can damaging body organs.

The weakened immune system increases the host's vulnerability to a wide range of diseases that include but are not limited to:

- **Meningitis:** The inflammation of the meninges is known as meningitis. The meninges are membranes covering the spinal cord and the brain. When the fluid surrounding the three membranes is infected, it results in meningitis.

- **Pneumonia:** When either or both of the lungs are infected, the infection leads to pneumonia. It is usually caused by viruses, bacteria and fungi.

Chapter Eight: Physics

Physics is a branch of natural science that focuses on the study of matter, its behavior and its motion.

It can also be defined simply as the study of matter and energy and the relationship between the two.

Some of the major topics in physics that the HESI exam will cover are:

Fundamentals of Motion

Motion is defined as the change of the position of a body with respect to time. Motion can be studied in two different ways: dynamics and kinematics.

In the former, the study of motion involves the study of the impact of forces on motion while the latter doesn't involve the forces responsible for the change in motion.

Types of Motion

Motion is classified into four categories. These are:

- Random motion

Random motion refers to the movement of objects at random orientation or direction. Thus, the moving object moves around haphazardly. The motion of particles in gas is an example of random motion.

Other examples include the movement of a football in play, an insect flying and others.

- Translational linear motion

Translational linear motion is the movement of a rigid body from one place to another. The body doesn't rotate during the motion. For instance, a runner moving from the starting point to the finish line, a ball thrown upward and a train moving are typical examples of this type of motion.

- Rotational motion

As the name implies, this motion type focuses on the movement of a body in a circle. The movement takes place on an axis or center.

The wheel of a car in motion and the earth's rotation about its axis are some examples of rotational motion.

- Periodic motion

Periodic motion is the motion of a body in a circular path while maintaining a uniform speed. A watch's balance wheel, a pendulum, a vibrating tuning fork and a rocking chair are all in periodic motion.

- Motion and Speed

In physics, speed is defined as the distance traveled per unit of time. Thus, it is a measure of how fast an object is.

Speed is a scalar quantity: it doesn't have a direction. Thus, the speed of an object can be calculated irrespective of direction.

When you clean a room within a specific period of time or type at a specific rate, your speed can be calculated. Take a look at your speedometer while driving. It shows your speed at each point in time.

Motion refers to the change in an object's position over time. When you move from one place to another, you are in motion.

Motion is usually expressed mathematically in terms of distance, speed, displacement, velocity, time and acceleration. If an object's position doesn't change relatively to a time, such object is said to be stationary or at rest.

There are four fundamental types of motion. These are:

1. Linear motion

This is often referred to as translational motion. It refers to the change of location of an object from one point to another.

Examples of linear motion abound in nature. When you drop an object from a height, it moves linearly. The same applies to a swimmer going in a straight line. A bullet shot at a target also moves on a straight line.

All these examples will continue in their motion unless external forces change their path or direction.

2. Oscillatory motion

When an object assumes to-and-fro movement while standing in a mean position, it is said to undergo oscillatory motion. An example of this motion is a swinging pendulum that moves to-and-fro without changing its position.

Without an external force such as friction, the object will repeat the movement forever. However, that's impossible in the real world because the body will eventually go into equilibrium.

Sound waves, seismic waves and ocean waves undergo oscillatory motion as well. The same can be said of bridges and buildings.

Other typical examples of oscillatory motion are:

- The movement of a spring
- An alternating current
- A musical instrument's vibrating springs.
- Atoms' movement
- Earthquake-triggered movements of the earth's crust
- A tuning fork.

3. Rotary motion

Rotary motion is characterized by the movement of a body around a circle or an axis.

This motion can occur in two different ways. The axis may pass through the body or not. Consider the examples of a skater who rotates on an ice rink and a gymnast who swings on rings. While the axis of the former doesn't pass through the body, that of the latter does.

This is also known as rotational motion.

4. Reciprocating motion

Reciprocating motion is similar to oscillating motion. It involves the linear movement of an object in a direction and back in the opposite direction along the same path until the object returns to its original point. It then repeats the cycle for as long as possible.

Notable examples of this type of motion are material testing devices, piston pumps and compressors, and insertion machines, among others.

Parameters of Motion

When a motion is carried out in a straight line, the following parameters can be used to describe the motion:

- Speed

The speed of a body refers to the rate of change of the body's distance with respect to time.

Speed (v) = change of distance (s) within a time (t)

Thus, $v = s/t$.

The SI unit of speed is meters per second or m/s.

- Average Speed

The average speed of an object is a function of the time it takes to cover a distance. Thus, mathematically, you can calculate the average speed as the total distance covered divided by the time taken to cover the distance.

Average speed = total distance covered/time taken. Average speed has magnitude without a direction. Hence, it is a scalar quantity.

Consider these examples:

1. What is the average speed of a sports car that covered 60 miles in 2 hours?

Average speed = total distance/time taken

= 60 miles/2 hours

= 30 miles per hour.

Note that the time taken should be converted into hours when performing the calculation.

For instance, a car traveling from one city to another covered 90 miles in 1 hour 30 minutes. Calculate its average speed.

Solution:

Total distance: 90 miles.

Time taken: 90 minutes.

Convert minutes to hours = 1 hour 30 minutes or 1.5 hours.

Hence, average speed = 90 miles/1.5 hours

= 60 miles/hour.

Note that a traveling vehicle can't maintain a constant speed throughout the duration of the journey. It may exceed the average speed at some points and drop far below it at others. Hence, the average speed gives a general idea of the vehicle's speed, irrespective of how fast or slow it is at different points in the journey.

Question:

A train leaves point A to point C in segments. It covers the 60 miles between points A and B in 2 hours and the 45 miles between points B and C in 1 hour. What is the train's average speed?

Solution:

Total distance traveled = 60 miles + 45 miles

= 105 miles.

Total time taken = 2 hours + 1 hour

= 3 hours.

Average speed = total distance traveled / total time taken

= 105 miles / 3 hours = 35 miles /hour

Thus, the average speed of the train is 35 miles per hour.

Uniform Speed

A body is said to be at uniform speed if the rate of change of distance with respect to time remains constant.

Thus, for uniform speed, $v = s/t$ = constant.

For instance, if a vehicle moves along a straight line without changing its speed, it is said to be at uniform speed. The same is said of a sewing machine's vibrating springs and a train moving from one location to another at a steady speed.

Velocity and Acceleration

Velocity is the rate of change of displacement per time. It can also be defined as the measurement of speed in a specific direction.

The difference between speed and acceleration is that speed focuses on the change of direction per time while velocity factors in the direction of the motion. Thus, speed is a scalar quantity while velocity is a vector quantity.

Acceleration is the rate of change of velocity per time. Thus, $a = v/t$. The SI unit is acceleration per meter squared or m/s^2. Since acceleration refers to the change of velocity, it is also a vector quantity.

While acceleration and velocity are used for describing motion, that's where the similarities end. Velocity is a measure of the rate of change of position with time. On the other hand, acceleration measures the rate of change of velocity. While acceleration is measured in meters per second squared, the SI unit of velocity is meters per second.

Uniform Acceleration

A body is said to be in uniform acceleration if the rate of change of velocity of the body remains constant. Thus, $a = v/t = $ constant.

A body that travels at a constant pace doesn't accelerate but has a velocity. However, if the pace changes from time to time, it accelerates. Hence, the body has both velocity and acceleration.

However, if the body's velocity decreases over time, the body is said to be decelerating. Negative acceleration is also called retardation. This usually occurs when a body in motion slows down after the application of the brakes.

Deceleration is expressed mathematically as:

Deceleration = [Final velocity (v) – Initial velocity (u)]/Time taken (t)]

Hence, deceleration = $(v - u)/t$

It can also be expressed as $(v^2 - u^2)/2s$ if the distance, initial velocity and final velocity are given. Note that the formula doesn't take the time taken into consideration but factors in the distance covered.

Example:

1. If a vehicle moving with a uniform velocity of 60 km/hr is brought to rest after traveling a distance of 15 meters, calculate its deceleration.

Solution:

Initial velocity = 60 km/hr

Final velocity = 0

Distance covered, s = 15m

Deceleration = (v2 – u2)/2s

= (0² – 60²)/2 * 15

= (0 – 3600)/30 = -3600/30

Thus, deceleration = -120 m/s².

2. If an object accelerates from rest for 20 seconds at 3 m/s², how much deceleration can bring the object to rest in just 5 seconds?

Solution:

A = v/t

Therefore, v = at.

= 20 * 3 = 60 meters.

Step 2:

Initial velocity u = 60 meters.

Final velocity, v = 0 meters.

Time, t = 5 seconds.

Deceleration = (v² – u²)/2s

= (0² – 60²) /2 * 5

= (0 –3600)/10 = -3600/10

Thus, the deceleration is -360 m/s².

While acceleration is denoted by a, deceleration is denoted by -a.

Sometimes, velocity is misunderstood for speed. However, remember that speed is a scalar quantity while velocity is a vector quantity. For instance, if an object travels 30 meters per second, it has magnitude without a direction. That's speed. Conversely, if the same object travels at 30 meters per second in a specific direction, it becomes a vector quantity. That's velocity.

Velocity is also a measure of the distance traveled divided by time taken.

Hence, Velocity = Distance Traveled/Time Taken.

Thus, $V = D/T$

If you are traveling continuously in the same direction and at the same speed, you are said to have constant velocity in which case the acceleration is zero.

There may be constant acceleration as well. You will experience constant acceleration when your velocity keeps changing by the same value every second. A common example of an object undergoing constant acceleration is an object falling from a height. The object starts with low velocity but keeps increasing by the value of acceleration (9.8 m/s²) every second as it falls under gravity.

Equations of Motion

The four commonly used equations of motion are:

1. $S = [(v + u)/2] * t$
2. $v = u - at$
3. $v2 = u^2 + 2as$
4. $s = ut + \frac{1}{2}(at^2)$

You can use any of the four equations above to solve uniform accelerated motion problems. Your choice should be determined by the available variables.

For instance, the first equation doesn't contain a, while s is missing in the second equation. Equations 3 and 4 are missing t and v respectively. Hence, memorize these formulas and learn how to apply the most appropriate one when necessary.

Newton's Laws of Motion

There are three Newton's Laws of Motion, also known as the Three Laws of Physics. These are:

1. First Law of Motion (Newton's First Law)

This law states that a body will remain in uniform motion or at rest in a straight line unless a force acts on it. Thus, if a body is traveling in a straight line at a constant speed or is at rest, its status won't change unless an external force creates a change that moves it from its stationary position or alters its speed. This law is also referred to as the law of inertia.

For instance, when you are in a moving vehicle and the vehicle stops suddenly, you tend to move forward because your body is initially in motion in the direction of the car. When the car stops suddenly, your body can't adjust as abruptly as the vehicle and tends to continue in motion.

Airbags are designed to stop the body's forward motion when a vehicle is suddenly stopped when it hits an object or is involved in an accident.

The law also explains the importance of seat belts. A fastened seat belt will hold you in place when a vehicle stops suddenly. Otherwise, you may be thrown through the windshield as your body continues the forward motion.

2. Second Law of Motion

The rate of change of momentum of a body is proportional to the force causing the change. Invariably, a body's rate of change of momentum is equal in both direction and magnitude to the force responsible for the change. Thus, if an external force is applied to a body, it may change its direction or its magnitude. It may also change both values as well.

Mathematically, $F = ma$, where:

- F = Force.
- m = mass of the body.
- a = acceleration.

It will take more force to move or accelerate a body with a bigger mass than a smaller object.

Both acceleration and force are vector quantities since they have both direction and magnitude.

3. Third Law of Motion

For every action, there is always an equal and opposite reaction. Thus, when two bodies interact with each other, they will apply forces that are opposite in direction and equal in magnitude to one another. The third law is also known as the law of conservation of momentum or the law of action and reaction.

A typical example of the application of this law is the action and reaction of a book resting on a table. The book applies a force on the table that is equal to the book's weight. In response, the table will also apply a force on the book. According to Newton's third law of motion, the applied force is equal to the force applied on the table by the book but in the opposite direction. The book's force is applied downward on the table while the table applies its force upward.

Have you ever dived off a diving board? The third law is also in action in this situation. When you jump on the board, you push it down. It responds with an equal but opposite force that throws you into the air.

Work, Energy and Power

The two terms, work and energy, are used extensively. Their scope includes farmwork, playing and mental activity. Thus, a huge amount of human activities require a great deal of energy.

Humans depend on combustible organic matters such as coal, wood, sunshine, petroleum and wind as their primary source of energy.

The sources of energy can be classified into:

- **Renewable resources**: In the renewable group are the likes of wind, solar energy and hydroelectricity. These sources of energy can be used in many ways. For instance, wind can be used to turn windmills and produce electricity. Solar energy also produces electricity for both domestic and industrial uses. What is more, it is also a very important element of photosynthesis for the production of carbohydrates used by plants.
Hydroelectricity is produced in dams where generators are driven by water to generate electricity.

- **Nonrenewable resources**: In this category are coal, petroleum and nuclear energy. Petroleum produces electricity in power stations. Its cousin, kerosene, is likewise a source of energy for domestic cooking while other members of the family such as diesel and petrol are used as a source of energy for vehicles.
Coal, on the other hand, can undergo combustion to produce heat for driving ships and trains. This is in addition to being a source of heat for cooking.
In the same vein, nuclear energy produces enormous heat that can be used for operating turbines and driving aircrafts and ships.

When energy is transferred to an object, work is said to be done on the object. Thus, generally speaking, work is simply considered a transfer of energy.

However, in physics, a body is said to be at work when the body applies a force on another body and it moves the receiving body a certain distance, in the specific direction of the applied force. Thus, if object A transfers energy to object B and moves B in the direction of the applied force, the former is said to work on the latter. Thus, work done is equal to the product of the applied force and the distance it moves the receiving object.

Work is also said to be done when force is applied over a distance. You are working when you move your table from one location in your room to another. Lifting a heavy object from the ground to another location is another example of work. In each case, the object's weight is the force while the distance covered is from the pickup location to the destination.

A vehicle that covers a distance between A and B is also said to work. The work done in all the examples above is the product of the applied force and the distance moved in its direction.

Hence, work = force * distance.

$W = f * s$.

Work Done on a Plane

While the above formula is used for calculating work done on a flat surface, work can also be calculated on an inclined plane with the formula:

$W = F * s\cos\theta$

The joule is the SI unit of work. It is the work done by a force of one Newton through a distance of one meter. Thus, it can also be represented as Newton-meter where meter is the distance and Newton is the force.

When calculating work, the force must cause a displacement over a distance. Otherwise, work is not done because the distance equals zero.

If a man keeps pushing a wall for hours but the wall doesn't budge, the distance covered is zero. Thus, the work done is zero.

The same rule applies to a ball thrown at a wall which comes back. The total distance covered is zero. You haven't done any work with the ball.

However, if you drop an object, work is done if the dropped object travels a distance before reaching the destination. This underscores the importance of distance when calculating work.

W = F * S

W = work done

F = force

S= displacement

For example, the work done if a force of 15 Newton moves an object a distance of 3 meters is calculated as follows:
W = F * S

= 10 * 3

= 30 joules.

Consider some other examples:

1. A man pulled a body up an inclined plane at a 60-degree angle with a force of 15 N. Calculate the work done if he covers 30 meters.

Solution:

Force = 15 N.

Angle = 60 degrees.

Work = force * distance * $\cos\theta$

= 15 * (30 * 0.5)

= 15 * 15 = 225 joules.

2. Calculate the work done if the man pulled the body on a horizontal ground for 30 meters.

Force = 15 N.

Distance = 30 m.

Work = force * distance

= 15 * 30m

= 450 joules.

Work can also be done in a force field such as the gravitational field. To lift a load a specific height, the weight of the body can be overcome by applying a pulling force on it. Thus, work will be done against gravitational force to lift the weight vertically.

Thus, the work done can be calculated with the formula:

$W = mgh$ where:

- m = mass of the body in kg
- g = gravitational force or acceleration due to gravity. It is 9.8 m/s^2
- h = height in meters.

Consider these examples:

1. A pregnant woman weighing 75 kg carries a 5-kg grocery basket up a 10-meter long vertical ladder. Calculate the work done by the woman. Take g = 9.8 m/s^2.

Solution:

Mass of woman: 75 kg

Mass of grocery basket: 5 kg.

Total mass = mass of woman + mass of basket

= 75 kg + 5 kg

Total mass = 80 kg.

Distance covered = 6 m.

Work done = mgh

= 80 * 9.8 * 6

= 4704 joules.

= 4.7 kJ.

2. Calculate the work done by a 50-kg stone falling from a height of 20 m if acceleration due to gravity is taken as 9.8 m/s^2.

Solution:

Mass of stone: 50 kg.

Distance: 20 m.

$g = 9.8 \text{ m/s}^2$.

Work done = mgh.

$= 50 * 9.8 * 20$

$= 9,800\text{J}$ or 9.8 kJ.

Energy

Energy is defined as the capacity to do work. Your capacity to move an object from one point to another by applying force is energy.

Energy doesn't exist strictly in a single form. It can exist in different forms and can transform from one form to another when necessary.

Forms of Energy

Energy can exist in any of these forms:

- **Kinetic energy**: An object in motion is said to possess kinetic energy. A typical example is a swinging pendulum.
- **Electrical energy**: This type of energy is derived from electrons, protons ions, and other charged particles.
- **Potential energy**: This the opposite of kinetic energy. It is energy an object possesses due to its position. A stationary object possesses potential energy.
- **Heat energy**: This is otherwise called thermal energy. When molecules or atoms are in motion, they generate heat energy.
- **Nuclear energy**: Interactions with the neutrons and protons of an atom generate nuclear energy. This type of energy is usually released by chemical processes such as fusion and fission.
- **Chemical energy**: Chemical reactions release this form of energy. It is usually produced when chemical bonds between molecules and atoms are either formed or broken.
- **Magnetic energy**: Magnetic energy is produced by magnetic fields.

Law of Conservation of Energy

The law of conservation of energy states that although energy may change from one form to another, the total energy in a system will always remain constant. During the transformation, energy can neither be created nor destroyed. This also supports the idea of the constant value of the total energy in a system.

When you kick a ball, it moves from the point where you kick it until it reaches a point where it stops. While in motion, the ball possesses kinetic energy. This energy is transformed into potential energy when it eventually stops. In either case, the total energy in the ball, both while in motion and while at rest, remains the same. This is irrespective of its change in form.

Hence, all the different forms of energy listed above can change from one form to another. The burning of fuel in a vehicle generates heat energy. This energy is converted into mechanical energy that keeps the vehicle moving.

When brakes are applied, the mechanical energy in the vehicle changes to sound and heat energy as the vehicle comes to a halt.

The nuclei of atoms contain energy that produces heat energy. The heat energy is subsequently changed to electrical energy. Thus, transformation of energy from one form to another is a common phenomenon.

Mechanical Energy

A body can have the ability to work or possess mechanical energy as a result either of a body's motion or position. These are called kinetic energy and potential energy, respectively.

Kinetic Energy

This is the energy possessed by a body in motion. Kinetic energy is represented as KE. Some examples of kinetic energy are:

- An object falling
- A moving bullet
- A rolling ball
- A flying plane.

If a body of mass, M, is acted upon by a force, F, that brings it to rest from a speed, V, the kinetic energy is calculated by the formula:

$KE = \frac{1}{2}(mv^2)$ where:

M= mass of the body.

V = speed.

Examples:

1. A 50-kg kid runs around a playground at a speed of 10m/s. Calculate his kinetic energy.

Solution:

Mass: 50 kg

Speed v = 10 m/s

KE = ½(mv²)

Therefore, KE = ½ (50 * 10²)

= ½ (50 * 100) = ½ (5000)

KE = 2500 joules or 2.5 kJ.

2. Calculate the kinetic energy of a 50-gram bullet moving at a speed of 300 km per hour.

Solution:

Mass of bullet: 50 g

Convert mass to kg = 50/1000

Therefore, mass of the body = 0.05 kg

Speed of the body = 300 km/hour

Convert speed from kilometer per hour to meters per second. Therefore,

300 km/hour = (300 * 1000)/3600

= 300,000/3600

= 83.33 m/s.

Note that KE= ½ (mv²)

= ½ (0.05 * 83.33²)

= ½ (0.05 * 6943.8889)

= 347.20 joules.

Potential Energy

A stationary object possesses potential energy (PE)

Potential Energy = Work done = Force * Distance.

If a body of mass m is raised to a height, h, above the ground, it possesses potential energy represented by PE = mgh.

Consider this example:

A 50-kg person falls from a height of 500 meters. Calculate the energy with which the person strikes the ground.

Solution:

Mass m= 50 kg

Distance h= 500 m.

Acceleration due to gravity g = 9.8 m/s²

The gravitational potential energy is mgh.

= 50 * 9.8 * 500

= 245,000 joules or 2.45 kJ.

Note that the PE will be immediately converted into kinetic energy as the body moves toward the ground.

Power

Power is work done per unit time. Thus, it measures how fast work is done.

Average Power = (energy expended or work done) /time taken.

This is equal to work or energy per second.

It can be represented mathematically as:

- W/t
- (F * s)/t
- F * v.

The SI unit of power is watt (W). This is the rate of transfer of 1 joule of energy per second.

Hence, 1 w = 1 J/s

Power is measured in watts or joules/second. Larger units of power are kilowatts (kW) and megawatts (mW). Sometimes, though, power is measured in horsepower where 1 horsepower = 746 watts or 0.75 kW.

Sometimes when calculating electrical energy, kilowatt-hour is used. This refers to the energy that an appliance with a power of 1 kW uses in 1 hour.

Hence, 1 kWh = 1,000 W * 3,600 s

= 3600000 J

= 3.6 * 10^6 J or 3.6 MJ.

The equation for power is Power = Work/Time

Other mathematical formulae for calculating power are:

Power = (Force * Displacement)/ Time

Power = Force * Velocity

Examples:

1. A pump lifts 600 kg of water to a height of 6 meters in 10 seconds. Assuming g = 9.8 m/s², calculate the pump's power.

Solution:

When lifting the water, the pump works against gravity.

Thus, power = (work done) / time

= (forced used * distance)/time.

Force used = 600 * 9.8 (weight of load * acceleration due to gravity)

Thus, power = (600 * 9.8 * 6)/10

= 35, 280/10 = 3,528 watts or 3.5 kW.

2. While traveling at a constant speed of 40 m/s, a car overcomes 500 N of constant frictional force. Calculate the engine's horsepower. (1 horsepower = 3/4 kW).

Solution:

Engine power = work done/time.

= F * v

= 500 * 40 = 20,000 watts or 20 kW.

However, 1 horsepower = 3/4 kW or 1 kW = 4/3 horsepower.

Therefore, 20 kW = (20 * 4)/3 horsepower

= 80/3 horsepower or 26.7 horsepower.

Thus, the vehicle's engine is 26.7 horsepower.

Friction

Friction is said to exist between two objects moving in relation to each other if there is a resistance to the motion.

Friction can also be defined as the resistance between a fluid's moving layers. In this case, the friction is referred to as viscosity. The viscosity of a fluid determines its thickness and that explains the rationale behind honey's higher fluid friction than that of other lighter liquids such as water.

Applications of Friction

Friction is responsible for the wear and tear on an object's mechanical parts. The friction between the parts will eventually take its toll as the parts are gradually worn out. This explains the reason behind the use of liquids or lubricants to reduce friction and wear and tear between moving parts.

Although friction is sometimes considered a nuisance, it actually has a wide range of useful applications. It is useful in the following areas:

1. Without friction, holding an item is practically impossible.
2. Walking and driving are impossible without friction. Friction between your feet and the ground prevents you from slipping and helps you walk. The friction between the ground and tires also makes it possible for vehicles to move. Otherwise, the tires would keep spinning.

Laws of Friction

Friction is governed by several laws. These include:

1. Sliding friction is independent of speed

2. Friction is determined by the nature of the materials which come in contact
3. Sliding friction is less than static friction
4. Friction is directly proportional to the force pressing the surfaces together
5. Friction doesn't depend on the area of the surfaces in contact
6. Friction is reduced at high speeds in sliding friction but increases with increased relative speed in fluid friction.

Friction can be classified into:

1. **Static friction**: This form of friction exists between two interfaces whose motions are not in relation to each other. When an object rests on a surface, static friction acts upon it. It helps you to walk without slipping and that explains why walking on ice is difficult, because ice has little friction. People can also climb rock walls thanks to static friction between the wall and their feet and hands.
2. **Sliding friction**: This type of friction exists between two objects that are in motion or between an object sliding over a surface and the surface. Static friction is stronger than sliding friction and usually requires more force to overcome. If you try to slide a heavy object over a floor surface, making the object move requires more effort than keeping it in motion after the initial resistance has been overcome.
3. **Rolling friction**: Another name for this type of friction is rolling resistance. This resistive force acts on a rolling object and slows it down.
This friction is easier to overcome than other types and that explains its wide application in roller skates, bicycles, scooters, four-wheelers, skateboards and cars.
4. **Fluid friction**: This form of friction exists between an object moving in air and the air through which the object is in motion.
Fluid friction depends on several factors that include the material, the object's shape, the fluid's viscosity and the moving speed of the object. The fluid friction in opposition to an object's motion increases with its size and speed.
A bullet fired from a gun, a launched aircraft and other related objects won't slow down naturally without this friction.

Note that sliding, static and rolling friction can be found between solid surfaces. On the other hand, fluid friction is found between gases and liquids.

Waves

A wave can be considered an oscillation or a disturbance that travels through space. The travel is usually accompanied by energy transfer. A wave transfers energy and doesn't move mass.

Types of Waves

Waves can be classified into:

a. Matter waves

Matter waves are otherwise known as De Broglie waves. The frequency of matter waves is a function of their kinetic energy.

b. Electromagnetic waves

These types of waves are created by the fusion of magnetic and electric fields. Some examples of such waves are colors and light.

A clear distinction between mechanical and electromagnetic waves is that the latter don't require a traveling medium. All electromagnetic waves travel through a vacuum at a speed of 300,000 kilometers per hour or $3 * 10^8$ m/s.

Electromagnetic waves are classified into different groups. These are:

➤ **X-rays**: X-rays are considered one of the most energetic forms of electromagnetic waves. They are used for taking images of the human body for medical purposes. That takes advantage of the rays' ability to see through a human body, helping medical professionals to see external organs.

➤ **Microwaves**: Microwaves are another form of electromagnetic ration. They have a wide range of wavelength, ranging from one meter to one millimeter. The frequency can also range between 300 MHz and 300 GHz. EHF and UHF bands are some examples of microwaves.

➤ **Ultraviolet waves**: Ultraviolet waves are electromagnetic radiation. Their wavelength falls between 10 nm and 400 nm. The wavelengths are shorter than those of X-rays but are not as long as visible light.
Ultraviolet radiation makes up a tenth of all electromagnetic radiation from the sun, its primary source.

➤ **Radio waves**: These wavelengths are longer infrared light waves.
Their frequencies are between 30 Hz and 300 GHz. Their wavelength at 300 GHz is 1 mm and 10,000 kilometers at 30 Hz.

➤ **Gamma rays**: Gamma rays are an electromagnetic radiation with penetrating power. These rays can be observed when atomic nuclei undergo radioactive decay.
In comparison with other electromagnetic waves, gamma rays have the shortest wavelength and provide the highest photon energy.

➤ **Infrared rays**: This form of radiation consists of electromagnetic waves with wavelengths between 700 nanometers and one millimeter.

Infrared rays are usually emitted by most of the warm objects we come in contact with every day. About 50% of the total energy the sun produces is infrared.

➤ **Visible light**: This is the form of electromagnetic radiation that human eyes can see.

c. Mechanical waves

Mechanical waves are classified into longitudinal or transverse, depending on their oscillation's direction.

Transverse waves

When the disturbance of a wave causes oscillations that are at right angles or perpendicular to the direction of energy transfer or propagation, the wave is considered transverse.

Examples of transverse waves abound in nature. Some examples of this type of wave are:

1. The vibrations on a guitar string
2. Electromagnetic waves such as microwave, light waves and radio waves.
3. Ripples on water
4. S-wave earthquake waves
5. Torsion waves.

The crest is the highest point of a transverse wave while the trough is the lowest part.

➤ **Longitudinal waves**

In longitudinal waves, the direction of energy transfer and oscillation are parallel to each other. This implies that the wave moves in the same direction as the displacement of the wave's medium.

Pressure waves and sound waves are two examples of longitudinal waves. Note that water waves are special kind of waves. They are an example of a combination of both longitudinal and transverse waves.

Properties of Electromagnetic Waves

Electromagnetic waves have some properties that distinguish them from other wave types. Some of their properties are:

- They can be polarized
- They travel at the speed of light in a vacuum

- They don't need a medium for propagation
- They are mostly transverse
- Electromagnetic waves have momentum.

Thermal radiation, radio waves and light waves are common examples of electromagnetic waves.

Sound

Sound is a form of energy that is transmitted as wave, a vibration that is transmitted through liquid, solid or gas.

Characteristics of Sound

Sound has five major characteristics. These are:

1. Wavelength

When two waves are beside each other, the distance between their corresponding points is the wavelength. When sound is produced, the air is rarified or compressed in waves. The waves travel out from the source in different directions. When the compressed area hits your eardrum, it undergoes vibration with the compression waves in the air. You can then hear the produced sound.

The frequency is inversely proportional to the distance between each successive rarification or compression in the sound wave approaching you. The distance between the successive compressions is the wavelength.

2. Amplitude

Amplitude refers to the measure of a sound's power. Sound can be soft or loud. The amplitude of a sound wave shows how low or high the wave is. In other words, it is a measure of how loud or soft a sound is.

3. Frequency

The frequency of oscillation is a measure of the number of oscillations that occur per second. It refers to the number of complete cycles or waves sound produces in a second. Thus, if an object makes 50 oscillations per second, its frequency is 50 Hz.

A cycle is completed each time a wave peaks, troughs, and peaks again. In other words, it refers to the wave going up, down, and up again. How fast the cycle is completed is the wave's frequency. Frequency is also called pitch.

Sound frequency is measured in cycles per second or Hertz (Hz), named after German physicist Heinrich Rudolf Hertz, who is credited with proving the existence of electromagnetic waves.

Frequency is an important attribute of sound. It explains the rationale behind why we hear some sounds differently. For instance, the cry of a baby sounds different from the cry of an adult because the sounds exhibit different frequencies.

The frequency of the vibrating body is the determinant of the shrillness of the sound produced by a body. Pitch is a term used to define and explain shrillness. Pitch is directly proportional to frequency. This implies that the higher or lower the frequency of the vibrating body, the higher or lower its pitch. When the pitch is low, the sound will appear gruff or deep while shrill sounds are high-pitched.

4. Period

The period of a wave refers to the time between two adjacent troughs or peaks. The time is always the same regardless of the adjacent troughs or crests. This is usually the time it takes a wavelength to pass.

5. Loudness

Loudness is another major characteristic of sound. It is dependent on the amplitude of the vibration that produces the sound. The loudness of sound depends on the amplitude. Another important factor that determines sound is the quantity of the air that vibrates in response to the sound.

The SI unit of sound loudness is a decibel (dB).

6. Velocity

The velocity of sound refers to the speed and direction at which it travels. This is dependent on different factors that include density, humidity and temperature.

The relationship between the speed of sound, its wavelength and frequency is represented by the equation:

$V = f\lambda$ where:

V = the speed of sound.

F = frequency of sound

λ = wavelength of sound

Let's consider some examples of how to calculate the speed of sound with the relevant information.

1. The speed of sound is 340 m/s. Find the wavelength of sound if its frequency is 25 cycles per second.

Velocity: 340 m/s

Frequency: 20 cycles/s

$V = f \lambda$

Therefore, $\lambda = V/f$

$= 340/25 = 13.6$ m.

2. What is the frequency of a sound wave with speed 340 m/s and 2.0 Hz wavelength?

Velocity: 340 m/s

Wavelength: 2.0 Hz

$V = f \lambda$

Therefore, $f = V/ \lambda$

Frequency $= 340/2.0$

Frequency $= 170$ Hz.

3. A motorboat's wave travels across a lake at a velocity of 2.5 m/s. The distance between successive wave crests is 3.5 m. Calculate the frequency of the waves.

Wave velocity $= 2.5$ m/s

Wavelength $= 3.5$ m

$V = f \lambda$

$F = v/ \lambda$

Frequency $= 2.5/3.5 = 0.714$ Hz.

4. A wave has a frequency of 80 Hz and its wavelength is 30 cm. How fast is the wave moving?

This question asks you to find the speed of the wave, given its frequency and wavelength.

$V = f\lambda$

Frequency = 80 Hz.

Wavelength = 30 cm.

Convert wavelength to meters = 30/100

Wavelength = 0.3 m.

$V = 0.3 * 80$

$V = 24$ m/s

Frequency is inversely proportional to time. Hence, the frequency of a wave can be calculated as the inverse of its time, and vice versa.

Hence, $f = 1/t$

For instance, if the period of a pendulum is 5 seconds, calculate its frequency.

T = 5 seconds

$F = 1/t$

Hence, frequency = 1/5

$F = 0.2$ Hz.

Properties of Waves

So far, we have discussed the characteristics of waves extensively. What are the properties of waves? These attributes are discussed extensively in this section.

Waves have five properties. They are:

1. Reflection

Reflection occurs when waves hit a barrier. This implies that waves don't penetrate hard surfaces but bounce off from them. For instance, light waves are known for bouncing off mirrors, and sound waves are reflected by walls, while planes cause the reflection of radar waves.

The reflection process is affected by several factors. One is the angle at which the wave hits an obstacle.

If the hitting is done at the right angle to the object's surface, the wave will be reflected backwards. However, if the wake strikes at an angle to the surface, it won't be reflected backwards directly. The angle at which the wave hits the obstacle (known as the incident angle or angle of incidence) is the same as the angle at which it is reflected back (known as the reflected angle or angle of reflection).

Reflection of sound waves has some practical applications. Consider a few of them:

- It is used for measuring the speed and distance of underwater objects through a method called SONAR
- It is the underlying principle behind how a stethoscope works
- It is the foundation for the soundboard
- Horns, megaphones and trumpets use the principle of reflection of sound.

2. Refraction

Waves sometimes move across a medium. A medium is a substance through which waves are transported. A change in the properties of a medium can have a huge effect on the wave. Consider the case of water changing from one depth to another.

Refraction of waves occurs when waves change their direction when passing from one medium to another. This is also referred to as the bending of a wave's path. When a wave changes its direction, its wavelength and speed will change accordingly. This explains why water waves slow down when moving from deep water into shallow water.

3. Interference

Interference refers to the superimposition of two waves with the objective of forming a wave of lower, greater or equal amplitude. All types of waves display this trait including acoustic, light, radio, gravity waves, surface water waves, matter waves and other wave types.

Interference of waves can be divided into:

- *Constructive interference*: Constructive interference is a feature of two identical waves that are superimposed to either form a peak or a trough. If the waves have the same amplitude, wavelength and frequency, the height of the peak formed is the sum of the two waves' heights. If they form a trough, the depth is also the sum of the two waves' troughs.

- *Destructive interference*: On the other hand, when two non-identical waves are superimposed, they cause destructive interference. When one wave wants to form a peak and the other desires to form a trough, they cancel themselves out rather than achieve their different objectives. In that case, the waves produced have a reduced amplitude.

4. Diffraction

The diffraction of waves also involves a change in a wave's direction. However, unlike reflection that involves a change in direction when a wave bounces off a barrier, and refraction that involves change in direction triggered by passing from one medium to another, diffraction focuses on a change in the direction of any wave as the wave passes through a barrier or an opening in its path.

Water waves are known for their ability to pass through openings and around barriers. This property distinguishes water waves from most other waves.

The sharpness of the bending or the amount of diffraction is determined by the wavelength. When the wavelength increases, the amount of diffraction will increase too and vice versa. You can't notice the occurrence of diffraction if the wave has a smaller wavelength than the obstacle.

5. Standing wave

A standing wave is a special type of interference. This occurs when two identical waves are traveling in opposite directions through the same medium. In this type of interference, the wave will have antinodes or regions of constructive interference, and nodes, regions of destructive interference. Standing waves are otherwise referred to as stationary waves.

Characteristics of Stationary Waves

Some characteristics of stationary waves are:

- They form stationary waveforms
- The antinodes and nodes are formed alternately
- There are maximum pressure changes at the nodes while the pressure changes are minimum at the antinodes
- With the exception of the nodes, all the particles of stationary waves have simple harmonic motions with the same period
- At the nodes, the particles don't have a velocity

- No energy transfer takes place in stationary waves.

Test 1 Questions

Math Test 1 – 50 Questions

1. The addition of two or more numbers to form a new number is known as …
   a. Summation.
   b. Addition.
   c. Division.
   d. Multiplication.

2. The numbers added together are individually known as the …
   a. Addends.
   b. Added parts.
   c. Additional elements.
   d. Add-ons.

3. One-digit numbers in addition are referred to as …
   a. Tens.
   b. Digitals.
   c. Units.
   d. One-digit additional elements.

4. Hundreds are … numbers between … and …
   a. Three-digit numbers between 100 and 999.
   b. Two-digit numbers between 10 and 99.
   c. Two-digit numbers between 0 and 100.
   d. Multiple-digit numbers between 0 and 999.

5. What is the first step in adding multiple-digit numbers?

    a. Finding their common values.

    b. Rearranging the numbers according to the number of digits.

    c. Summing up the numbers regardless of their order of arrangement.

    d. None of the above.

6. When adding multiple-digit numbers using column addition, the operations are started from ...

    a. The column farthest to the right.

    b. The column farthest to the left.

    c. The middle column.

    d. Any convenient column.

7. When do you get a 'carry-over' during an addition operation?

    a. When the sum of the addends exceeds 20.

    b. When the sum of the addends exceeds 10.

    c. When the sum of the addends exceeds 9.

    d. When the sum of the addends is less than 50.

8. Which of the following will have a 'carry-over' during addition?

    a. 20 + 15

    b. 34 + 12

    c. 28 + 12

    d. 87 + 10

9. What do you do with the carry during an addition operation?

    a. Add the carry to any number on the left.

    b. Add the carry to the middle number.

    c. Add the carry to the next number to the left.

    d. Add the carry to the next number to the right.

10. What effect does subtraction have on the bigger number?

    a. It increases the bigger number.

    b. It has no significant effect on the bigger number.

    c. It decreases the bigger number.

    d. It increases the smaller number.

11. When subtracting using column subtraction, the operations are started from ...

    a. The column farthest to the right.

    b. The column farthest to the left.

    c. The most convenient place.

    d. The middle column.

12. Which of the following subtraction operations gives a positive difference?

    a. Subtract 333 from 124.

    b. Subtract 764 from 239.

    c. Subtract 239 from 664.

    d. Subtract 123 from 098.

13. When adding the carry to a number during addition, it has a value of ...

    a. 1 or a multiple of 1.

    b. 8 or a multiple of 8.

    c. 50 or a multiple of 50.

    d. 20 or a multiple of 20.

14. When subtracting numbers, which of the following holds true?

    a. You can't subtract numbers of equal value from each other.

    b. You can subtract numbers of equal value from each other.

    c. You should start the subtraction from the biggest to the smallest number.

    d. The order of arrangement is immaterial once you understand the concept.

15. Under what condition is borrowing necessary during column subtraction?

    a. If you must subtract a smaller digit from a bigger digit.

    b. When both digits in a column are of equal value.

    c. When subtracting a bigger digit from a smaller digit.

    d. When both digits in a column are bigger than 20.

16. What is the value of the borrowed number?

    a. 20.

    b. 10.

    c. 5.

    d. 2.

17. Which of the following operations involves repeated subtraction?

    a. Cross-multiplication.

    b. Addition of even numbers.

    c. Division.

    d. Multiplication.

18. The most appropriate place to start in short division is from ...

    a. The right-hand column.

    b. The middle column.

    c. The left-hand column.

    d. Any side of the numbers.

19. What is the result of dividing 324 by 4?

    a. This operation cannot be performed.

    b. 024.

    c. 81.

    d. 320.

20. Which of the following operations start from the left?
    a. Addition and subtraction.
    b. Subtraction and multiplication.
    c. Addition and multiplication.
    d. Division only.

21. Which of these operations requires repeated addition?
    a. Multiplication.
    b. Addition of integers.
    c. Division of odd numbers.
    d. Multiplication of perfect squares.

22. The whole part and the fractional part of a decimal number are separated by ...
    a. A decimal divider.
    b. A decimal point.
    c. A decimal demarcator.
    d. None of the above.

23. Which of these correctly describes 0.50?
    a. The digit 5 represents a whole number preceded by 0 for clarity.
    b. The number .50 is a multiple of 5 with the appropriate reference.
    c. The digit 5 represents a fractional part of a whole number.
    d. The digit 5 is a divisor for 1.

24. All of the following operations can be performed on decimal numbers except ...
    a. Multiplication.
    b. Division.
    c. Addition.
    d. None of the above.

25. A guiding rule when adding decimal numbers is …

    a. The decimal points must align.

    b. The decimal points must be ignored.

    c. Regardless of where the decimal point is, you can start adding anywhere.

    d. Addition can't be performed on even numbers.

26. Which of the following expressions accurately represents "add 234.56 and 12.6"?

    a. 234.56 + 12.60

    b. 234.56 + 12.06

    c. 234.56 + 12.006

    d. 234.56 + 12.600

27. What is the value of 0 in 257.90?

    a. It makes the number look more presentable.

    b. It makes the number look divisible by 5.

    c. It makes the number divisible by 10.

    d. It adds value to the number.

28. How do you handle two numbers with different numbers of decimal places?

    a. Arrange them as they are.

    b. Add the corresponding number of zeros to balance the number of decimal places.

    c. Arrange them in your order of preference.

    d. Do nothing about them.

29. Two important factors you must focus on when multiplying decimal numbers are:

    a. The positions and number of the decimal values.

    b. The number and importance of the decimal values.

    c. The number of the decimal values and the position of the multiplier.

    d. None of the above.

30. What determines the location of the decimal point after multiplication?
    a. The decimal in the smaller number.
    b. The decimal in the bigger number.
    c. The addition of the decimals in both numbers.
    d. The subtraction of the smaller decimal from the bigger decimal.

31. A better understanding of ... will enhance your multiplication and division skills.
    a. Four-figure tables.
    b. Calculators.
    c. Multiplication tables.
    d. Abacus machines.

32. A number is expressed as a percentage when it is expressed as ...
    a. A fraction of another number with respect to 50.
    b. A part of a whole number with respect to 100.
    c. An improper fraction with respect to 20.
    d. A whole derived from a part with respect to 50.

33. *Percent* is derived from the Latin words ....
    a. *Per centage.*
    b. *Per centenary.*
    c. *Per centum.*
    d. *Per central.*

34. Percent means ...
    a. For 100 or basically 100.
    b. Per 100 or around 100.
    c. Per 100 or approximately 100.
    d. Per 100 or through 100.

35. It is important to convert a given number into a/an ... before converting it into a percentage.

    a. Fraction.

    b. Roman numeral.

    c. Improper fraction.

    d. None of the above.

36. The second step in finding the percentage of a given number is ...

    a. Finding the decimal value of the given number.

    b. Rearranging the given number.

    c. Multiplying the fractional value by 100.

    d. Expressing the given number as a fraction of the whole.

37. The bottom value in a fraction is called a ...

    a. Numerator.

    b. Divisor.

    c. Divider.

    d. Denominator.

38. The top value in a fraction is called a ...

    a. Numerator.

    b. Divisor.

    c. Divider.

    d. Denominator.

39. Add 345.67, 236.9 and 167.0

    a. 657.34.

    b. 875.90.

    c. 749.57.

    d. 7495.7.

40. A man bought five pairs of shoes at $50 per pair. How much did he spend altogether?

    a. $230.

    b. $350.

    c. $240.

    d. $250.

41. In the question above, the man got a 5% discount. How much did he spend for the five pairs after the discount?

    a. $235.50.

    b. $233.50.

    c. $237.50.

    d. $238.80.

42. Represent the store discount as a fraction of the original cost of the five pairs.

    a. 2/12.

    b. 3/15.

    c. 1/20.

    d. 4/15.

43. What is the place value of the digit 5 in 235?

    a. Unit.

    b. Hundred.

    c. Thousand.

    d. Tens.

44. If only 80 out of 300 students passed an entrance exam, what percentage of the students failed the examination?

    a. 26.66%.

    b. 46.22%.

    c. 87.23%.

    d. 73.33%.

45. Subtract 45.6 from the sum of 67.80 and 99.12.

    a. 57.80.

    b. 34.99.

    c. 121.32.

    d. 22.20.

46. The Roman numeral M stands for ...

    a. 500.

    b. 400.

    c. 1,000.

    d. 100.

47. LXXX stands for what figure?

    a. 400.

    b. 300.

    c. 80.

    d. 800.

48. Which of the following Roman numerals represents 800?

    a. DCCC.

    b. LXXX.

    c. CXXX.

    d. MDDD.

49. XV times VI is ...

    a. CDDD.

    b. XCC.

    c. XDM.

    d. XC.

50. Add 23, 47 and 12. Give the answer in Roman numerals.

    a. LXXII.

    b. CXII.

    c. LXXXII.

    d. CXIII.

Reading Test 1 – 47 Questions

Read the following passages and answer the questions that follow.

Passage 1 – Multitasking: Is it for You?

We all multitask at one point or another, either consciously or unconsciously. Perhaps you may be listening to your favorite music on your earphones while reading this book, or perhaps you pick up phone calls while watching your favorite sports team or TV show. Your ability to engage in multiple activities or tasks simultaneously is multitasking.

Many people consider multitasking to be a perfect way to get a lot done within a short time. However, researchers disagree with that school of thought. According to some researchers, the human brain is not all that great at handling multiple tasks simultaneously. On the contrary, multitasking is believed to reduce, rather than boost, productivity.

According to these studies, the idea of working on several tasks at the same time is nothing but a myth, a self-delusion. Individuals who believe they are good multitaskers are actually not achieving as much as they believe they are. Let's look at some reasons that may make you reconsider your view of multitasking.

The human brain is not designed to multitask: In opposition to the general belief, the human brain is not designed as an efficient multitasking machine. Rather, it is designed to focus on one task at a time. Thus, when handling more than one task concurrently, the brain won't function at maximum capacity because it is not designed to efficiently and successfully handle more than one task at a time.

Multitasking is a myth: No one actually multitasks, we only task-switch. Thus, your brain focuses on what you are working on at that time while it sends the other tasks to the background.

Multitasking reduces productivity: Contrary to your expectation, multitasking doesn't help you achieve more; rather, it wastes your time. When switching from one task to another, it takes the brain some time to get used to the new task you switch to. Thus, repeatedly moving from one task to another will actually waste your time and reduce your productivity.

Edward Hallowell, MD, found that simultaneously working on two tasks will impair your ability to focus on one task and give it your best attention. The result is always a substandard performance.

Multitasking may harm your brain: Trying to handle more than one task at a time won't only reduce your productivity; it may harm your brain as well. A 2011 study by a group of scientists at the San Francisco-based University of California shows that switching from one task to another may trigger short-term memory loss.

In the report of the research published in *Proceedings of the National Academy of Sciences*, researchers revealed that multitasking negatively affects the short-term memory (also known as the working memory). Imagine the huge impact that multitasking regularly can have on your brain in the long run.

Why should you Single-Task?

While multitasking is appealing, there is overwhelming evidence to support that it not only wastes time but can also have a negative impact on your productivity and memory. Thus, you should consider single-tasking as a better alternative. Why is single-tasking a worthy option?

Less stress: Single-tasking is less stressful than multi-tasking. By focusing on one task, you don't expend extra energy by handling more than one task. Thus, you are less stressed and won't be under too much pressure that may jerk up your work-related stress levels.

Ability to focus on a task: When you multitask, task-switching is the order of the day. It is practically impossible to give your undivided attention to a task because you want to handle multiple tasks at a time. On the other hand, single-tasking enables you to focus on a task and get it done swiftly before moving to the next task.

Improved creativity: Your creativity will also receive a massive boost if you concentrate all your efforts on one task. Focusing on a task helps you fashion out the best way to get the job done quickly and effectively. That will put your creative skills to task. The more you hone your creative skills, the better you become.

1. What is multitasking?
    a. Multitasking is the ability to complete a couple of tasks daily.
    b. Multitasking is the ability to perform two or more tasks at the same time.
    c. Multitasking is the ability to operate several machines simultaneously.
    d. None of the above.

2. What is the general belief about multitasking?
    a. It is generally believed that multitasking is time-wasting.
    b. It is generally believed that multitasking is exclusively for amateur workers.
    c. It is generally believed that multitasking boosts productivity.
    d. It is generally believed that multitasking is expensive.

3. What is the realistic view of multitasking?

    a. Multitasking is a waste of time.

    b. Multitasking is good for professional multitaskers.

    c. Multitasking is useful for some tasks and not good for others.

    d. Multitasking is addictive.

4. People who believe they are multitasking are actually doing what?

    a. They are actually playing around their tasks.

    b. They are actually being realistic.

    c. They are actually task-switching.

    d. They are actually indecisive.

5. What is the potential effect of multitasking on the human brain?

    a. It has a positive impact on short-term memory.

    b. It has a negative impact on short-term memory.

    c. Its impact depends on the multitasker.

    d. It has no impact on the human brain.

6. What is the connection between multitasking and productivity?

    a. Multitasking boosts productivity.

    b. Multitasking reduces productivity.

    c. Multitasking has no effect on productivity.

    d. Multitasking's impact on productivity has not been determined.

7. Which is more stressful: single-tasking or multitasking?

    a. Multitasking is more stressful.

    b. Single-tasking is more stressful.

    c. It depends on the amount of time dedicated to it.

    d. None of the above.

8. How does single-tasking affect creativity?

    a. Single-tasking helps people to be more focused and more creative.

    b. Single-tasking has no significant impact on creativity.

    c. Creativity and single-tasking are dependent on each other.

    d. Single-tasking triples creative skill levels.

9. What is the connection between multitasking and the ability to focus on a task?

    a. Multitasking increases the difficulty of focusing on a task.

    b. Multitasking creates the right environment that makes focusing easier.

    c. Multitasking is impossible without the ability to focus on a task.

    d. All of the above.

10. The human brain is not designed to multitask. Explain.

    a. The human brain is designed with the ability to focus on one task at a time.

    b. The human brain is designed to process multiple tasks simultaneously and efficiently.

    c. The human brain stops multitasking at a specific age.

    d. None of the above.

11. Which of the following is not an example of multitasking?

    a. Chatting with a friend while cooking.

    b. Humming to a melodious song while driving.

    c. Knitting while dancing.

    d. Dreaming while sleeping.

12. Differentiate between multitasking and task-switching.

    a. Multitasking is the ability to perform two or more tasks simultaneously while task-switching is switching from one task to another.

    b. Multitasking is the perceived ability to perform two or more tasks efficiently while task-switching is switching from one task to another.

    c. Task-switching is the ability to perform two or more tasks simultaneously while multitasking is switching from one task to another.

    d. Multitasking and task-switching are synonyms.

13. On her list of tasks, Sheila has two options: handle two tasks simultaneously to get them done quickly or handle one task after the other. What's your advice?

    a. She should handle the two tasks simultaneously.

    b. She should handle the tasks one after the other.

    c. All of the above.

    d. None of the above.

14. What is another name for working memory?

    a. Active memory.

    b. Long-term memory.

    c. Short-term memory.

    d. Infinite memory.

15. What can you conclude from the article?

    a. That multitasking is a myth and a waste of time.

    b. That multitasking should be done by professionals.

    c. That multitasking is a necessary skill for everyone.

    d. That multitasking has no pros and cons.

Passage 2 – Motivation: The Key to Success

Motivation is a very powerful beast. Sometimes, though, it can be tricky. Some people are easily motivated while others have to struggle hard to get and stay motivated. If you find yourself in the latter category, you may find it easy to give way to procrastination.

If you have been struggling with motivation recently, some practical ideas that will help you get motivated and avoid needless procrastination are discussed here.

Motivation has been defined by scientists as an individual's general willingness to act or do something. It is that psychological force that moves people to take necessary action at the appropriate time.

If you need a major boost for self-motivation, consider the easy and practical tips below:

Set Realistic Goals

Setting realistic goals is the key to achieving them. To succeed at setting realistic goals, be practical. Understand the amount of work required to hit your target and plan your goals around it. Don't set the bar so high that you can't hit your target. That will set you up for failure, and invariably, will remove the last iota of motivation you have left.

Understanding your limitations is another important factor that will contribute immensely to setting realistic goals. For instance, some can study for hours in one sitting, while others do better when they read at intervals, with short breaks in between. If you are not cut out for marathon reading, that's your limitation. If you can't study more than a few pages at one time, understand that limitation and set your goals with such limitations in mind.

Write Down Your Goals

What goals do you have with respect to your nursing career? Do you know them? Have you written the goals down? Start from your dream of passing the nursing entrance exam. Write that goal down. Then, think about the other goals you have. Keep a list of such goals as a reminder of what you must do to get to where you want to be. Rearrange them in order of importance so that you know which to focus on.

When you write your goals down, it is easier to work towards achieving them because writing makes them concrete rather than abstract ideas. More so, you are less likely to forget the goals and how you intend to achieve them. Put your goals down in writing and regularly monitor them. With a regular reminder, your chances of forgetting what you set out to achieve are drastically reduced. That gives you the motivation to keep working until you hit your target.

Break Your Goals into Smaller Chunks

If you want to climb a mountain, you don't just jump right up it. Rather, you take it one calculated step at a time. Each step you take brings you closer to your dream. Do the same for your goals.

Breaking down goals into smaller chunks makes them easier to achieve. Think of it this way. You want to become a nurse. What's the first step? Take the nursing school entrance exam, right? When you recognize that fact, you already have your goal of becoming a nurse broken down.

How do you achieve that goal? Prepare adequately for the examination. The next step is to pass the test. What's the next step? Apply for nursing school, etc. This is how you break your goals down into workable steps. You can imagine how much easier it is if you focus on one stage at a time rather than focusing on the one very large goal of 'becoming a nurse.'

If you can't drive, you don't just buy your dream car and jump inside it, start the engine and hope for some superpower to drive the vehicle to your destination. The first step is to learn to drive and take it from there.

Practice Self-Reflection

During self-reflection, go through your written plans and goals. Take a critical look at how much you have done so far. Consider the areas where improvements are needed and practical ways you can improve your performance and achieve your goals faster.

Your self-reflection shouldn't be mere routine. Rather, it must be done with the purpose of learning from it every single time. Whatever information you gather during your self-reflection will contribute immensely to your success.

Find Time for Yourself

Finding time for yourself is another effective way to get motivated. When you overwork yourself, stress may keep you from doing a good job. When you are stressed, not only will you suffer from physical fatigue, but you will also lose your motivation. You won't be motivated to work when you lack the physical and mental capacity to do so.

Thus, it is imperative that you find time for yourself. Hang out with friends and family when necessary, go to the movies when you feel like it and generally ensure that you have enough time to destress.

Sometimes, the best way to create time for yourself is to celebrate your achievements. That's another benefit of breaking your goals down into smaller chunks. When you achieve each chunk, celebrate it. Give yourself a treat as a celebration of how far you have come.

According to motivation experts, the celebration will boost your dopamine release. The feel-good feeling will serve as motivation to keep pushing forward until you achieve whatever you have set your mind on. That's a reliable source of motivation. Remember, each stage of your goal deserves a celebration. When you look forward to the next celebration, you will be fired up to keep going. That's the essence of motivation.

Read Motivational Materials

This is a no-brainer. Motivational books, novels, movies, talks, etc., are designed to motivate people to keep going, regardless of their impulses. Most of these materials are produced by individuals who have succeeded in life despite all odds and distractions, including a lack of motivation.

From their personal experiences, they share effective tips that can help you to overcome your challenges and be motivated to pursue your dreams.

You can leverage motivational quotes as well. Reflect on at least one motivational quote daily and see how acting on it will have a huge impact on your ability to overcome procrastination and be motivated.

Do Not Compare Yourself to Others

You do yourself a great disservice when you compare yourself to others. Measuring your achievements and abilities against others is unproductive. Remember that you are not identical to the people you compare yourself with. Your make-up is different. You don't share the same DNA. You are wired differently.

While you may have friends and family that are brilliant and can ace exams and tests with ease, you may have to put in more effort to do the same. Rather than engaging in unnecessary and demoralizing comparisons, identify your personal strengths and leverage them.

If you can't read more than five pages daily, that's fine. Use that knowledge and limitation to your advantage. Do that consistently and you will still be amazed at the outcome within a few months. However, if you make careless comparisons and decide to read two or three chapters daily, you won't only hurt yourself physically due to exhaustion and stress, you will hurt yourself emotionally too. Your strengths and limitations are what make you unique. Learn to work with what you have rather than feeling bad about what you don't.

Leverage Your Strengths

Regardless of your personal opinions of yourself, you do have strengths. Sadly, most people focus on their weaknesses and see nothing good about themselves. That's wrong. You are setting yourself up for failure if that's the only thing you know about yourself.

However, when you identify your strengths, you are on your way to developing the needed motivation to excel in life. You will be more motivated to act if you plan your affairs around your strengths. You can't work with the same mindset and vigor if you focus solely on your weaknesses.

Work on Your Weaknesses

While taking advantage of your strengths with a view to using them to be more motivated in life, don't overlook the importance of working on your weaknesses. If you don't find a way to get the best out of your weaknesses, they will undermine whatever you achieve with your strengths.

Thus, know where you are weak and how that impacts your life. Try to find out some practical ways you can minimize the impact by improving specific areas of your life.

As you work on one weakness after another and you realize that your weaknesses can be leveraged for your benefit, your struggles with motivation will gradually fade.

Find a Coach or Mentor

If everything else fails or if you wish to complement your other efforts, getting a coach isn't a bad idea. Look for someone with a track record of success.

Experienced mentors understand the importance of motivation. They know what it takes to succeed in life in view of the barrage of distractions around you. From their personal experiences, they can offer you the assistance you need to get out of your comfort zone and become fired up.

As you're preparing for nursing school, the best mentor to boost your motivation level is unarguably an experienced medical practitioner. Aside from helping you to overcome procrastination, the mentor can also assist you to obtain the best from your nursing school years and beyond.

1. Which of the following is true?
    a. Everyone is equally motivated.
    b. People become easily motivated as they age.
    c. Some people are easily motivated while some struggle with lack of motivation and procrastination.
    d. Meditation is a thing of the mind and can easily be triggered.

2. The key to setting realistic goals is ...
    a. Setting yourself up to be at par with others.
    b. Having a realistic view of yourself and your limitations.
    c. Believing that you have the ability to do anything.
    d. Doing things at your convenience.

3. What benefit does writing your goals down offer?
    a. A reminder of what you need to do to make your dreams come true.
    b. A documentation of your abilities for future reference.
    c. It enables you to have something you can boast about.
    d. It offers no benefit.

4. Goals are best achieved when ...
    a. They are written in alphabetical order.
    b. They are broken down into smaller and easier-to-achieve chunks.
    c. They are attempted when you have all the resources to achieve them.
    d. You wait for the most appropriate time to attempt them.

5. ... is a form of performance appraisal that helps you to identify how much you have achieved and where improvements are needed.
    a. Goal appraisal.
    b. Personal abilities and limitations assessment.
    c. Self-reflection.
    d. Personal appraisal.

6. Finding time for yourself enables you to ...

    a. Manage stress effectively.

    b. Celebrate each achievement at a time.

    c. Develop and analyze your next plan of action.

    d. All of the above.

7. You will always find the motivation to realize your dreams if you ...

    a. Compare yourself to successful people.

    b. Resist the urge to compare yourself to others.

    c. Respond to challenges without giving them a second thought.

    d. Try as many things as you can.

8. Which of the following is true?

    a. Working on your weaknesses is as beneficial as leveraging your strengths.

    b. Your weaknesses will always hamper your progress regardless of your efforts to improve them.

    c. You are less likely to be motivated if you include your weaknesses in your plans.

    d. Concentrating only on your strengths will help you to achieve your goals in life.

9. Which of these people can best impact your motivation?

    a. Angel investors.

    b. Venture capitalists.

    c. Experienced coaches.

    d. Religious and political leaders.

10. What should you bear in mind when writing your goals down?

    a. Set goals that are realistic.

    b. Write the goals down in order of importance.

    c. The written-down goals should serve as a guide.

    d. All of the above.

Passage 3 – Medical Marijuana: Health Benefits and Side Effects

Since its adoption into mainstream medicine, medical marijuana has continued to generate debates and arguments among scientists, doctors, policy makers, and researchers. There are questions about its safety and whether it should be legalized or not. In this article, we take a look at the potential health benefits and side effects of using medical marijuana.

Although the US government is yet to declare it legal, it is currently considered legal in 29 states, including Washington DC. This is in addition to the millions of users across the country.

Marijuana contains cannabinoids or CBD in short. This component is responsible for the hallucinogenic effects of marijuana on users. CBD reportedly can prevent the central nervous system from inflammation, thanks to its anti-inflammatory effects on the system. For this and other reasons, marijuana has a ton of medical purposes.

Medical marijuana's list of benefits includes the following.

Pain management: Through its cannabinoids content, marijuana is used medically to alter pain perception in the human brain. Physicians take advantage of this benefit to treat some medical conditions such as fibromyalgia, arthritis, migraines, and endometriosis, medical conditions that are known for their pain-causing effects.

Reduced inflammation: Irritable bowel syndrome, Crohn's disease, and rheumatoid arthritis are some medical conditions that may cause inflammation. Marijuana's CBD content is a powerful antidote that helps with inflammation reduction in people with the medical conditions listed above. Thus, such individuals can enjoy improved health without going through the excruciating pain that may result from the inflammation.

Sleep management: Victims of sleep disorders may heave a sigh of relief as they benefit from the relaxing effect of using marijuana. Thanks to its anti-inflammation and pain management properties, patients that are treated with medical marijuana can also sleep better.

Mental disorders management: Marijuana also affects the limbic system positively. Medical doctors are taking advantage of this property when treating patients with mental or neurological disorders. Thus, it is extensively used in treating post-traumatic stress disorder (PTST), multiple sclerosis, Tourette's syndrome, and anxiety. It is also recommended for treating Parkinson's disease and epilepsy.

While the numerous benefits of using medical marijuana as highlighted below have contributed to its increasing use in the medical world, there are concerns over its potential side effects on users too. Some of the reasons why a growing number of individuals and experts are calling for its ban are:

Marijuana is also known for its ability to trigger some medical problems such as rapid breathing, hyperactivity, and increased heart and blood pressure rates. If these conditions are not properly managed, they may be the harbinger for more serious health concerns.

While marijuana may have a depressant-like effect on a user, such users may also become more prone to concentration and coordination issues. When left untreated, they are at the risk of suffering from other physical health challenges aside from the depressive symptoms that marijuana users display from time to time.

Marijuana is a two-sided coin. It offers tons of benefits that are leveraged by a physician to treat different medical conditions. Nevertheless, its users are not immune to several side effects that are mentioned above.

1. Replace "mainstream" with any of the words below.

    a. Medical.

    b. Important.

    c. Conventional.

    d. Special.

2. How does the US respond to medical marijuana?

    a. It shows a nonchalant attitude.

    b. It forbids its use.

    c. It encourages its use.

    d. There are insufficient data to determine the country's response.

3. Which of the following marijuana component is responsible for its hallucinogenic effect on users?

    a. Cannabis.

    b. Cannabidines.

    c. Cannabinoids.

    d. Cannabis acid.

4. What feature of medical marijuana makes it ideal for treating arthritis?
    a. Inflammation reduction.
    b. Pain management.
    c. Sleep management.
    d. All of the above.

5. Identify the list that contains medical conditions that may trigger inflammation.
    a. Arthritis and irritable bowel movement.
    b. Irritable bowel movement and type-1 diabetes.
    c. Crohn's disease and Parkinson's disease.
    d. Peptic ulcer and high blood pressure.

6. What is the connection between CBD and inflammation?
    a. It increases inflammation.
    b. It creates an enabling environment for inflammation.
    c. It reduces inflammation.
    d. It doesn't have any connection with inflammation.

7. What properties of medical marijuana help its user overcome sleeping issues?
    a. Its anti-inflammation and pain management properties.
    b. Its pain management and hallucinogenic properties.
    c. Its aphrodisiac and anti-inflammation properties.
    d. Its aphrodisiac and pain management properties.

8. What is marijuana's effect on the limbic system used for?
    a. It is used for sleep management.
    b. It is used for pain management.
    c. It is used for mental disorder management.
    d. It is used for glucose management.

9. From the list below, select the pair of medical conditions that can be triggered by the use of marijuana.

    a. Hyperactivity and low blood pressure.

    b. Rapid breathing and increased heart pressure rate.

    c. Insomnia and amnesia.

    d. Peptic ulcer and type-2 diabetes.

10. What are the side effects of marijuana's depressant-like effect on users?

    a. Concentration and coordination issues.

    b. Sleeplessness and peptic ulcer.

    c. Concentration and high blood pressure issues.

    d. None of the above.

11. Why is the use of medical marijuana considered a two-sided coin?

    a. It can be harmful and beneficial.

    b. It can be harmful and expensive.

    c. It can be beneficial and addictive.

    d. It can be addictive and expensive.

Passage 4 – Common Causes of Mental Disorders

Mental disorders are also known as mental illnesses. These are medical conditions that may affect the victim's feelings and thoughts, aside from their behavior and mood. Sometimes, mental disorders may be temporary while some people suffer from chronic mental illnesses.

There are different types of mental disorders. They include eating disorders, anxiety disorders, post-traumatic stress disorders, personality disorders, and psychotic disorders. Others are bipolar disorder, depression, and mood disorder.

It is noteworthy that no single cause can be attributed to mental disorders. Rather, it can be triggered by a wide range of factors. People with the following conditions and experiences are more vulnerable to mental illnesses than others:

Heredity: People from families that have a history of mental illnesses are more at risk of this medical condition than others. The descendants of families will have the ailment passed down to them through their genes.

Exposure to toxic chemicals or viruses during pregnancy: When a pregnant woman is exposed to viruses or chemicals during pregnancy, they expose the fetus to prenatal damage such as the disruption of fetal brain development or some related health problems. For instance, autism spectrum disorder and some conditions may be triggered by reduced oxygen to the brain.

Stress and trauma: People who go through traumatic life events from time to time are prone to developing mental disorders. The same can be said of some who suffer domestic violence, social isolation, work-related problems, and relationship breakdowns, among other stress-inducing problems. For instance, post-traumatic stress disorder is common among people who grow up or live in war zones. The constant sound of war and war-related experiences may unbalance their mental strength, making them prone to all forms of mental health challenges.

Biological factors: Some victims of mental illnesses develop mental issues while experiencing some hormonal changes. These changes may affect their mentality and increase their vulnerability to mental problems. Some medical conditions also trigger this medical condition. Childbirth, menopause, and thyroid problems are some hormonal changes that are associated with depression, according to WebMD.

Traumatic childhood experience: An individual's early life experience and environment may have a huge impact on their mental state. People who are exposed to child abuse or neglect are always at the risk of developing some mental problems later in life. Since they are denied that love that a child needs to grow properly, especially, mentally, they lack the basic ingredients for mental health and that may affect their mentality adversely.

Excessive use of recreational drugs or alcohol: Overdependence on alcohol or recreational drugs may also increase an addict's susceptibility to mental health challenges. Prolonged substance abuse has been linked to depression, anxiety, and paranoia. Thus, individuals who have been abusing drugs such as marijuana, cocaine, and amphetamines, and alcohol for years may become depressed or express undue anxiety occasionally. They are also prone to psychosis or bipolar disorder.

Mental problems can be caused by a wide range of factors as mentioned above. Individuals who have any of these factors may struggle with mental issues in life.

1. What are mental disorders?
    a. They are medical conditions that affect its victim's feelings and thoughts.
    b. They are medical conditions that encourage bipolarism.
    c. They are medical conditions that affect the human's motor skills.
    d. None of the above.

2. Identify the odd one.
    a. Bipolar disorder.
    b. Personality disorder.
    c. Psychotic disorder.
    d. Organic disorder.

3. What is the primary cause of mental illnesses?
    a. Smoking and alcohol.
    b. Heredity and exposure to infection.
    c. None of the above.
    d. All of the above.

4. What is the connection between heredity and mental ailment?
    a. Mental illness can be inherited.
    b. Mental illness cannot be inherited.
    c. Heredity creates opportunity for other factors to creep in.
    d. None of the above.

5. What ailment can a reduced amount of oxygen to the brain cause?

    a. Post-partum disorder.

    b. Autism spectrum disorder.

    c. Autism special disorder.

    d. Irritable brain disorder.

6. What type of disorder can be traced to stress and trauma?

    a. Pre-traumatic stress disorder.

    b. Post-traumatic stress disorder.

    c. Pre-stress traumatic disorder.

    d. Post-stress traumatic disorder.

7. Which of the following biological factors can trigger depression?

    a. Menopause and hair growth in the pubic areas.

    b. Broken voice and menopause.

    c. Thyroid problems and acne.

    d. Childbirth and menopause.

8. Which one of these factors can't trigger mental ailment?

    a. Heredity.

    b. Stress and trauma.

    c. Biological factor.

    d. Adulthood.

9. Pregnant women that are exposed to viruses or toxic chemicals are vulnerable to which health problem?

    a. Addiction to smoking.

    b. Disruption of fetal brain development.

    c. Disruption of fetal growth.

    d. Stillbirth.

10. Replace "vulnerable" with the appropriate word or group of words from the list below.

    a. Endangered.

    b. Exposed.

    c. Protected from.

    d. At the risk of.

11. What expression from the passage is synonymous with "prone to?"

    a. Vulnerable to.

    b. Associated with.

    c. Also trigger.

    d. Triggered by.

Vocabulary Test 1 – 50 Questions

1. As one of the most important parts of the test, the vocabulary section will test your ...
   a. Medical vocabulary only.
   b. General vocabulary only.
   c. Medical and general vocabulary.
   d. None of the above.

2. What is an effective way to upgrade your vocabulary?
   a. Memorize all types of vocabulary at once.
   b. Read medical journals.
   c. Read a wide range of materials.
   d. All of the above.

3. Each medical student is expected to have a comprehensive knowledge of ...
   a. Pathology.
   b. Parasitology.
   c. Psychology.
   d. Syndrome.

4. After receiving treatment for months, the patient gradually went into ...
   a. A coma.
   b. Remission.
   c. Cardiac arrest.
   d. Myocardial infarction.

5. After conducting a series of tests, plaque deposits were found on the patient's ...
   a. Coronary veins.
   b. Coronary shells.
   c. Coronary walls.
   d. Coronary cells.

6. The old man was diagnosed with low blood pressure, medically known as ...

    a. Hypertension.

    b. Hypotension.

    c. Hypothermal expansion.

    d. Hypothermal contraction.

7. A heart attack is a common health problem caused by a wide range of factors. It is also known in the medical field as ...

    a. Cardiac arrest.

    b. Cardiac failure.

    c. Myocardial infarction.

    d. Myocardia failure.

8. His ailment was considered ... because it would be quite difficult to cure it.

    a. Intractable.

    b. Unsolvable.

    c. Chronic.

    d. Terminal.

9. Epistaxis is one of the common health problems associated with the ...

    a. Nose.

    b. Coronary arteries.

    c. Wall between the nose and the eyes.

    d. Special place between the eyebrows.

10. ... is a medical suffix that indicates pain in a specific part of the body.

    a. -ectasis

    b. -algia

    c. -lysis

    d. -plasty

11. A hollow organ in the body can dilate or expand. This condition is usually represented with words with the … suffix.

    a. -lysis

    b. -algia

    c. -tensive

    d. -ectasis

12. The blood condition or a certain substance in the blood can be identified in medical terms with the … suffix.

    a. -rrhagia

    b. -centesis

    c. -itis

    d. -emia

13. … is a process that involves the puncturing of a body organ or cavity with a hollow needle.

    a. Centesis.

    b. Acupuncture.

    c. Gnosis.

    d. Plexy.

14. The removal of wrinkles on the abdomen and the tightening of the skin covering the stomach can be done through cosmetic surgery known as …

    a. Abdominocentesis.

    b. Abdominalcentensis.

    c. Abdomenia.

    d. Abdopuncture.

15. The old patient was referred to a ... for the treatment of his severe heart-related disease.

    a. Cardiologist.

    b. Heartologist.

    c. Chemotherapist.

    d. General physician.

16. A tear or break in any soft issue or organ such as the spleen is known as ...

    a. A rupture.

    b. Cystitis.

    c. Atrophy.

    d. Wear and tear.

17. A patient can't remember any of her past experiences. She is said to be suffering from ...

    a. Amnesia.

    b. Brainesia.

    c. A concussion.

    d. Atrophy.

18. The prefix for double or twice is ...

    a. Bi-

    b. Dual-

    c. Arthro-

    d. Mast-

19. The prefix for before, in front of and forward is ....

    a. Ultra-

    b. Extro-

    c. Ante-

    d. Lactro-

20. After several years as a professional boxer, he was diagnosed with ...

   a. Mild traumatic brain injury.

   b. Serious traumatic brain injury.

   c. Severe traumatic brain injury.

   d. Damaging traumatic brain injury.

21. The medical attention given to an urgently sick or injured person is ...

   a. First attention.

   b. Emergency medical assistance.

   c. First aid.

   d. Pre-diagnosis test.

22. The footballer had to undergo an urgent surgical operation to repair the ... he sustained during a football match.

   a. Rupture.

   b. Sprain.

   c. Cystitis.

   d. Strain.

23. An inflammation of the vein that commonly occurs in the legs is ...

   a. Phlebitis.

   b. Veinicular inflammation.

   c. Inflammatory concussion.

   d. None of the above.

24. Pepsia is usually caused by...

   a. Gallbladder disease.

   b. Ulcers.

   c. Gastroesophageal reflux.

   d. None of the above.

25. All of the following are found in a first aid box except …

    a. Tweezers.

    b. Disposable sterile gloves.

    c. Sterile eye dressings.

    d. A pair of pliers.

26. An anomaly in the body can be corrected through which medical procedure?

    a. Artificial Intelligence.

    b. Surgery.

    c. Medications.

    d. Removal.

27. People who suffer from one form of blood disease or the other are usually referred to what specialists?

    a. Blood experts.

    b. Dermatologists.

    c. Hematologists.

    d. Psychiatrists.

28. Physicians find clues to an ailment through what?

    a. The ailment's syndromes.

    b. The ailment's medical history.

    c. The patient's medical history.

    d. None of the above.

29. What ailment can be triggered when the heart stops supplying the body with blood?

    a. Cardiac arrest.

    b. Heart attack.

    c. Low blood pressure.

    d. Hypothermia.

30. Which of the following blood pressures are a symptom of hypertension?
    a. 120/80.
    b. 145/90.
    c. 125/85.
    d. 100/80.

31. Define the pulse rate.
    a. It is the amount of times the heart beats per minute.
    b. It is the amount of times the heart beats per second.
    c. It is the amount of times the heart beats per hour.
    d. It is the amount of times the heart beats per month.

32. What are the symptoms of epistaxis?
    a. Swollen legs and trauma.
    b. Increased blood pressure and peptic ulcers.
    c. Trauma and increased blood pressure.
    d. Hypertension and hypotension.

33. What does the suffix "ectomy" signify?
    a. It signifies the surgical removal of a part of the body.
    b. It signifies the surgical removal of a part of the brain.
    c. It signifies the surgical removal of the kidney.
    d. It signifies the surgical removal of the pancreatic.

34. What medical condition can arise from indigestion?
    a. Ectasis.
    b. Pepsia.
    c. Lypasis.
    d. Barognoosis.

35. What medical condition does "Rrhagia" stand for?

    a. It prefixes medical ailments that involve excessive blood flow.

    b. It prefixes medical ailments that involve excessive menstrual flow.

    c. It prefixes medical ailments that involve excessive blood shortage.

    d. It prefixes medical ailments that involve mental disorder.

36. Although Kelly isn't pregnant, she hasn't seen her menstrual flow for a couple of months. What ailment does she suffer from?

    a. She suffers from abdominocentesis.

    b. She suffers from vaginismus.

    c. She suffers from amenia.

    d. She suffers from lymphadenitis.

37. Which of the following conditions require dialysis?

    a. Acute Respiratory Distress Syndrome.

    b. Anuric.

    c. Atherosclerotic Cardiovascular Disease.

    d. At lib.

38. Under what condition is an ailment considered to be bibasilar?

    a. If it affects the bases of the kidneys.

    b. If it affects the base of the left ventricle.

    c. If it affects the bases of the lungs.

    d. If it affects the base of one of the lungs.

39. What does CABG mean?

    a. It means Coronary Artery Bilateral Graft.

    b. It means Colon Artery Bilateral Graft.

    c. It means Coronary Artery Bypass Graft.

    d. It means Colon Artery Bypass Graft.

40. Which of the following is commonly known as stroke?

    a. Cerebrovascular accident.

    b. Cerebrum accident.

    c. Colon accident.

    d. None of the above.

41. What is neurofibroma?

    a. It is a fibrous tumor that covers the peripheral nerve.

    b. It is a fibrous tumor that covers the small intestine.

    c. It is a fibrous tumor that covers the large intestine.

    d. It is a fibrous tumor that covers the lungs.

42. Define atrophy.

    a. It is a medical condition that affects the bones and joints.

    b. It is a medical condition associated with pregnancy.

    c. It is a medical condition that is common to the aged.

    d. It is a medical condition that affects the body tissue.

43. What is a medical treatment that involves using powerful chemicals called?

    a. Chemical reaction.

    b. Chemical radioactivity.

    c. Chemotherapy.

    d. None of the above.

44. What factors can trigger bradycardia?

    a. Age and lifestyle.

    b. Physical condition and gender.

    c. Physical condition and age.

    d. All of the above.

45. How frequently should medications that are recommended as B. I. D be taken?

    a. They should be taken three times daily.

    b. They should be taken twice daily.

    c. They should be taken once daily.

    d. As recommended by the physician.

46. How do you identify an ACL?

    a. If the ACL is sprained or ruptured.

    b. If the ACL swells.

    c. If the ACL keeps reducing in size.

    d. All of the above.

47. Which of the following types of diabetes is difficult to treat?

    a. Type-1 diabetes.

    b. Type-2 diabetes.

    c. Type-3 diabetes.

    d. Type-4 diabetes.

48. What does "pan" mean as a prefix?

    a. It means entire.

    b. It means a section of.

    c. It means in favor of.

    d. It means against.

49. Which of the following suffixes is used for medical conditions that involve inflammation?

    a. Rrhagia.

    b. Cyte.

    c. Itis.

    d. Aemia.

50. What are the factors that can trigger lysis?
    a. Osmotic or viral mechanisms.
    b. Osmotic or internal mechanisms.
    c. Viral or simple mechanisms.
    d. All of the above.

Grammar Test 1 – 50 Questions

1. There are ... parts of speech.

    a. Five.

    b. Eight.

    c. Seven.

    d. Three.

2. These are words used to represent people, places or things.

    a. Pronouns.

    b. Nouns.

    c. Adjectives.

    d. Verbs.

3. Which of the following is not an example of a noun?

    a. Mary.

    b. School bus.

    c. New York City.

    d. None of the above.

4. Nouns can be classified into ... groups.

    a. Six.

    b. Four.

    c. Eight.

    d. Ten.

5. A type of noun that is commonly used for naming a group of similar objects or a general item is a ...

    a. Collective noun.

    b. Common noun.

    c. Proper noun.

    d. Group noun.

6. Specific single entities are …

   a. Proper nouns.

   b. Collective nouns.

   c. Group nouns.

   d. Single nouns.

7. Which of the following is not an example of a common noun?

   a. Teacher.

   b. Deliveryman.

   c. Footballer.

   d. None of the above.

8. In the expression "Lucas is a successful boxer," what is the difference between Lucas and boxer?

   a. Lucas is a common noun while boxer is a proper noun.

   b. Lucas is a proper noun while boxer is a common noun.

   c. Lucas is a group noun while boxer is a single noun.

   d. Lucas is a single noun while boxer is a group noun.

9. With the exception of …, the following are some examples of proper nouns.

   a. Christmas.

   b. New Year.

   c. Halloween.

   d. College graduation party.

10. A noun used for representing non-physical nouns is a/an …

   a. Abstract noun.

   b. Invisible noun.

   c. Fundamental noun.

   d. Proper noun.

11. Substances and objects we can feel with our senses are otherwise known as …

    a. Concrete nouns.

    b. Proper nouns.

    c. Physical nouns.

    d. Abstract nouns.

12. Which of the following is an outlier?

    a. Animals.

    b. Flowers.

    c. Clouds.

    d. Emotions.

13. Concrete nouns can be classified into … groups.

    a. Two.

    b. Three.

    c. Four.

    d. Five.

14. A collection of objects is known as a …

    a. Collection noun.

    b. Merged noun.

    c. Collective noun.

    d. Combination noun.

15. A word or a phrase that is used as a replacement for a noun is a/an …

    a. Replacement word.

    b. Pronoun.

    c. Adjectival clause of replacement.

    d. Adjunct of noun replacement.

16. The major importance of a pronoun is that …
    a. It helps to avoid needless repetition.
    b. It doesn't have a significant impact on sentences.
    c. It is easier to remember than a noun.
    d. Pronouns are collectively better than nouns.

17. A type of pronoun used for recognizing the ownership of an object is a/an …
    a. Ownership pronoun.
    b. Possession pronoun.
    c. Possessive pronoun.
    d. All of the above.

18. You can indirectly reference a noun by using a/an …
    a. Referencing pronoun.
    b. Connecting pronoun.
    c. Indefinite pronoun.
    d. Particular pronoun.

19. You can connect a phrase or clause to a proper noun or proper pronoun with …
    a. Connecting pronouns.
    b. Relative pronouns.
    c. Apparent pronouns.
    d. None of the above.

20. You can emphasize or intensify nouns and pronouns with …
    a. Intensive pronouns.
    b. Intensity pronouns.
    c. Emphasizing pronouns.
    d. Combination pronouns.

21. What is an auxiliary verb?

    a. It is an inanimate thing.

    b. It is a form of verb that makes its clause more meaningful.

    c. It is a form of verb that can be used for isolating important things.

    d. It is a descriptive form of verb.

22. Verb modification or description can best be done with ...

    a. Adverbs.

    b. Pronouns.

    c. Modification pronouns.

    d. Connecting adverbs.

23. You can describe nonspecific things and people by using ...

    a. Articles.

    b. Possessive adjectives.

    c. Indefinite adjectives.

    d. Possessive verbs.

24. A noun can best be modified or described with the help of ...

    a. Adjectives.

    b. Adverbs.

    c. Conjunctions.

    d. Interjections.

25. The form of adjective that is commonly used to describe the specific features or qualities of an object is a/an ...

    a. Attributive adjective.

    b. Demonstrative adjective.

    c. Indefinite adjective.

    d. Quantitative adjective.

26. Identify the noun in this sentence: "This is a very fast car."
    a. This.
    b. Fast.
    c. Very fast.
    d. Car.

27. Which of the following is not a proper noun?
    a. New Year.
    b. Halloween.
    c. Argungu Fishing Festival.
    d. None of the above.

28. One of the lists below is a list of abstract nouns. Identify it.
    a. Intelligence, social concepts, and traits.
    b. Qualities, festivals, and Halloween.
    c. Both of the above.
    d. Neither of the above.

29. Milk, water, and salt are examples of what type of noun?
    a. Uncountable noun.
    b. Countable noun.
    c. Abstract noun.
    d. Collective noun.

30. I, she, him, and they are examples of what type of pronoun?
    a. Possessive pronoun.
    b. Attributive pronoun.
    c. Personal pronoun.
    d. Relative pronoun.

31. What are verbs that refer to the action performed by the subjects known as?

    a. Infinite verbs.

    b. Finite verbs.

    c. Irregular verbs.

    d. Auxiliary verbs.

32. What is the major difference between "flout" and "flaunt"?

    a. Flout means showing off while flaunt means scornful defying.

    b. Flaunt is a verb while flout is an adjective.

    c. Flaunt means showing off while flout means scornful defying.

    d. Flaunt and flaunt are synonyms.

33. What type of verbs provide more information about the main verb?

    a. Auxiliary verbs.

    b. Modal verbs.

    c. Primary auxiliary verbs.

    d. Regular verbs.

34. Which of the following adjectives can answer the question "How many?"

    a. Interrogative adjective.

    b. Possessive adjective.

    c. Numbers adjective.

    d. Question adjective.

35. What type of adverb provides information about the regularity of an action or event?

    a. Adverbs of regularity. '

    b. Adverbs of manner.

    c. Adverbs of frequency.

    d. Adverbs of event.

36. "We got home at around 10 p.m." is an example of what type of preposition?
    a. Preposition for place.
    b. Preposition for instrument.
    c. Preposition for time.
    d. Preposition for possession.

37. Differentiate between "on" and "in."
    a. "On" is a preposition that is used to provide information about the surface of an object while "in" is used to define a physical or virtual boundary.
    b. "In" is a preposition that is used to provide information about the surface of an object while "on" is used to define a physical or virtual boundary.
    c. "On" is a conjunction that is used to provide information about the surface of an object while "in" is used to define a physical or virtual boundary.
    d. "In" is a conjunction that is used to provide information about the surface of an object while "on" is used to define a physical or virtual boundary.

38. What is the head of a school called?
    a. Principle.
    b. Principal.
    c. Principles.
    d. School leader.

39. "They are going towards the bus stop" is an example of which of the following prepositions?
    a. Preposition for place.
    b. Preposition for instrument.
    c. Preposition for direction.
    d. Preposition for numbers.

40. How can you identify a sentence that contains a preposition of agent?
   a. If it contains whoever, whatever, and whosoever.
   b. If it contains words such as by or with.
   c. All of the above.
   d. None of the above.

41. Under what condition are subordinating conjunctions used?
   a. For connecting two dependent clauses.
   b. For connecting two independent clauses.
   c. For connecting a dependent and an independent clause.
   d. For connecting a dependent clause to two or more independent clauses.

42. Sentences with the same grammatical values are best connected with what type of conjunction?
   a. Adverbial conjunctions.
   b. Coordinating conjunctions.
   c. Subordinating conjunctions.
   d. Correlative conjunctions.

43. Differentiate between "toward" and "towards."
   a. "Toward" is commonly used for academic purpose while "towards" is acceptable in regular conversations.
   b. "Toward" is formal while "towards" is informal.
   c. Americans are in favor of "towards" while "toward" is acceptable in British English.
   d. Americans are in favor of "toward" while "towards" is acceptable in British English.

44. "The girl is both tall and intelligent" is an example of a …
   a. Correlative conjunction.
   b. Correlative interjection.
   c. Subordinating conjunction.
   d. Adjectival clause.

45. What is a clause?
   a. A clause is a group of words without a verb.
   b. A clause is a group of words with a verb and a subject.
   c. A clause is a group of adjectives.
   d. A clause is a group of figures of speech.

46. Which of the following words is used to show appreciation for someone's efforts or achievements?
   a. Remarks.
   b. Complements.
   c. Compliments.
   d. Feedbacks.

47. Identify the passive sentence from the list below.
   a. The boy is going home.
   b. They are swimming in the large pool.
   c. The food has been eaten by the cat.
   d. The lion jumped over its prey.

48. Words with the same meaning are referred to as what?
   a. Homophones.
   b. Antonyms.
   c. Synonyms.
   d. Synecdoche.

49. What are a set of expressions that have a different meaning from their individual words known as?

    a. Onomatopoeia.

    b. Paradox.

    c. Idiom.

    d. Phrasal verbs.

50. What is the major difference between "breathe" and "breath"?

    a. "Breath" is a verb while "breathe" is a noun.

    b. "Breathe" is a verb while "breath" is a noun.

    c. "Breathe" and "breath" are synonyms.

    d. "Breathe" and "breath" are antonyms.

Biology Test 1 – 25 Questions

1. Biology is derived from two Greek words: … and …
    a. *Bios* and *logos*.
    b. *Logos* and *logy*.
    c. *Bio* and *logics*.
    d. None of the above.

2. Some major branches of biology include all of the following except…
    a. Botany.
    b. Molecular Biology.
    c. Cellular Biology.
    d. Informatics Biology.

3. The study of the origins of species is a branch of biology known as …
    a. Evolutionary Biology.
    b. Darwinian Biology.
    c. Origin Biology.
    d. Genesis Biology.

4. The complex system through which plants and some complex organisms convert light into energy is called …
    a. Conversion.
    b. Photosynthesis.
    c. Food production.
    d. Energy converting system.

5. The first stage of photosynthesis is ….
    a. Radiant energy collection.
    b. Radiant energy harvest.
    c. Radioactive energy collection.
    d. Radioactive energy harvest.

6. The light from the sun is converted into chemical energy in the ... stage.

   a. Radiant energy processing.

   b. Radioactive energy processing.

   c. Radiant energy conversion.

   d. Radioactive energy conversion.

7. NADPH and adenosine triphosphate are usually converted by plants using ... and ... as raw materials.

   a. Sunlight and water.

   b. Water from soil and sunlight.

   c. Atmospheric carbon dioxide and water from the soil.

   d. A combination of any of the materials above.

8. What takes place during the Calvin-Benson cycle?

   a. The energy produced by light reactions is used for producing protein in the body.

   b. The energy produced by the light reactions is used for carbohydrate production for plants.

   c. The conversion of light energy into chemical energy in plants.

   d. The metabolism of fats and oil in the body.

9. ... and ... are the products of the Calvin-Benson cycle.

   a. Carbohydrates and glucose.

   b. Glucose and proteins.

   c. Carbohydrates and light energy.

   d. Glucose and fatty acids.

10. Which of the following is not a benefit of photosynthesis?
    a. It is the primary source of oxygen for both humans and animals.
    b. It makes the symbiotic relationship between animals and humans possible.
    c. It is the primary source of energy for both humans and animals.
    d. It is the only source of energy for both humans and animals.

11. Two plants that are photosynthesis-independent for energy production are ... and ...
    a. Indian pipe and beechdrops.
    b. Chinese pipe and beechdrops.
    c. Indian tube.
    d. Beechdrops and Indian tube.

12. Some non-parasitic and photosynthesis-independent plants are ...
    a. Molds, mushrooms and yeasts.
    b. Yeasts and molds only.
    c. Mushrooms and molds only.
    d. Mushrooms and yeasts only.

13. The amount of calories an individual's body needs for proper functioning of some body parts is known as the ...
    a. Resting Metabolism Gauge.
    b. Functional Metabolic Rate.
    c. Resting Metabolic Rate.
    d. Required Metabolic Rate.

14. Metabolism is divided into ... and ...
    a. Primary metabolism and secondary metabolism.
    b. Catabolism and metabolism.
    c. Catabolism and anabolism.
    d. Metabolism and anabolism.

15. Which of the following is not one of the benefits of metabolism?

    a. It supplies the needed energy as calories.

    b. It provides the substance needed by the body for its upkeep.

    c. It ensures the body functions properly.

    d. It aids photosynthetic processes.

16. Which of the following is not a function of fats in the body?

    a. Protecting the vital organs in the body.

    b. Reserving energy for future use.

    c. Assisting with the absorption of fat-soluble vitamins.

    d. Speeding up metabolic rates.

17. Hemoglobin formation for oxygen transportation is supported by ... in the body.

    a. Carbohydrates.

    b. Fats and oil.

    c. Minerals and water.

    d. Proteins.

18. All of the following are common amino acids except ...

    a. Leucin.

    b. Isoleucine.

    c. Lysine.

    d. Valeline.

19. Food regulation in the body is the primary responsibility of ...

    a. Minerals.

    b. Amino acids.

    c. Proteins.

    d. Fats and oil.

20. Some of the important vitamins needed for metabolism are...
    a. Nicotinic acid and pantothenic acid.
    b. Fatty acids and vitamin A.
    c. Riboflavin and arctic acid.
    d. None of the above.

21. Humans can get carbohydrates by consuming ...
    a. Starch, protein and fiber.
    b. Sugar, fiber and vitamins.
    c. Sugar, starch and fiber.
    d. Fiber, fats and oil and essential minerals.

22. Cellular respiration can be defined as ...
    a. Respiration through cellular organisms.
    b. Oxidation of fats and oils to glucose and starch.
    c. Oxidation of organic compounds for energy production.
    d. A chemical reaction that supports respiration.

23. Cellular respiration is a ... process.
    a. Three-stage.
    b. Multi-stage.
    c. Five-stage.
    d. Infinite-stage.

24. The final stage of cellular respiration is ...
    a. Electron absorption.
    b. Electron usage.
    c. Electron transport.
    d. Electron storage.

25. The major difference between anaerobic and aerobic cellular respiration is ...

    a. Anaerobic cellular respiration requires oxygen while aerobic cellular respiration does not.

    b. Aerobic cellular respiration requires oxygen while anaerobic cellular respiration does not.

    c. Anaerobic cellular respiration supports anabolic metabolism while aerobic cellular respiration supports catabolic metabolism.

    d. Anaerobic cellular respiration takes place in plants while aerobic cellular respiration takes place in animals.

Chemistry Test 1 – 25 Questions

1. The simplest form of any matter is ...
    a. Molecules.
    b. Elements.
    c. Atoms.
    d. Compounds.

2. Protons, neutrons and electrons are the three parts of ...
    a. Mixtures.
    b. Elements.
    c. Compounds.
    d. Atoms.

3. Which of the following reside inside an atom's nucleus?
    a. Protons and neutrons.
    b. Neutrons and electrons.
    c. Electrons and protons.
    d. Electrons only.

4. When atoms bond together, the result is ...
    a. Molecules.
    b. Atoms.
    c. Compounds.
    d. Elements.

5. Two major factors that determine the differences in molecules are ...
    a. Complexity and atoms.
    b. Boiling and freezing points.
    c. Size and complexity.
    d. None of the above.

6. ... are made up of atoms of different elements that are bound together.

    a. Compounds.

    b. Elements.

    c. Reactants.

    d. Molecules.

7. ... are made up of two or more elements that are physically combined together.

    a. Physical elements.

    b. Chemical elements.

    c. Compounds.

    d. Mixtures.

8. ... is/are anything that has mass and occupies space.

    a. Weight.

    b. Matter.

    c. Physical attributes.

    d. Chemical attributes.

9. The properties of matter are classified into ...

    a. Physical and chemical properties.

    b. Chemical and metabolic properties.

    c. Combustion and evaporation.

    d. None of the above.

10. ... are associated with matter's transformation.

    a. Primary properties.

    b. Secondary properties.

    c. Chemical properties.

    d. Physical properties.

11. A common difference between physical and chemical changes is ...

    a. New substances are formed in chemical changes but not in physical changes.

    b. New substances are formed in physical changes but not in chemical changes.

    c. Physical changes support combustion while chemical changes support fusion.

    d. Physical changes require enzymes while chemical changes require hormones.

12. Which of the following is not an example of physical change?

    a. Evaporation.

    b. Demagnetization/magnetization of iron.

    c. Mixture separation through fractional distillation.

    d. Changes in electrochemical cells.

13. A substance that can't be broken down into simpler units by regular chemical processes is a/an ...

    a. Element.

    b. Impenetrable substance.

    c. Indestructible substance.

    d. Special substance.

14. Transition metals can be found in ...

    a. Groups 3 to 12 of the periodic table.

    b. Groups 3 and 4 of the periodic table.

    c. Groups 1 and 2 of the periodic table.

    d. Groups 5 and 6 of the periodic table.

15. Transition metals that are used as industrial catalysts include ...

   a. Oxygen and nitrogen.

   b. Neon and argon.

   c. Manganese and nickel.

   d. Sulfur and benzene.

16. Metals with a very strong oxidation tendency are ...

   a. Radioactive metals.

   b. Oxidative metals.

   c. Reactive metals.

   d. All of the above.

17. Naturally occurring elements that conduct neither heat nor electricity are ...

   a. Oxidative metals.

   b. Radioactive metals.

   c. Reactive metals.

   d. Non-metals.

18. Some common examples of non-metals on the periodic table are ...

   a. Nitrogen, oxygen and carbon.

   b. Carbon dioxide, oxygen and sulfur.

   c. Oxygen, carbon dioxide and benzoic acids.

   d. Nitrogen oxide, carbon dioxide and ammonium sulfate.

19. ... are known as rare-earth elements.

   a. Lanthanides.

   b. Pure metals.

   c. Naturally occurring metals.

   d. Oxygen-based metals.

20. A class of metals that do not contain atoms of multiple metallic elements are ...

    a. Special metals.

    b. Pure metals.

    c. Contaminated metals.

    d. Monogamous metals.

21. Which group of elements does not react with other elements under standard conditions?

    a. Lanthanides.

    b. Actinides.

    c. Noble gases.

    d. Rare elements.

22. The process by which one or more substances, known as reactants, are converted into different substances or products is a/an ...

    a. Oxidation reaction.

    b. Redox reaction.

    c. Catalytic reaction.

    d. Chemical reaction.

23. A single reactant can produce two or more products in a chemical process known as ...

    a. Decomposition.

    b. Fusion.

    c. Coordinate covalent bond.

    d. Dative covalent bond.

24. A redox reaction that involves the combination of an oxidizer and a combustible material is a ...

    a. Chemical reaction.

    b. Reduction and oxidation reaction.

    c. Combustion reaction.

    d. Fission reaction.

25. A/an ... reaction is a chemical reaction where electrons are transferred between the reactants.

    a. Redox reaction.

    b. Transfer reaction.

    c. Electron transmission reaction.

    d. Simple metabolic reaction.

Anatomy and Physiology Test 1 – 25 Questions

1. A branch of biology that focuses on the structure of animals is ...
   a. Zoology.
   b. Anatomy.
   c. Botany.
   d. Animal science.

2. What is the primary function of the circulatory system?
   a. Transporting oxygen throughout the body.
   b. Transporting blood into the capillaries.
   c. Transporting oxygen and blood throughout the body.
   d. Transporting oxygen into the capillaries.

3. The parts of the circulatory system responsible for transporting blood into the capillaries are ...
   a. Arteries.
   b. Capillaries.
   c. Transporting veins.
   d. Circulatory transporters.

4. The circulatory system is a combination of ... systems working together to achieve a common goal.
   a. Two.
   b. Four.
   c. Three.
   d. Five.

5. What are the major components of human blood?

    a. Blue blood cells, plasma, white blood cells and red blood cells.

    b. Red blood cells, plasma, platelets and white blood cells.

    c. Plasma, white blood cells, blue blood cells and platelets.

    d. White blood cells, red blood cells and plasma.

6. The veins, arteries and blood vessels form a network of ...

    a. Systemic circulation.

    b. Anabolic circulation.

    c. Transporting circulation.

    d. None of the above.

7. The components of the nervous system are ...

    a. Electrons and complex nerves.

    b. Protons and complex nerves.

    c. Neurons and complex nerves.

    d. Simple and complex nerves.

8. The nervous system has two subdivisions which are the ...

    a. Autonomic and somatic nervous systems.

    b. Somatic and manual nervous systems.

    c. Simple and complex nervous systems.

    d. Primary and secondary nervous systems.

9. Which of the following is not a function of the somatic system?

    a. It connects the spinal cord and the brain with the sensory receptors and muscles.

    b. It relays responses to the skeletal muscles.

    c. It relays information from the sense organs, skin and muscles to the central nervous system.

    d. None of the above.

10. The ... is responsible for regulating several body processes.
    a. Special nervous system.
    b. Manual nervous system.
    c. Primary nervous system.
    d. Autonomic nervous system.

11. A nervous system disorder that triggers the degeneration of the brain's nerve cells is ...
    a. Alzheimer's disease.
    b. Parkinson's disease.
    c. Cerebral palsy.
    d. Chronic dementia.

12. A brain disorder that causes tremors is ...
    a. Alzheimer's disease.
    b. Parkinson's disease.
    c. Cerebral palsy.
    d. Chronic dementia.

13. A patient was diagnosed with an ailment that affects both brain function and the nervous system. The patient is suffering from ...
    a. Chronic amnesia.
    b. Chronic dementia.
    c. Cerebral palsy.
    d. Parkinson's disease.

14. The human digestive system consists of the ... and the ...
    a. Gastrointestinal tract and accessory organs of digestion.
    b. Gastrointestinal tract and primary organs of digestion.
    c. Gastrointestinal tract and secondary organs of digestion.
    d. Gastrointestinal tract and auxiliary organs of digestion.

15. The digestion stage that starts with the secretion of gastric acid is the ...

    a. Primary phase.

    b. Cephalic phase.

    c. Launching phase.

    d. Preparatory phase.

16. The two digestive enzymes in saliva that support digestion are ... and ...

    a. Fructose and lingual lipase.

    b. Lingual lipase and sucrose.

    c. Amylase and lingual lipase.

    d. Lingual lipase and saccharide.

17. We respond to the smell or thought of food through the ...

    a. Cerebral cortex.

    b. Olfactory organs.

    c. Rudimentary organs.

    d. Dietary organs.

18. What reaction occurs in the stomach after food consumption?

    a. The stomach contracts and activates the stretch receptors.

    b. The stomach expands and immediately activates the stretch receptors.

    c. The food goes through the vagus before reaching the stomach.

    d. The food combines with other chemicals in the stomach.

19. Swallowed food activates gastric activity in the ... of digestion.

    a. Lipase phase.

    b. Opening phase.

    c. Gastric phase.

    d. Processing phase.

20. Gastric secretion in the stomach is stimulated by ... chemicals.
    a. Three.
    b. Four.
    c. Two.
    d. Five.

21. ... triggers the intestinal phase of digestion.
    a. The arrival of chyme in the esophagus.
    b. The arrival of chyme in the secretive organs.
    c. The reaction between chyme and amino acids.
    d. The arrival of chyme in the duodenum.

22. Which of the following are components of the muscular system?
    a. Skeletal muscles, smooth muscles and cardiac muscles.
    b. Cardiac muscles, reflex muscles and smooth muscles.
    c. Smooth muscles, skeletal muscles and reflex muscles.
    d. Reflex muscles, cardiac muscles and skeletal muscles.

23. The muscles that are present in the stomach, intestines and blood vessels are ...
    a. Reflex muscles.
    b. Cardiac muscles.
    c. Skeletal muscles.
    d. Visceral muscles.

24. What is the primary function of the cardiac muscle?
    a. It carries oxygen to the heart.
    b. It transports blood to the brain.
    c. It pumps blood throughout the body.
    d. It makes it easier for the body to move.

25. Which of the following is not a function of the muscular system?

    a. It protects vital organs.

    b. It guides the pelvic floor muscles during childbirth.

    c. It makes urination possible.

    d. It makes the body stronger.

Physics Test 1 – 25 Questions

1. Physics can be defined as a branch of natural science that studies ...
    a. Matter, its behavior and its motion.
    b. The composition of matter.
    c. The physical and chemical attributes of matter.
    d. The distinct features of matter.

2. ... is the study of the impact of forces on motion.
    a. Law of Electrodynamics.
    b. Newton's Laws of Motion.
    c. The Principle of Centripetal and Centrifugal Motion.
    d. Dynamics.

3. An object rolls down a rough surface. It is said to undergo ...
    a. Centripetal motion.
    b. Cyclic motion.
    c. Random motion.
    d. Linear cum cyclic motion.

4. A runner runs in a straight line from the starting point to the finish line. That is an example of ...
    a. Translational linear motion.
    b. Cyclic linear motion.
    c. Linear translational motion.
    d. None of the above.

5. The wheel of a car in motion and the rotation of the blades of an electric fan are two examples of ...

    a. Straight line motion.

    b. Circular motion.

    c. Rotational motion.

    d. Rotation cum circular motion.

6. A body undergoing ... maintains a uniform speed throughout the duration of the motion.

    a. Uniform motion.

    b. Long distance motion.

    c. Periodic linear motion.

    d. Periodic motion.

7. A measure of the distance you covered within a duration of time is ...

    a. Speed.

    b. Acceleration due to gravity.

    c. Acceleration due to distance.

    d. Uniform acceleration on a straight line.

8. The difference between a scalar quantity and a vector quantity is that ...

    a. A scalar quantity has both magnitude and direction while a vector quantity only has direction.

    b. A scalar quantity has both magnitude and direction while a vector quantity only has magnitude.

    c. A vector quantity has both magnitude and direction while a scalar quantity only has direction.

    d. A vector quantity has both magnitude and direction while a scalar quantity only has magnitude.

9. Differentiate between speed and motion.

    a. Speed is distance traveled per unit of time while motion is a change in an object's speed over time.

    b. Speed is distance traveled per unit of time while motion is a change in an object's direction over time.

    c. Speed is distance traveled per unit of time while motion is a change in an object's position over time.

    d. Motion is distance traveled per unit of time while speed is a change in an object's position over time.

10. Which of the following are examples of vector quantities?

    a. Speed and force.

    b. Speed and velocity.

    c. Acceleration and force.

    d. Acceleration and distance.

11. Oscillatory motion can be defined as ...

    a. The to-and-fro movement of an object while standing in a mean position.

    b. The to-and-fro movement of an object while rotating along an axis.

    c. The movement of an object over an inclined plane at 90 degrees.

    d. The to-and-fro movement of an object from a given height.

12. Which of the following is not an example of oscillatory motion?

    a. A swinging pendulum.

    b. Ocean waves.

    c. Sound waves.

    d. None of the above.

13. A boy moves from point A to point B and retraces his step from point B to point A. This is ...

    a. Random motion.

    b. Oscillatory motion.

    c. Reciprocating motion.

    d. Circular motion.

14. Which of the definitions below describes average speed?

    a. Total distance covered multiplied by total time taken.

    b. Total distance covered divided by total time taken.

    c. Total distance covered minus total time taken.

    d. Total distance covered plus total time taken.

15. Ms^{-1} or meters per second is the SI unit of ...

    a. Speed.

    b. Acceleration due to gravity.

    c. Uniform acceleration on a plane.

    d. Acceleration.

16. The average speed of a vehicle can be calculated with which of the following formulas?

    a. Average speed = total distance covered / time taken

    b. Average speed = total distance covered / half of the time taken

    c. Average speed = total distance covered / average acceleration

    d. Average speed = total distance covered · time taken

17. A driver covers 120 kilometers in 3 hours. Calculate his average speed.

    a. 360 kilometers per hour.

    b. 60 kilometers per hour.

    c. 30 kilometers per hour.

    d. 40 kilometers per hour.

18. Calculate the average speed of a train that travels 200 kilometers from point A to point B in 4 hours.

    a. 60 kilometers per hour.

    b. 30 kilometers per hour.

    c. 20 kilometers per hour.

    d. 50 kilometers per hour.

19. A vehicle that moves without changing its speed is moving at ...

    a. Uniform speed.

    b. Uniform velocity.

    c. Uniform acceleration.

    d. Uniform deceleration.

20. In which of the following does distance/time remain constant?

    a. Uniform speed.

    b. Uniform motion.

    c. Uniform acceleration.

    d. Uniform velocity.

21. Differentiate between speed and acceleration.

    a. Acceleration is the change of speed per unit of time while speed is the change of distance per unit of time.

    b. Acceleration is the change of velocity per unit of time while speed is the change of distance per unit of time.

    c. Acceleration is the change of distance per unit of time while speed is the change of velocity per unit of time.

    d. Acceleration is the change of movement per unit of time while speed is the change of velocity per unit of time.

22. A vehicle travels from London to Buckingham at a constant pace. Which of the following does the vehicle have?

    a. Velocity.

    b. Acceleration.

    c. Negative acceleration.

    d. Deceleration.

23. A vehicle moving with a uniform velocity of 120 km/hr is brought to rest after traveling a distance of 30m. Calculate its deceleration.

    a. 30 m.

    b. 50 kilometers per hour.

    c. 240 ms^{-2}.

    d. 18.52 ms^{-2}.

24. Newton's first law of motion states that ...

    a. Actions and reactions are always equal and opposite.

    b. A body will remain in uniform motion in a straight line or will remain at rest unless a force acts on it.

    c. Although energy can be transformed from one form to another, it can't be destroyed.

    d. The value of kinetic energy is equal to the value of potential energy for a body moving at uniform speed.

25. Some of the primary sources of combustible organic matter used by humans are ...

    a. Sunlight, wood and coal.

    b. Petroleum, wood and water.

    c. Sunlight, plastic and water.

    d. Dry hay, plastic and sunlight.

Learning Style Test 1 – 14 Questions

1. If you hear the word *injection*, what do you instantly do?

a. Picture an injection

b. Speak the word *injection*

c. Imagine injecting someone

d. Write the word *injection*

2. Which books do you prefer for studying?

a. Books with fewer pages

b. Books with a lot of graphics and pictures

c. Books with a lot of text

d. Books with separated chapters

3. When the doctor is explaining something new to you, what do you do?

a. Listen attentively

b. Read the book during the explanation

c. Make notes

d. Get lost in your own thoughts

4. Which is your preferred place in a class?

a. At the front

b. At the back

c. In the middle

d. On the corners alongside the windows

5. Which of the following is a key component of your notes?

a. Drawn images

b. Detailed sentences

c. Summaries

d. A lot of boxed details

6. If a teacher takes you to a laboratory and performs an experiment before teaching the particular topic to you, what would your response be?

a. Not understand anything and feel lost

b. Complain to the teacher

c. Ask the teacher to repeat things again and again

d. Immediately understand the concepts

7. If you are in a group of people, what would you most likely do?

a. Talk with the people around you

b. Observe the people and their behaviors

c. Try to leave the place as soon as possible

d. Indulge yourself on the phone

8. If a doctor explains a process in detail but does not give a practical demonstration of it, how will you deal with that?

a. Find it difficult

b. Understand it either way

c. Mess things up when asked to do that

d. Ask the doctor to repeat things again and again

9. How do you prepare for a test?

a. Memorize the matter of the book by heart

b. Ask someone to ask you questions

c. Read the notes and pictures you have created for your understanding

d. Read the content out loud

10. If you attend an event, what are you most likely to remember after a week?

a. The faces of people you saw at the event

b. The food you ate

c. The songs that were played

d. The dance steps that you saw

11. If someone wants to impress you with something, what can best convince you to like it?

a. The price

b. The brand name

c. Big names of people who have used it

d. A picture of it

12. If the doctor asks you to explain a report, how would you do that?

a. Show the x-ray or the picture and then explain

b. Narrate the components of the report as a story

c. Find it difficult to explain it verbally

d. Summarize the report in a few sentences

13. If a patient's family member tells you about a medicine or therapy and asks you about of the patient's condition, what will you do?

a. Ask them to book an appointment

b. Prescribe the medicine

c. Ask them to bring the patient first

d. Send them to the doctor

14. If a patient describes a medical condition, what will you do at first?

a. Picture the condition in your mind

b. Note the condition on a piece of paper

c. Listen with complete attention

d. Cut the patient off and send him to the doctor

Personality Style Test 1 – 15 Questions

1. If you just fought with your colleague, and a visitor in the hospital asks you about the location of a bedroom, how will you respond?

a. Ignore him

b. Tell him, politely

c. Pour the frustration on him

d. Tell him, but angrily

2. If a senior nurse is always taunting you about your skills, how will you react?

a. Move aside silently and avoid conflict

b. Lose control and start fighting

c. Taunt her back

d. Complain about her in the department

3. If a doctor has asked you to accompany them on their rounds, how will you behave?

a. Closely watch and observe the doctor's way of dealing with the patients

b. Interfere and give suggestions

c. Communicate with the doctor

d. Be lost in your thoughts

4. When will you complete your assignment if the deadline is in a month?

a. The next day

b. The same day

c. One night before the submission date

d. In a week or two

5. If a patient is very talkative and does not keep quiet, how will you deal with this as a nurse?

a. Ask the patient to shut up after a time

b. Listen compassionately

c. Ask some other nurse to take over

d. Start talking with someone else in the room so the patient eventually shuts up

6. What will you do if a doctor assigns you an important responsibility and wants to leave you as the in-charge of the clinic at night?

a. Politely refuse

b. Take the responsibility

c. Make a fake excuse

d. Request a senior nurse from the staff to take responsibility

7. What will you do if you are studying in a group?

a. Be the most interactive member

b. Be the non-contributing member

c. Be the most studious member

d. Be a distracting member

8. If a kid is resisting when you are injecting him, how will you treat him?

a. Scold him

b. Convince him in a friendly way

c. Ask another nurse or his parents to hold him forcefully

d. Not inject him and leave him to the doctor

9. If an elderly patient is refusing to eat, how will you treat him?

a. Forcefully make him eat

b. Leave him on his own

c. Politely convince him to eat

d. Scold him

10. You are alone in the hospital, there is no doctor on duty, and a patient is brought to the emergency room. What will be your immediate reaction?

a. Calm down and deal with things in a relaxed manner

b. Start panicking

c. Call the doctor

d. Ask the patient's family to take him to some other hospital

11. How will you react to the news of a junior nurse getting a promotion in the hospital?

a. Get angry and resign from the job

b. Cut off ties with the nurse

c. Complain to management

d. Not say anything and continue with the job

12. If a doctor scolds you over a mistake that was not yours, how will you react?

a. Get angry and possibly resign

b. Take the blame yourself

c. Politely tell the doctor that it was not your mistake

d. Bring the real culprit in front of the doctor to be scolded

13. If you are in a room with someone who is a complete stranger, how will you behave?

a. Keep quiet until asked a question

b. Initiate a conversation

c. Leave the room

d. Get involved in your phone

14. Your professor has asked the class to write an answer to a question. You are done writing the answer. What will you do next?

a. Take it to the professor to get it checked

b. Ask a classmate to proofread it

c. Read it out loud to the class

d. Stay silent after finishing your task unless the professor calls you up

15. If you are given a break for a month, how will you spend most of your time during the vacation?

a. Reading books

b. Taking part in nursing internship programs

c. Sleeping

d. Planning a trip

Test 1 Answers

Math Test 1 Answers

1) b: Addition.

Addition is the sum of two or more numbers. New numbers are formed during addition. The new number is usually bigger than any of the different parts.

2) a: Addends.

The numbers that are added together to form a new number are individually known as addends. For instance, in 2 + 4 = 6; 2 and 4 are the addends while 6 is the sum.

3) c: Units.

One-digit numbers are referred to as units. Units are numbers between 0 and 9.

4) a: Three-digit numbers between 100 and 999.

While numbers between 0 and 9 are referred to as units, numbers between 100 and 999 fall into the hundreds group.

5) b: Rearranging the numbers according to the number of digits.

Adding up multiple-digit numbers is a bit more technical than adding units. Hence, the first step you should take to ensure you arrive at the right answer is to rearrange the numbers according to their number of digits.

6) a: The column farthest to the right.

As a rule of thumb, the addition of multiple-digit numbers should be started from the right-hand side. When there are carry-overs, you can easily add them to the appropriate numbers with ease.

7) c: When the sum of the addends exceeds 9.

When you are adding up numbers, consider the sum of the digits in each column. Only totals between 0 and 9 don't have carry-overs. Once the sum exceeds 9, you will have a carry-over whose value depends on the digit in the tens place value.

8) c: 28 + 12.

According to the rule, there will be a carry-over if the sum of the addends is more than 9. In options A, B and D, the sum of the numbers in the units column is less than 10. However, in option C, the addition of 2 and 8 gives 10.

9) c: Add the carry to the next number to the left.

When you start your addition operation from the right and have a carry, add the carry to the number to the left. If this new number has a carry too, add it to the number to its left. Continue the process until you are done.

10)   c: It decreases the bigger number.

When you subtract a small number from a bigger number, the bigger number will be reduced in value by the value of the number subtracted from it. For instance, when you subtract 2 from 10, 10 is reduced to 8.

11)   a: The column farthest to the right.

Just as with addition, subtraction is also started from the farthest digits to the right. Then, you work progressively to the left side until you have no digits left to subtract.

12)   c: Subtract 239 from 664.

For the difference to be positive, you must subtract a smaller number from a bigger number, not the other way around. In all the other answer options, bigger numbers are subtracted from smaller numbers, leaving a negative difference. In option c, 239 is smaller than 664, making the difference positive.

13)   a: 1 or a multiple of 1.

When adding a carry to a number, its value depends on whether you are adding 1 or a bigger number as a carry. If you are adding one, the value of the carry is 1. Otherwise, its value is a multiple of 1.

14)   b: You can subtract numbers of equal value from each other.

When performing subtraction operations, several rules apply. One of them is to start the subtraction from the right-hand side. Another important rule is that you can subtract numbers of equal value from each other and the answer will be zero.

15)   c: When subtracting a bigger digit from a smaller digit.

You can't subtract a smaller number from a bigger number to give a positive answer. However, you can find your way around the rule by borrowing a figure that represents 10.

16)   b: 10.

The value of the borrowed number is 10. When you add 10 to the smaller number, it becomes bigger. Thus, subtracting the previously larger number won't be an issue. For instance, in the equation 21 – 19, you can't subtract 9 from 1, but you can subtract it from 11.

17)   c: Division.

Division is the common name for repeated subtraction. Every division operation you perform can also be performed by subtracting the denominator from the numerator repeatedly. For instance, in 12/4, you can subtract 4 from 12 repeatedly until you reach zero, counting the number of times you subtract to arrive at the answer. This applies to all division operations.

18)   c: From the left-hand side column.

While addition and subtraction are usually started from the right-hand side, division is the opposite. Division operations are usually started from the left while you work progressively towards the right until there is nothing left to divide.

19)   c: 81.

When you divide 324 by 4, the answer is 81. Following the rule, start your division from the left. Try to divide 3 by 4. You can't do that, so divide 32 by 4. The answer is 8. Then, divide 4 by 4. The answer is 1. Hence, 324/4 is 81.

20)   d: Division only.

As previously explained, addition and subtraction of multiple-digit numbers are started from the far right. The same applies to multiplication operations too. Otherwise, you will arrive at the wrong answer. Conversely, division operations are started from the left.

21)   a: Multiplication.

While division is repeated subtraction, multiplication can also be performed by adding a number to another one for a specified number of times. For instance, to get the value of $2 \cdot 8$, add 2 to itself repeatedly 8 times.

22)   b: A decimal point.

The whole part and the fractional part of a decimal number are usually separated by a decimal point. To the left of the decimal point are the whole numbers while the fractional parts are to the right, for example, in 123.45, the whole is 123 and the fractional part is 45 hundredths.

23)   c: The digit 5 represents a fractional part of a whole number.

In the expression 0.50, since 5 is to the right of the decimal point, it is a fractional part of a whole number. In this case, it is 5 tenths of 1 whole.

24)   d: None of the above.

A wide range of operations can be performed on decimal numbers. You can add decimal numbers, subtract them from each other, divide them and multiply them just as you would with regular numbers.

25)   a: The decimal points must align with the arrangement of the numbers.

You may have to add decimal numbers with different numbers of decimal places. You must arrange the numbers in such a way that their decimal points align, irrespective of their decimal places.

26)   a: 234.56 + 12.60.

You can only perform an accurate addition operation on numbers if they have the same number of decimal places. To add 234.56 and 12.6, you can add an imaginary 0 to 12.6 to balance up the decimal places without affecting the real value of the number.

27)   a: It makes the number look more presentable.

The 0 has zero impact on the number. It neither adds nor subtracts from its value. Hence, it only makes it more presentable and may be necessary to ensure the addends share a uniform number of decimal places. This is especially necessary during addition operations.

28) b: Add the corresponding number of zeros to balance the number of decimal places.

Adding the corresponding number of zeros to balance the number of decimal places is sometimes necessary. For instance, if you add 123.456 and 15.6, the arrangement won't be okay without adding two extra zeros to 15.6 for it to have a uniform number of decimal places.

29) a: The positions and number of the decimal values.

The multiplication of decimal numbers can be tricky. Before multiplying, it is imperative that you align the decimal values to be in the correct place value column. After multiplying, the number of decimal places is used to determine how many decimal places the answer should have.

30) c: The addition of the decimal places in both numbers.

Decimal places are treated differently in multiplication than in other operations. Hence, after multiplying two decimal numbers, count the number of decimal places in both numbers to tell you where to place the decimal point in the final result.

31) c: Multiplication tables.

Division and multiplication are repeated subtraction and addition, respectively. Hence, knowing the multiplication table will make it easier to divide and multiple whole numbers. It is a good idea to memorize multiplication tables for 1-20.

32) b: As a part of a whole number with respect to 100.

A number is expressed as a percentage with respect to 100. For example, 55% means 55 out of 100. The same rule applies to every other number with the % sign. 100 is the reference point, irrespective of the presentation.

33) c: Per centum.

Percent is a derivative of the Latin words per centum, which literally means for 100 or through 100.

34) d: Per 100 or through 100

Any number expressed as a percentage literally means per 100 or through 100 in reference to the fact that the number is a fraction of 100. Thus, 50% simply means 50 per 100 or 50 through 100. In a nutshell, 50% means 50 out of 100.

35)   a: Fraction.

Converting a given number to a percentage is a very simple mathematical operation. The first step is to convert the number to a fraction. Then, multiply the result by 100 to get the actual value as a percentage. When necessary, you may express the number as a decimal instead, before turning this into a percentage by multiplying by 100.

36)   c: Multiplying the fractional value by 100.

As discussed earlier, after converting a number to a fraction, the next stage is multiplying the result by 100 to express it as percentage. Don't forget that this is also the next step if you convert the expression into a decimal. Either way, you will arrive at the percentage value of the converted number.

37)   d: Denominator.

The bottom value in a fraction is called the denominator. A fraction can also be considered a division. The denominator shows how many parts the numerator is divided into, so it acts as the divisor. In 4/5, 5 is the denominator.

38)   a: Numerator.

While the number below the fraction represents the denominator, the one above it is the numerator. The fraction can also be considered a division, with the numerator as your starting number or dividend. In 4/5, 4 is the numerator.

39)   c: 749.57.

The addition of 345.67, 236.9 and 167.0 will give you 749.57 if properly calculated. Note that one of the numbers has two decimal places while the others don't. Balance the decimal places with the appropriate number of zeros.

40)   d: $250.

This is a multiplication problem. Each pair of shoes cost $50. Thus, 5 pairs of the same shoes will cost $50 · 5. That is $250.

41)   c: $237.50.

The total cost of the five pairs of shoes is $250. Calculate the discount amount by finding 5% of $250. This is $0.05 \cdot 250$. Thus, the discount is $12.50. Deduct it from the total amount: $250 – $12.50. You will get $237.50. That's the cost after the discount.

42)   c: 1/20.

The discount as a fraction of the original cost can be calculated thus: 12.5/250. To make it easier, multiply both numbers by 10 to give an equivalent fraction of 125/2500. Both are multiples of 5, so divide these both by 5 until you can no longer do so. You will get the final fraction of 1/20.

43)   a: Unit.

In 235, the digit 5 is in the unit position. When you start from the right, 5 is in the units place value, 3 is in the tens place value and 2 is in the hundreds place value.

44)   d: 73.33%.

Simply subtract the number of students that passed from the total number of students to get the number of students that failed. Then, divide the number that failed by the total number of students. Multiply the result by 100.

45)   c: 121.32.

This question combines addition and subtraction. Add before you subtract.

67.80 + 99.12 = 166.92

166.92 – 45.6 = 121.32.

46)   c: 1,000.

In Roman numerals, M stands for 1,000. Other important Roman numerals you should know by heart are I for 1, V for 5, X for 10, L for 50, C for 100, D for 500 and M for 1,000. You can combine these numerals to form any Arabic number.

47)   c: 80.

LXXX stands for 80. You will recall that L stands for 50 and X for 10. Thus, triple X is 30. 50 + 30 = 80. It is the important to memorize the Roman numerals for this style of question.

48)   a: DCCC.

Find the largest components that add to make 800. These are 500 and 300. These are D and CCC respectively. Thus 800 = 500 + 300 = DCCC.

49)   d: XC.

Rewrite the numbers in Arabic numerals first. XV is 15 while VI is 6. Thus, 15 * 6 = 90. Convert the result into Roman numerals. 90 is XC, that is, remove 10 from 100. Note that when the smaller Roman numeral comes first, you should subtract it from the greater one.

50)   c: LXXXII.

The addition of 23, 47 and 12 gives 82. Find the different components that add to make 82. You have 50, 30 and 2. These are L, XXX and II respectively. Thus, 82 = 23 + 47 + 12 = LXXXII.

Reading Test 1 Answers

Passage 1 Answers and Explanations

1. b: Multitasking is the ability to perform two or more tasks at the same time.

Your ability to engage in multiple activities or tasks simultaneously is multitasking. You multitask when you are chewing gum while jogging, or singing while doing the dishes.

2. c: It is generally believed that multitasking boosts productivity.

Many people consider multitasking to be a perfect way to get a lot done within a short time. To them, it is a good way to boost their productivity levels.

3. a: Multitasking is a waste of time.

Because multitasking doesn't actually boost productivity, it is a waste of time. Thus, moving from one task to another repeatedly will actually waste your time and reduce your productivity.

4. c: They are actually task-switching.

When people think they are multitasking, they are actually switching from one task to another because the human brain isn't designed to handle multiple tasks simultaneously.

5. b: It has a negative impact on short-term memory.

A 2011 study by a group of scientists at the San Francisco-based University of California shows that switching from one task to another may trigger short-term memory loss.

6. b: Multitasking reduces productivity.

Contrary to your expectation, multitasking doesn't help you achieve more. When switching from one task to another, it takes the brain some time to get used to the new task. This increases the time it takes to complete each task; therefore, it reduces productivity.

7. a: Multitasking is more stressful.

Single-tasking is less stressful than multi-tasking. By focusing on one task at a time, you don't expend extra energy handling more than one task. Thus, you are less stressed and won't be under too much pressure that may jerk up your work-related stress levels.

8. a: Single-tasking helps people to be more focused and more creative.

Focusing on a task helps you to fashion out the best way to get the job done quickly and effectively. This will put your creative skills to task. The more you hone your creative skills, the better you become.

9. a: Multitasking increases the difficulty of focusing on a task.

When you multitask, you have to switch between tasks. On the other hand, single-tasking enables you to focus on a single task and get it done swiftly before moving to the next task.

10.   a: The human brain is designed with the ability to focus on one task at a time.

Contrary to the general belief, the human brain is not designed as an efficient multitasking machine. Rather, it is designed to focus on one task at a time. Thus, when handling more than one task at a time, the brain won't function at maximum capacity.

11. d: Dreaming while sleeping.

While the other options are voluntary actions performed by humans, dreaming and sleeping are involuntary actions. Thus, humans don't choose whether to do them or not because they are natural and in-built.

12.   b: Multitasking is the perceived ability to perform two or more tasks efficiently while task-switching is switching from one task to another.

Task-switching is generally misconceived as multitasking. Task-switching refers to switching from one task to another while multitasking refers to the perceived ability to handle more than one task at a moment. In practice, multitasking is actually task-switching, because the brain cannot cope with multiple tasks simultaneously.

13.   b: She should handle the tasks one after the other.

If she decides to handle the two tasks simultaneously, she exposes herself to the inherent danger of multitasking, especially reduced productivity. She will be more productive if she focuses on one task at a time.

14. c: Short-term memory.

In a report published in *Proceedings of the National Academy of Sciences*, researchers revealed that multitasking negatively affects the short-term memory (also known as the working memory).

15. a: That multitasking is a myth and a waste of time.

As can be seen from the article, people don't actually multitask, they only task-switch. Multitasking also reduces productivity and thus wastes people's time. It is not a good option for improving productivity.

Passage 2 Answers and Explanations

1. c: Some people are easily motivated while some struggle with lack of motivation and procrastination.

Motivation is quite challenging for some and such people aren't motivated unless they are pushed to do so. On the other hand, others may find it easy to find the motivation to get stuff done.

2. b: Having a realistic view of yourself and your limitations.

You can't set realistic goals if you have zero knowledge of yourself and your limitations. Self-discovery is an effective tool for setting achievable goals. When you are fully aware of your limitations and skills, you can set goals that factor in such weaknesses and strengths.

3. a: A reminder of what you need to do to make your dreams come true.

Writing goals down is one of the most recommended ways to derive motivation to keep going. When you write your goals down, you have a reminder of what you have achieved and what you need to do to make your dreams come true. That will create the desire and motivation you need.

4. b: They are broken down into smaller and easier-to-achieve chunks.

The sheer size of a huge task such as preparing for an entrance exam may weigh you down and sap you of your energy. On the other hand, when you break such a task down, you can easily get each small piece done. This motivates you to do more.

5. c: Self-reflection.

Self-reflection is a form of performance appraisal that helps you to identify how much you have achieved and where improvements are needed. During a self-reflective period, you can reflect on what you intend to achieve and how much you have already done. This can increase motivation.

6. d: All of the above.

Sometimes, you must create time for yourself. You can seize the opportunity to celebrate your achievements, manage stress that may arise from overworking, and develop and analyze your next plan of action. When you are in the best frame of mind after enough rest, motivation will naturally come.

7. b: Resist the urge to compare yourself to others.

You should resist the destructive urge to compare yourself to others. More often than not, you won't measure up to the standards or achievements of the individuals you make such comparisons with. Rather than focusing on what you can achieve, you will lose the little motivation you have.

8. a: Working on your weaknesses is as beneficial as leveraging your strengths.

If left unchecked, your weakness will hamper your success. Being mindful of your weaknesses when planning your goals is another effective way to be motivated.

9. c: Experienced coaches.

You will do yourself a lot of good if you seek mentorship from experienced individuals in your profession.

10. d: All of the above.

When writing down your goals, they should be realistic in order for you to stay motivated. It is imperative that you write them down in the order of importance and attempt them one at a time. Also, remember that the written-down goals should serve as a guide you consistently follow.

Passage 3 Answers and Explanations

1. c: Conventional.

"Conventional" can replace "mainstream" as used in the passage. They refer to opinions or ideas that people consider to be normal due to their popularity.

2. c: It encourages its use.

The US encourages the use of medical marijuana in view of its millions of users in the country. More so, it is currently considered legal in 29 states, including Washington DC.

3. c: Cannabinoids.

Although it has several potent components, marijuana contains cannabinoids or CBD in short. This component is responsible for the hallucinogenic effects of marijuana on its users.

4. b: Pain management.

Marijuana is used medically to alter pain perception in the human brain. Physicians take advantage of this benefit to treat some medical conditions such as fibromyalgia, and arthritis.

5. a: Arthritis and irritable bowel movement.

Irritable bowel syndrome, Crohn's disease, and rheumatoid arthritis are some medical conditions that may cause inflammation.

6. c: It reduces inflammation.

Marijuana's CBD content is a powerful antidote that helps with inflammation reduction in people with the medical conditions that can result in inflammation, such as arthritis.

7. a: Its anti-inflammation and pain management properties.

Thanks to marijuana's anti-inflammation and pain management properties, patients that are treated with medical marijuana can also sleep better.

8. c: It is used for mental disorder management.

Marijuana also affects the limbic system positively. Medical doctors are taking advantage of this property when treating patients with mental or neurological disorders.

9. b: Rapid breathing and increased heart pressure rate.

Marijuana is also known for its ability to trigger some medical problems such as rapid breathing, hyperactivity, and increased heart and blood pressure rates. If these conditions are not properly managed, they may be the harbinger for more serious health concerns.

10. a: Concentration and coordination issues.

While marijuana may have a depressant-like effect on a user, such users may also become more prone to concentration and coordination issues. When left untreated, they are at the risk of suffering from other physical health challenges.

11. a: It can be harmful and beneficial.

As highlighted in the passage, medical marijuana has tons of positive uses and is highly beneficial. Nevertheless, it can also be harmful as it can trigger a wide range of health problems if not used properly.

Passage 4 Answers and Explanations

1. a: They are medical conditions that affect its victim's feelings and thoughts.

Mental disorders are also known as mental illnesses. These are medical conditions that may affect the victim's feelings and thoughts, aside from their behavior and mood.

2. d: Organic disorder.

There are different types of disorders such as personality disorder, bipolar disorder, and psychotic disorder. There is no such thing as an organic disorder.

3. c: Neither of the above.

It is noteworthy that no single cause can be attributed to mental disorders. Rather, it can be triggered by a wide range of factors. Thus, none of the listed causes can single-handedly trigger mental disorder.

4. a: Mental illness can be inherited.

People from families that have a history of mental illnesses are more at the risk of this medical condition than others. The descendants of such families will have the ailment passed down to them through their genes.

5. b: Autism spectrum disorder.

Exposure to some toxic chemicals or viruses during pregnancy can lead to reduce oxygen supply to the brain. This can result in autism spectrum disorder.

6. b: Post-traumatic stress disorder.

People who go through traumatic life events from time to time are prone to developing mental disorders. The same can be said of some who suffer other stress-inducing problems such as domestic violence and job-related stress.

7. d: Childbirth and menopause.

Childbirth, menopause, and thyroid problems are some hormonal changes that are associated with depression. This explains why some women experience post-partum depression after giving birth.

8. d: Adulthood.

Among the several factors that can cause mental illnesses are heredity, biological factors, and stress and trauma. It is noteworthy that not all adults struggle with mental disorders. Thus, adulthood isn't a factor.

9. b: Disruption of fetal brain development.

When a pregnant woman is exposed to viruses or chemicals during pregnancy, they expose the fetus to prenatal damage such as the disruption of fetal brain development or some related health problems.

10. d: At the risk of.

"Vulnerable" as used in the passage means to be at the risk of something. Thus, "At the risk of" can replace the word in the passage.

11. a: Vulnerable to.

According to the passage, "prone to" is synonymous with "vulnerable to." Hence, the latter can replace the former and convey the same message.

Vocabulary Test 1 Answers

1) c: Medical and general vocabulary.

The vocabulary test isn't a test of *either* your general *or* medical vocabulary. Rather, it is a test of how conversant you are with medical vocabulary *and* your ability to communicate effectively during your day-to-day activities. This ensures that you won't only understand medical materials but other materials as well.

2) c: Read a wide range of materials.

There are several ways to upgrade your vocabulary. You can do this by listening to expert vocabulary users, specifically authorities in both the medical world and other fields. However, a very effective technique is to read a wide range of materials. You will come across unfamiliar words you can include in your vocabulary.

3) a: Pathology.

As a medical or nursing student, it is not only expected, but advantageous, that you have a good knowledge of pathology. When you have top-notch knowledge of the causes and effects of injury and disease, you are on the path to becoming a successful medical practitioner.

4) b: Remission.

Remission occurs when a patient responds so much to treatment that there is either a gradual reduction of the symptoms and signs of a disease or a total disappearance of the signs and symptoms. At that stage, the patient is on the way to full recovery from the ailment.

5) c: Coronary walls.

When plaque is deposited on the wall of the blood-carrying coronary arteries, the arteries are narrowed, preventing the heart from receiving sufficient oxygen. This may trigger a wide range of heart-related ailments or death in some cases if not swiftly treated.

6) b: Hypotension.

Low blood pressure is medically known as hypotension. This occurs when the blood pressure reads below 90/60. Note that low blood pressure can lead to inadequate blood flow to some body parts such as the brain, heart and some other vital body organs.

7) c: Myocardial infarction.

A heart attack is medically known as a myocardial infarction. This ailment affects the coronary arteries. When plaque blocks the arteries that supply blood to the heart muscles, there is a gradual reduction in the amount of blood transported to the heart muscles. This damages the heart as the muscles die.

8) a: Intractable.

An ailment is considered intractable if there are reduced or zero chances of curing it. Most ailments of the type are rare diseases resulting from unidentifiable causes. In some cases, there are no records of established effective treatments.

9) a: Nose.

Epistaxis is one of the common health problems associated with the nose. It occurs when blood comes out of the nose. It is usually caused by trauma or may sometimes be triggered by increased blood pressure.

10) b: -algia.

Algia is a medical suffix that refers to pain in a specific part of the body. Some examples include myalgia, or muscle pain; mastalgia, or breast pain; arthralgia, or joint pain; and neuralgia, or nerve pain.

11) d: -ectasis.

The dilation or expansion of the hollow organs in the body is represented by the -ectasis suffix. There are several medical conditions suffixed with -ectasis, including esophagectasis, dilation of the esophagus; bronchiectasis, dilation or expansion of the lungs' bronchi; and pyopyelectasis, dilation of the renal pelvis.

12) d: -emia.

Blood-related conditions are identified by the -emia suffix. For instance, hypoglycemia refers to the presence of little glucose or sugar in the blood. Other examples include hypervolemia and anemia, which refer to an excess volume of blood and lack of blood, respectively.

13) a: Centesis.

Centesis is a curative medical process. The process involves the puncturing of a body organ or cavity with a hollow needle with the aim of drawing out fluid. An example is paracentesis, removing belly fluid for diagnosis.

14) a: Abdominocentesis.

Abdominocentesis is a surgical procedure which removes wrinkles on the abdomen. The skin covering the stomach can also be tightened through the surgical operation. The procedure is otherwise known as abdominal paracentesis, or paracentesis.

15) a: Cardiologist.

A cardiologist is a medical practitioner who specializes in heart and heart-related ailments and abnormalities, such as coronary heart disease, congenital heart disease, high blood cholesterol, hypertension and others.

16) a: A rupture.

A rupture is a tear or break in any soft issue or organ of the body. For example, the spleen and Achilles tendon can rupture.

17) a: Amnesia.

Amnesia is commonly known as memory loss. The memory deficit may be caused by a disease or brain damage. Other uncommon causes include the excessive use of hypnotic drugs or sedatives. The extent of damage done determines whether the memory loss is partial or total.

18) a: Bi-

Bi- is the prefix for 'double' or 'twice.' Examples are *bicuspid*, two cusps or flaps; *biceps*, two-headed muscle; or *bisexual*. Others are *binary vision, bifocal, biarticulated* and *bifurcation*.

19) b: Extro-

Extro- or extra- is a prefix that means in front of, before and forward. *Extrospection, extrovert* and *extrude* are some common examples of words with this prefix.

20) a: Mild traumatic brain injury.

Mild traumatic brain injury is a serious injury to the brain that can be triggered by a serious blow to the head, or violent head or body shaking. Its signs and symptoms include fatigue, headaches, anxiety, impaired cognitive functions, depression and irritability.

21) c: First aid.

The medical attention given to an injured or sick person is first aid.

22) b: Sprain.

A sprain occurs when the ligaments are stretched or torn. The ligaments are fibrous tissues in the joints for connecting two bones together. Sprains mostly happen in the ankle. Sprains are common in people who engage in physically demanding activities.

23) a: Phlebitis.

This is a vein inflammation that commonly occurs in the legs. When the veins are inflamed, they block the blood and thereby cause marked swelling in the leg.

24) d: None of the above.

Pepsia is a recurrent or persistent discomfort or pain in the upper abdomen caused by issues with the digestive tract or indigestion. Dyspepsia, otherwise known as indigestion, may be triggered by another health problem such as ulcers, gastroesophageal reflux or a gallbladder disease.

25) d: A pair of pliers.

A first aid kit must have the following items: Band-Aids, disposable sterile gloves, triangular bandages, sterile eye dressings, safety pins, tweezers and a host of other items that make it easier to render the needed assistance without delay.

26) b: Surgery.

Surgery is a medical operation procedure that is usually done to correct some anomaly in a patient's body.

27) c: Hematologists.

Hematology is the treatment of malignancies and blood diseases. Thus, experts who treat blood diseases and malignancies are usually known as hematologists.

28) a: The ailment's syndromes.

Syndrome refers to a disease or a condition's set of symptoms. A disease's syndromes give a clue into its nature and help medical professionals to find a solution to the problem.

29) a: Cardiac arrest.

A cardiac arrest occurs when the heart stops its primary function of supplying the body with blood. While this is similar to a heart attack, someone may suffer a cardiac arrest without an apparent cause.

30) b: 145/90.

Someone with a blood pressure reading of 140/90 and above is said to suffer from high blood pressure. Thus, 145/90 is a symptom of high blood pressure or hypertension.

31) a: It is the amount of times the heart beats per minute.

Pulse rate refers to the number of times the heart beats each minute. Simply put, this is a measure of the number of times an individual's heart beats each minute.

32) c: Trauma and increased blood pressure.

Simply put, epistaxis is a type of ailment characterized by blood discharge from the nose. It is usually caused by trauma, or sometimes, may be triggered by increased blood pressure.

33) a: It signifies the surgical removal of a part of the body.

Ectomy signifies the surgical removal of a part of the body. It is attached to any form of surgical operation with the objective of removing a body part.

34) b: Pepsia.

A recurrent or persistent discomfort or pain in the upper abdomen caused by issues with the digestive tract or indigestion is known as pepsia or indigestion.

35) a: It prefixes medical ailments that involve excessive blood flow.

Rrhagia means rapid or excessive blood flow and is thus used for medical conditions that involve excessive blood flow. Some common examples of such medical conditions are metrorrhagia and rhinorrhagia.

36) c: She suffers from amenia.

Amenia is the suppression or absence of a normal menstrual flow. This is otherwise known as amenorrhea.

37) b: Anuric.

Anuric means not producing urine. It is a critical health condition where dialysis may be urgently required. This makes it a serious medical condition.

38) c: If it affects the bases of the lungs.

Bibasilar means happening at both lungs' bases. It refers to a health problem that affects the bases of both lungs.

39) c: It means Coronary Artery Bypass Graft.

CABG means Coronary Artery Bypass Graft: This is a form of surgery performed on the heart to clear an obstructed coronary artery and ensure normal blood flow to it.

40) a: Cerebrovascular accident.

A cerebrovascular accident is a health condition that is commonly referred to as stroke. It is commonly known by its shortened form, CVA.

41) a: It is a fibrous tumor that covers the peripheral nerve.

Neurofibroma refers to the fibrous tumor that covers the peripheral nerve. The ailment can develop in any minor or major nerve in any part of the body.

42) d: It is a medical condition that affects the body tissue.

Atrophy is a medical condition that is characterized by the wasting away or the decrease in size of a body tissue or part. The ailment is usually caused by the degeneration of the patient's cells.

43) c: Chemotherapy.

Chemotherapy refers to treating ailments with powerful chemicals. This treatment method is mostly used for treating cancer and other fast-growing cells.

44) c: Physical condition and age.

Bradycardia is a medical condition that is characterized by extremely slow or abnormal heartbeat. This condition is determined by the patient's age and physical condition.

45) b: They should be taken twice daily.

B.I.D is a Latin word "bis in die" and is medically used to indicate that a medicine should be taken twice daily.

46) a: If the ACL is sprained or ruptured.

Anterior Cruciate Ligament or ACL is a common knee injury. It occurs when the ACL is completely torn or sprained.

47) a: Type-1 diabetes.

Insulin-Dependent Diabetes Mellitus is generally known as Type 1 diabetes. This form of a condition is more difficult to treat and maintain than the Type-2 variant of the ailment.

48) a: It means entire.

Pan means entire or all. For instance, pan-Africa means the policy or movement is designed for the entire African race.

49) c: Itis.

Itis is a medical condition that is characterized by inflammation. Examples are arthritis, appendicitis, and bronchitis.

50) a: Osmotic or viral mechanisms.

Lysis is the separation or destruction of the membrane or cell wall. This is usually caused by osmotic or viral mechanisms.

Grammar Test 1 Answers

1) b: Eight.

There are eight parts of speech. These are nouns, pronouns, adjectives, adverbs, verbs, prepositions, conjunctions and interjections. Each part of speech performs a different function. Understanding the parts of speech is crucial to your comprehension skills.

2) b: Nouns.

A noun is the name of a person, animal, place or thing. Thus, the name of anything around you is a noun.

3) d: None of the above.

From your previous knowledge, you should understand that Mary is the name of a person and is therefore a noun. The same applies to school bus and New York City, names of an object and a place, respectively.

4) a: Six.

Nouns can be classified into six groups. These are common nouns, concrete nouns, abstract nouns, proper nouns, collective nouns and possessive nouns. Improve your knowledge of these types of nouns to improve your reading skills.

5) b: Common noun.

A common noun is generally used for naming a group of similar objects. Examples of common nouns are people, cars, furniture, ideas, animals and newspaper.

6) a: Proper nouns.

A proper noun is used for identifying specific single entities. It can be used to identify the individual members of a group. For instance, the name of any person is a proper noun identifying the individual as a member of the common noun.

7) d: None of the above.

In the given examples, all of the options are examples of a common noun because they all refer to a group of similar people. A teacher can be anyone, as can a footballer or a deliveryman. They are members of a group.

8) b: Lucas is a proper noun while boxer is a common noun.

A proper noun refers to a member of a group of people, places or things. In this case, Lucas is a member of the boxing community, while boxer refers to any member of the community.

9) d: College graduation party.

New Year, Christmas and Halloween are some examples of proper nouns. Proper nouns are usually started with capital letters while common nouns are lowercased unless they start a sentence.

10) a: Abstract noun.

Non-physical things are referred to as abstract nouns. These are things you can't touch or see physically, but which still actually exist. Notable examples include ideas, concepts, feelings, emotions, knowledge, intelligence, love, hate and wisdom.

11) a: Concrete nouns.

Concrete nouns can be seen and felt. Examples include a house, car, shirt, phone and other physical objects.

12) d: Emotions.

Emotions are abstract nouns that can't be seen physically, although we are sure of their existence. The other members of the list—animals, clouds and flowers—are all concrete nouns.

13) a: Two.

Concrete nouns can be classified into countable and uncountable nouns. In the former class are objects you can pluralize such as houses and cars while the former group has members that can't be pluralized, such as salt.

14) c: Collective noun.

You can represent a collection of objects with collective nouns. Some examples of collective nouns include a team, pack and staff. This noun can't be used for a single member of a group, only for the group itself. That's why you have a team of footballers or a staff of employees.

15) b: Pronoun.

A pronoun is a word or phrase that is used to replace a noun. Thus, a pronoun will perform the same function as a noun in a sentence.

16) a: It helps to avoid needless repetition.

Needless repetition in a sentence makes a sentence look clumsy and boring. When referring to a noun for a second time in a sentence, using a pronoun instead helps to eliminate this problem.

17) c: Possessive pronoun.

Different types of pronouns serve different purposes. You can make reference to the ownership of an object with a possessive pronoun. Such pronouns include *hers, mine, yours, theirs* and *its.*

18) c: Indefinite pronoun.

You can reference nouns without specifying any noun by using indefinite pronouns such as *nobody, few, everyone, anything* and *everybody.*

19) b: Relative pronouns.

Relative pronouns are used for connecting a clause or phrase to a proper noun or proper pronoun. They are mostly used to provide more information about a noun or pronoun. *Which, who, whomever, whichever* and *that* are some examples of relative pronouns.

20) a: Intensive pronouns.

Intensive pronouns are used for intensifying or emphasizing pronouns and nouns. They are identified by their -self and -selves suffixes. *Yourself, myself* and *himself* are some examples of this type of pronoun.

21) b: It is a form of verb that makes its clause more meaningful.

An auxiliary verb is a form of verb that makes a clause more meaningful. Thus, it can express a wide range of concepts such as aspect, tense, emphasis and modality. Another name for this class of verbs is "helping verbs."

22) a: Adverbs.

Adverbs are words that are used to describe or modify another adverb, adjective, verb or a group of words. They provide more information about how an action is performed.

23) a: Articles.

Articles are used for describing nonspecific people and things. The three articles are *a, an* and *the*. Both *a* and *an* are indefinite articles while *the* is a definite article.

24) a: Adjectives.

Adjectives are used for describing or modifying a noun. When modifying a noun, an adjective provides more information as a way of shedding more light on the noun. Adjectives are also used for describing situations, personalities, amounts, and time.

25) a: Attributive adjective.

Attributive adjective are commonly used for describing the specific qualities or features of an object. They are used for modifying the age, shape, color, quality and other attributes of the target object. Real, interesting, delicious and beautiful are some attributive adjectives.

26) d: Car

With its definition as the name of any person, animal, place, or thing, "car" is the only noun in the sentence.

27) d: None of the above.

All the examples in this question are examples of proper nouns. All their words are initialized with a capital letter as a rule.

28) a: Intelligence, social concepts, and traits.

You can touch, smell, see, or hear abstract nouns. Some examples include social concepts, emotions, traits, and events, qualities, concepts, feelings, and political theories.

29) a: Uncountable noun.

You can't count grains of rice or sugar. Milk, water, electricity, and air are some other nouns you can't count as single elements.

30) a: Possessive pronoun.

They are examples of possessive pronouns, a pronoun that is used to show ownership or possession. *Mine, yours, hers, theirs, ours,* and *his* are other examples of possessive pronouns.

31) b: Finite verbs.

Finite verbs are types of verbs performed by the subjects. It can only serve as reference to the subject as well. They can exist in different forms and their status is determined by the number of people or the subject.

32) c: Flaunt means showing off while flout means scornfully defying.

While flaunt and flout are homophones, the former means showing off while the latter means scornfully defying.

33) b: Modal verbs.

A modal verb is another form of auxiliary verb. It sheds light on the main verb's attributes such as its ability, potential, expectation, and other attributes. Modal verbs are *may, might, can, could, shall, will, ought to, should,* etc.

34) c: Numbers adjective.

Numbers are mostly used as adjectives in sentences where a number provides the answer to the question "How many?".

35) c: Adverbs of frequency.

The frequency of the occurrence of a verb is the focus of this adverb type. You can easily identify them because they are usually written before a sentence's main verb. Examples are *always, normally, seldom, rarely, again, sometimes,* etc.

36) c: Preposition for time.

This is an example of preposition for time. This is the class of preposition that indicates the time when something occurs, occurred, or will occur. They focus on months of years, a particular day of the month, or any other time-related information.

37) a: "On" is a preposition that is used to provide information about the surface of an object while "in" is used to define a physical or virtual boundary.

Although "On" and "In" are prepositions, the former is used to provide information about the surface of an object while the latter is used to define a physical or virtual boundary.

38) b: Principal.

While this word sounds like "Principle," it is actually the word used for the head of a school while its homophone, "Principle," refers to a firmly held idea or belief.

39) c: Preposition for direction.

These are prepositions that are used to indicate the direction of a person or thing. Their presence in a sentence will give you a clue into the subject's direction without much ado. Some examples include: through, into, towards, and to.

40) b: If it contains words such as "by" or "with".

When expressing a causal relationship between the doer or noun and the action or verb, prepositions of agent are used. Notable examples are with, by, and so on.

41) c: For connecting a dependent and an independent clause.

Subordinating conjunctions are used for connecting two clauses with different grammatical values. They are typically ideal for connecting independent clauses and dependent clauses.

42) b: Coordinating conjunctions.

Coordinating conjunctions are connecting words that are used to connect sentence elements of the same grammatical type. Thus, they are used for connecting phrases with phrases, words with words, sentences with sentences, and clauses with clauses.

43) d: Americans are in favor of "toward" while "towards" is acceptable in British English.

Your choice depends on your audience. The Americans are in favor of the former while the latter is acceptable in British English.

44) a: Correlative conjunction.

Correlative conjunctions are used to show a contrasting or comparative relationship between ideas or words by connecting pairs. Thus, the relationship between "tall" and "intelligent" is expressed in the sentence.

45) b: A clause is a group of words with a verb and a subject.

A clause is a group of words with a subject and a verb or predicate. A word without either of the two isn't a clause.

46) c: Compliments

You compliment someone when making a good remark about them. This is quite different from "complement," its homophone with a distinct meaning.

47) c: The food has been eaten by the cat.

The passive voice refers to the use of a verb in a way that suggests that the verb's action is received by the subject. This is the opposite of the active voice that uses an expression that suggests that the subject performs the verb action.

48) c: Synonyms.

Words with the same meaning are known as synonyms. Examples are happy and joyful, rich and wealth, and knowledgeable and intelligent.

49) c: Idiom.

An idiom is a set of expressions with a different meaning than the individual words' literal meanings. An example is "shed crocodile tears." This simply means insincere sympathy.

50) b: "Breathe" is a verb while "breath" is a noun.

Breathe and breath are homophones. Breathe as a verb means to inhale or exhale while the noun, breath, refers to the air we inhale or exhale.

Biology Test 1 Answers

1) a: *Bios* and *logos*.

Biology is derived from two Greek words. These are *bios* and *logos*. They mean life and study, respectively. This explains the rationale behind biology's definition as the science of life.

2) d: Informatics Biology.

Botany is the branch of biology that deals with the study of plants while molecular and cellular biology deal with macromolecules and cells, respectively. Informatics biology, on the other hand, doesn't exist.

3) a: Evolutionary Biology.

Evolutionary biology deals with the study of the origins of species. It also covers the gradual changes that living organisms undergo over time.

4) b: Photosynthesis.

Photosynthesis is a complex system through which plants and some organisms convert light from the sun into useful energy. During the process, sunlight is used for the conversion of carbon dioxide, water and minerals into energy-rich chemicals and oxygen.

5) b: Radiant energy harvest.

Radiant energy harvest is the first stage of photosynthesis. This process is triggered when a green, leafy plant receives sunlight. Chlorophyll, a pigment in the plant cell, absorbs light photons from the plant cells' chloroplasts for photosynthesis to occur.

6) c: Radiant energy conversion.

A plant can't use sunlight in its raw form. Thus, before using the light for photosynthesis, the plant will convert the light energy into chemical energy, a usable form of energy it needs to fuel its cells.

7) c: Atmospheric carbon dioxide and water from the soil.

Plants convert NADPH and adenosine triphosphate by using water from the soil and atmospheric carbon dioxide as raw materials. The importance of the adenosine triphosphate is highlighted by its alias: "energy currency for all life."

8) b: The energy produced by the light reactions is used for carbohydrate production for plants.

During the Calvin-Benson cycle, the energy produced by the light reactions is used for the production of carbohydrates needed by the plants. NADPH is also produced during the reaction. NADPH is a special form of NADP with hydrogen ions and electrons, as well as adenosine triphosphate.

9) a: Carbohydrates and glucose.

The Calvin-Benson cycle produces carbohydrates and glucose. During the cycle, the plant uses both ATP and NADPH to fix the carbon dioxide while carbon from atmospheric carbon dioxide is used for the production of carbohydrates. Another product of the cycle is glucose.

10) d: It is the only source of energy for both humans and animals.

Photosynthesis is a beneficial process for both humans and animals. Among some of its numerous benefits is the production of oxygen.

11) a: Indian pipe and beechdrops.

While the majority of plants derive energy from photosynthesis, not all plants do. Some are photosynthesis-independent, deriving their energy from other sources. Two examples of such plants are beechdrops (*Epifagus americana*) and Indian pipe (*Monotropa uniflora*).

12) a: Molds, mushrooms and yeasts.

Not all photosynthesis-independent plants are parasitic. Some, such as mushrooms, molds and yeasts, source nutrients from their environment without hurting a host.

13) c: Resting Metabolic Rate.

A certain number of calories are needed for the body to function at maximum capacity. This amount of calories is known as the Resting Metabolic Rate (RMR).

Without it, the heart rate, brain and breathing will cease. RMR is responsible for 75% of the calories humans burn daily.

14) c: Catabolism and anabolism.

Metabolism is classified into catabolism and anabolism. While catabolism is the breakdown of molecules to obtain energy from molecules, anabolism refers to the synthesis of the compounds needed by the body's cells.

15) d: It aids photosynthetic processes.

Metabolism offers the human body many benefits. Some of these include providing the substance the body needs for its upkeep, supplying calories for energy and ensuring the body functions at optimum capacity. Metabolism, however, doesn't support photosynthesis.

16) d: Speeding up metabolic rates.

Fats play a vital role in the human body. Vital organs are protected by fats and they also help humans reserve energy for future use. Without fats, it is nearly impossible to absorb important fat-soluble vitamins. Nevertheless, they don't interfere with metabolism.

17) d: Proteins.

In the body, hemoglobin is formed for oxygen transportation. This is fully supported by protein. Proteins also assist with cell structure and functions, along with supplying the nitrogen needed by both DNA and RNA. Energy production is another important protein contribution in the body.

18) d: Valeline.

Amino acids come in different forms. Lysine, leucin and isoleucine are some important amino acids. Valeline is not an amino acid.

19) a: Minerals.

Minerals are primarily responsible for food regulation and are instrumental to the body's metabolic pathways.

20) a: Nicotinic acid and pantothenic acid.

Pantothenic acid and nicotinic acid, otherwise known as niacin, are some important vitamins that support metabolic reactions.

21) c: Sugar, starch and fiber.

Humans must consume a reasonable quantity of starch, sugar and fiber to get their daily dose of necessary carbohydrates.

22) c: Oxidation of organic compounds for energy production.

Cellular respiration refers to a process that involves the oxidation of organic compounds with the primary aim of producing energy. During the process, biochemical energy from nutrients is converted into ATP.

23) a: Three-stage.

A complete cellular respiration process will go through three stages. Glycolysis is the first stage, where glucose molecules are broken down into smaller molecules by enzymes. In the second stage, oxygen combines with the smaller molecules to form carbon dioxide as a waste product. The last stage is where electron transportation occurs.

24) c: Electron transport.

Electron transport is the last stage of cellular respiration. The energy stored from the previous two stages is used for the production of more ATP molecules. The oxygen combines with the hydrogen from the molecules storing energy to form water as a waste product.

25) b: Aerobic cellular respiration requires oxygen while anaerobic cellular respiration does not.

The major difference between the anaerobic and aerobic cellular respiration is that, while aerobic respiration requires oxygen, anaerobic doesn't.

Chemistry Test 1 Answers

1. c: Atoms.

Atoms are the simplest form of any matter and are the basic building blocks with which other things are built. Everything around you is made up of atoms.

2. d: Atoms.

Atoms are made up of three parts: protons, neutrons and electrons. While protons and electrons are positively and negatively charged, respectively, neutrons have no charge, hence their name.

3. a: Protons and neutrons.

The nucleus of an atom contains protons and neutrons while electrons revolve around the nucleus. Hence, the nucleus of an atom is positively charged due to the presence of the positively charged protons.

4. a: Molecules.

The bonding of atoms produces a molecule. A molecule is the smallest unit of an element or compound. The atoms in a molecule are combined together through chemical bonds. The bonds are formed when atoms share or exchange electrons with each other.

5. c: Size and complexity.

The differences in molecules are caused by the sizes and complexities of the molecules. Factors such as the boiling point, melting point and others have zero impact.

6. a: Compounds.

Compounds are made up of different elements. These elements are bonded together and can't be separated physically. They can only be broken down into their different constituents through a chemical means.

7. d: Mixtures.

Mixtures are made up of two or more elements that are physically combined together. Their physical combination is a major difference between them and compounds. Hence, they can be separated into their components by physical means. Most often, mixtures exhibit the properties of their individual components.

8. b: Matter.

Matter is anything that has mass and occupies space. Nearly everything around us is matter. Your phone, pen, desk, etc., are all examples of matter.

9. a: Physical and chemical properties.

Matter has both physical properties and chemical properties. Physical properties affect physical changes such as the boiling point and density while chemical properties such as rusting affect their transformation.

10. c: Chemical properties.

Chemical properties are associated with matter's transformation during the formation of new substances with distinct attributes. Chemical attributes include features such as rusting, toxicity, reactivity, and electromotive force.

11. a: New substances are formed in chemical changes but not in physical changes.

The most noticeable difference between a physical change and a chemical change is the formation of new substances in chemical changes. This explains why physical changes are reversible and chemical changes are often irreversible.

12. d: Changes in electrochemical cells.

Evaporation and demagnetization are physical changes. Mixture separation through fractional distillation and magnetization of iron is also a physical change. However, changes in electrochemical cells are an examples of a chemical change that results in the formation of a new substance.

13. a: Element.

An element is a substance that can't be broken down into simpler units by regular chemical processes. There are over a hundred elements that can be found in the earth's crust, in the air and in the sea. Ninety percent are natural, while the rest can be produced artificially.

14. a: Groups 3 to 12 of the periodic table.

In the third to twelfth groups of the periodic table, you can find the transition metals. The elements in these groups are all metals and display metallic properties such as high tensile strength and high melting points.

15.   c: Manganese and nickel.

The transition metals perform different functions as dictated by their properties. Among them are nickel and manganese, used extensively as industrial catalysts. On the other hand, iron, copper and silver are used for commercial purposes.

16.   c: Reactive metals.

Reactive metals are renowned for their high oxidation tendency. They are found on the left of the periodic table due to their high reactivity. Notable members of the group are sodium, lithium, potassium, cesium, rubidium, francium and barium.

17.   d: Non-metals.

Non-metals are naturally occurring elements that produce neither electricity nor heat. Structurally, they are brittle and thus can't be molded, rolled, pressed or extruded. Some non-metallic members of the periodic table are phosphorus, oxygen, nitrogen, selenium, carbon, sulfur and arsenic.

18.   a: Nitrogen, oxygen and carbon.

Nitrogen, oxygen and carbon are some examples of non-metals. They do not display the same characteristics as metals, and thus can't be molded and pressed. Other non-metals include selenium, phosphorus, arsenic and sulfur.

19.   a: Lanthanides.

Lanthanides are otherwise known as rare earth elements. These elements are found in the sixth group of the periodic table. The 15 members of this group include lanthanum (La), samarium, (Sm), cerium (Ce) and lutetium (Lu).

20.   b: Pure metals.

Metals that don't contain atoms of multiple metallic elements are referred to as pure metals. They have some useful properties. They are good electrical conductors, although most of them are too malleable and soft and thus can't be used for industrial purposes.

21. c: Noble gases.

Noble gases are usually colorless, odorless, have single atoms and are found in group 18 of the periodic table. Noble gases do not react with other elements under standard conditions. They only react when subjected to extreme conditions. Their high level of inertness contributes to their usefulness in applications with zero room for reactions.

22. d: Chemical reaction.

A chemical reaction is the process by which one or more substances are converted into different products or substances. The substances can be chemical elements or compounds. Decomposition and combustion are two examples of chemical reactions.

23. a: Decomposition.

Decomposition is a chemical reaction where a single reactant can produce two products. Thus, the reactant doesn't react with other reactants but undergoes the chemical reaction on its own to produce the products. Decomposition is otherwise known as a chemical breakdown or an analysis reaction.

24. c: Combustion reaction.

Combustion is a redox reaction that involves the combination of a combustible material and an oxidizer. The combustible material is usually oxidized while heat is generated during the reaction. This reaction is usually between a combustible material and oxygen to produce carbon dioxide and water.

25. a: Redox reaction.

A redox reaction is a chemical reaction that involves electron transfer between reactants. Thus, atoms, molecules or ions will experience a change in oxidation number as they gain or lose an electron during the reaction. When a reactant loses electrons, the other reactant gains it.

Anatomy and Physiology Test 1 Answers

1) b: Anatomy.

Anatomy is the branch of biology that is concerned with the study of the structure of animals. Zoology, botany and animal science are other branches that focus on other aspects of the subject.

2) b: Transporting blood into the capillaries.

The circulatory system is primarily designed to transport blood into the capillaries. In addition to this, it transports hormones within the body and removes waste products. It is primarily made up of blood, blood vessels or arteries, and the heart.

3) a: Arteries.

Arteries are the parts of the circulatory system that are responsible for transporting blood into the capillaries. They provide nutrients such as oxygen and a host of others to cells and tissues.

4) c: Three.

The circulatory system is a combination of three different systems that work together to achieve a common goal of making blood available to the capillaries. The three systems are the pulmonary, cardiovascular and systemic systems.

5) b: Red blood cells, plasma, platelets and white blood cells.

Plasma, red blood cells, white blood cells and platelets are the major components of human blood. They are responsible for between 4.7 and 5.6 liters or five to six quarts of blood in an average human.

6) a: Systemic circulation.

The arteries, veins and blood vessels form a network of systemic circulation. The network is responsible for transporting oxygenated blood to the heart. It also provides the body's cells with needed nutrients, and it transports deoxygenated blood back to the heart.

7) c: Neurons and complex nerves.

The nervous system is made up of neurons and complex nerves. They transmit signals between body parts. Thus, the nervous system acts as the electrical wiring for the body.

8) a: Autonomic and somatic nervous systems.

The two subdivisions of the nervous system are the somatic nervous system and the autonomic nervous system. The somatic system connects the spinal cord and the brain with the sensory receptors and muscles through the nerves while the autonomic system regulates the body's processes, such as blood pressure and breathing rate.

9) d: None of the above.

The somatic system performs several functions. These include connecting the spinal cord and the brain with the sensory receptors and muscles, relaying information from the skin and sense organs to the central nervous system, and relaying responses to the skeletal muscles.

10) d: Autonomic nervous system.

Body processes are regulated by the autonomic nervous system. It is responsible for regulating the breathing rate and blood pressure. It also regulates digestion, pupillary responses, sexual arousal and urination, among others.

11) a: Alzheimer's disease.

A disorder that triggers the degeneration of the brain's nerve cells is Alzheimer's disease. It is a common cause of dementia, another ailment that is characterized by a decline in social and behavioral skills.

12) b: Parkinson's disease.

Parkinson's disease is a brain disorder that causes tremors. Difficulty in movement and coordination, caused by the loss of control over some body parts, are two symptoms of this ailment. Other symptoms of the progressive disorder are constipation, impaired speech and rigid muscles.

13) c: Cerebral palsy.

Cerebral palsy is an ailment that affects the nervous system and brain function. Afflicted individuals have difficulty in learning, moving, seeing, learning and thinking.

14) a: Gastrointestinal tract and accessory organs of digestion.

The gastrointestinal tract and accessory organs of digestion are the two components of the human digestive system. The accessory organs include the pancreas, tongue, liver, salivary glands and gallbladder. They work together to aid digestion.

15) b: Cephalic phase.

The cephalic phase starts with the secretion of gastric acid, the body's response to the smell, thought or sight of food. The stimulation depends on your appetite. The cephalic phase includes the chemical breakdown of food by enzymes or chewing.

16) c: Amylase and lingual lipase.

Digestion is possible in the saliva through the contributions of two digestive enzymes, namely amylase and lingual lipase. Other accessory digestive organs that aid digestion are the gall bladder, liver and pancreas. The tongue, mouth, epiglottis, salivary glands and teeth play crucial roles in the digestive process as well.

17) a: Cerebral cortex.

When you imagine, smell, or see food, the cerebral cortex is stimulated. Through the vagus nerve, the stimulated organ sends messages to the medulla, the hypothalamus and the parasympathetic nervous system. It also sends a similar message through the gastric glands to the stomach.

18) b: The stomach expands and immediately activates the stretch receptors.

When food is consumed, the stomach expands and immediately activates the stretch receptors, which, in turn, send a message to the medulla and through the vagus nerve, back to the stomach.

19) c: Gastric phase.

Ingested food stretches the stomach and raises the pH of the stomach's contents to stimulate gastric activity. This triggers a chain of events that eventually causes the parietal cells to release hydrochloric acid. Parietal cells not only lower food's pH, but also help break apart the food.

20) a: Three.

Three chemicals in the stomach stimulate gastric secretion: histamine, acetylcholine and gastrin. The three trigger the secretion of hydrochloric acid by stimulating the parietal cells.

21) d: The arrival of chyme in the duodenum.

When chyme arrives in the duodenum, the intestinal phase is triggered. The phase ensures the moderation of gastric activities through nervous reflexes and hormones.

22) a: Skeletal muscles, smooth muscles and cardiac muscles.

Skeletal muscles, smooth muscles and cardiac muscles are components of the muscular system. The system allows humans to maintain the right posture, makes movement possible and supports blood circulation.

23) d: Visceral muscles.

Visceral muscles are present in the intestines, stomach and blood vessels. They are responsible for contracting organs for the transportation of substances through organs.

24) c: It pumps blood throughout the body.

The cardiac muscle pumps blood throughout the body so that it reaches where it is needed.

25) d: It makes the body stronger.

The muscular system performs several functions that include organ protection, guiding the pelvic floor muscles during childbirth and supporting urination. They are not responsible for an individual's strength.

Physics Test 1 Answers

1) a: Matter, its behavior and its motion.

Physics can be defined as a branch of natural science that studies matter, its behavior and its motion.

2) d: Dynamics.

Dynamics is the study of the impact of forces on motion. Kinematics is a branch of the study of motion that doesn't consider the forces responsible for the change in motion.

3) c: Random motion.

An object rolling down a rough surface is said to be in random motion. Random motion refers to the movement of objects at random orientation or direction. Thus, the moving object has no specific destination but moves around haphazardly, such as the particles of a gas.

4) a: Translational linear motion.

If a runner runs in a straight line from the starting point to the finish line, the runner demonstrates translational linear motion. Translational linear motion is the movement of a rigid body from one place to another. A train moving along a straight track is another example.

5) c: Rotational motion.

The wheel of a car in motion and the rotation of the blades of an electric fan are two examples of rotational motion. This motion type occurs when a body moves in a circle around an axis or center.

6) c: Periodic linear motion.

A body undergoing periodic linear motion maintains a uniform speed throughout the duration of the motion. Periodic motion is the motion of a body in a circular path or part of a circular path. During the motion, the body maintains a uniform speed. A watch's balance wheel, a pendulum clock, a vibrating tuning fork and a rocking chair are all examples of periodic motion.

7) a: Speed.

Speed is a measure of the distance a body covers within a certain time. The speed of a body refers to the rate of change of the body's distance with respect to time.

8) d: A vector quantity has both magnitude and direction while a scalar quantity only has magnitude.

The major difference between the two is direction. While vector quantities have direction in addition to their magnitude, scalar quantities don't have direction and only have magnitude.

9) c: Speed is distance traveled per unit of time while motion is a change in an object's position over time.

While speed and motion are concerned with distance, speed focuses on the time taken to cover a distance while motion is concerned with the change in the position of an object over time.

10) c: Acceleration and force.

Acceleration and force are two examples of vector quantities. In addition to their known magnitude, they also have a specific direction. Other examples include displacement, velocity and momentum.

11) a: The to-and-fro movement of an object while standing in a mean position.

Oscillatory motion can be defined as the to-and-fro movement of an object while standing in a mean position. The movements of atoms in a molecule, a tuning fork, simple pendulum, and the movement of the earth's crust triggered by an earthquake are examples of oscillatory motion.

12) d: None of the above.

Sound waves, ocean waves and a swinging pendulum are some other examples of oscillatory motion.

13) c: Reciprocating motion.

If a body moves from point A to point B and moves back to point A, following the same path, the body is said to undergo reciprocating motion. Examples of reciprocating motion are internal combustion in pumps and engines, and the movement in the coil of a loudspeaker.

14) b: Total distance covered divided by total time taken.

The average speed of a body can be calculated by dividing the total distance traveled by the total time taken to cover the distance. This is because, more often than not, a body in motion may change its speed; therefore, an average is calculated.

15) a: Speed.

The SI unit of speed is meters per second or ms^{-1}. It refers to the distance in meters covered by a body in one second.

16) a: Average speed = total distance covered / time taken.

The most appropriate formula for calculating the average speed of a vehicle is given as average speed = total distance covered / time taken.

17) d: 40 kilometers per hour.

The average speed of the vehicle can be calculated with the formula: Average speed = total distance covered / time taken. Total distance covered is 120 kilometers. Time taken is 3 hours. Average speed = 120 km/3 hr. Therefore, the vehicle's average speed is 40 kilometers per hour.

18) d: 50 kilometers per hour.

Average speed of the train = total distance covered / time taken. If it takes 4 hours for the train to cover a distance of 200 kilometers, its average speed = 200 km /4 hours. Therefore, the train's average speed is 50 kilometers per hour.

19) a: Uniform speed.

A vehicle that moves at a constant speed is moving at a uniform speed. Thus, the change of distance with respect to time remains constant during the journey.

20) a: Uniform speed.

When a body travels at uniform speed, it doesn't accelerate. Hence, the body's distance per unit time remains constant.

21) b: Acceleration is the change of velocity per unit of time while speed is the change of distance per unit of time.

Acceleration and speed are two distinct quantities under motion. Acceleration deals with a body's change in velocity with respect to time while speed defines change of distance per unit of time.

22) a: Velocity.

Although a body may move at a constant pace or uniform speed, the body may have a velocity if it has a direction alongside its magnitude.

23) d: 18.52 ms^{-2}.

The initial velocity of the vehicle (u) = 120 km/hr.

To find the initial velocity (u) in m/s, 120km/hr x 1000 = 120,000 m/hr

$$120,000 \text{ m/hr} \div (60 \cdot 60) = 33.33 \text{ m/s}$$

The final velocity (v) = 0

Distance covered (s) = 30m

Deceleration = $(v^2 - u^2)/2s$

$$= (0^2 - 33.33^2)/2 \cdot 30$$

$$= (0 - 1111.11)/60$$

$$= -1111.11/60$$

$$= -18.52$$

Thus, deceleration = 18.52 ms^{-2}.

24) b: A body will remain in uniform motion in a straight line or will remain at rest unless a force acts on it.

According to Newton's First Law of Motion, without an external force, a body will continue moving in a straight line. The same applies to a stationary body. If no external force works on the body, it will remain in that stationary position for as long as possible.

25) a: Sunlight, wood and coal.

Sunlight, wood and coal are some primary sources of combustible organic matter. Humans depend on these for a wide range of applications, such as using coal to fuel certain engines.

Learning Style Test 1 Answers

1. a: Picture an injection.

You will instantly imagine an injection.

2. b: Books with a lot of graphics and pictures

A book with pictures helps you maintain your focus while studying.

3. c: Make note

You write the explanations down for your memory.

4. a: At the front

You like to sit at the front to be able to pay complete attention.

5. a: Drawn images

You arrange your notes in the form of images, graphs, and charts.

6. d: Immediately understand the concepts

You can grasp the practical concepts more easily than the theory concepts.

7. b: Observe the people and their behaviors

You are the less talkative yet the more observant one in a group of people.

8. a: Find it difficult

This is because you will not have something to imagine correctly.

9. c: Read the notes and pictures you have created for your understanding

You skim through your notes and created images, and you memorize your concepts.

10. a: The faces of people you saw at the event

The faces will be etched in your mind, if nothing else.

11. d: A picture of it

If the picture of a thing is appealing and feels interesting, you will instantly buy it even if it is cheap and not a big brand.

12. a: Show the x-ray or the picture and then explain

You would have learned it with the help of the picture, so you will be able to explain it through the picture only.

13. c: Ask them to bring the patient first

You would want to see the patient and their condition before jumping to any conclusions.

14. a: Picture the condition in your mind

You will picture the condition and then describe to the patient what you have understood to confirm your understanding.

With the help of videos, you will be able to understand the topic completely. You will also not have to keep going back to them because you will not forget the information easily.

If all or a majority of the answers mentioned above are your responses to the questions we have asked, your learning style is VISUAL.

Your first instinct is to imagine the thing if a name is placed in front of you. You prefer drawing things instead of writing lengthy details about them. You have a habit of making notes, and for that, you make sure that you pay complete attention by mostly sitting at the front in the class.

Books with visual explanations of a theory are your favorite, and you watch videos if you are required to carry out research. For you, practical demonstrations are more important than theory because if a practical demonstration is given in front of you, you are easily able to link it with the theoretical parts of the chapter.

You prepare for tests by going through your prepared notes, and if you forget something, you will still certainly have an image of it in your mind. Also, you are more inclined to observe people, and you do not make impulsive decisions. Instead, you plan and take the action you think is the best.

Personality Style Test 1 Answers

1. b: Tell him, politely

No matter your anger, you will always try to be calm.

2. a: Move aside silently and avoid conflict

If you have an option, you will always choose to stay away from any conflict.

3. a: Closely watch and observe the doctor's way of dealing with the patients

If given an option, you will always prefer watching over working.

4. c: One night before the submission date

You are lazy and will study only when you feel the pressure.

5. b: Listen compassionately

You will kindly listen because you are a compassionate listener.

6. a: Politely refuse

You run away from responsibilities but will always directly say no because you do not like conflicts.

7. b: Be the non-contributing member

You are more inclined to watch than work.

8. b: Convince him in a friendly way

Because you are compassionate, you will try to make friends with him and convince him to get injected.

9. c: Politely convince him to eat

You will kindly encourage him by informing him of the consequences of not eating.

10. a: Calm down and deal with things in a relaxed manner

Since you have a calming personality, you will not panic, no matter the situation.

11. d: Not say anything and continue with the job

You are compromising and like to avoid conflicts.

12. b: Take the blame yourself

You have a compromising nature.

13. a: Keep quiet until asked a question

You are an introvert who does not like to speak a lot.

14. b: Ask a classmate to proofread it

You like to discuss your answers with your friends because you lack a certain degree of confidence within yourself.

15. c: Sleeping

You are not very goal-oriented.

If the answers above are your responses to the questions, it indicates that your personality is CALM.

If you have an option, you are more inclined to watch rather than work. You have a relaxing effect on your surroundings, and you are a kind and compassionate listener. You try to avoid conflicts and prefer staying silent in most situations. People often mistake you as lazy and unenthusiastic.

Moreover, you try to avoid responsibilities and need constant pressure to study. You learn better in a group but contribute the least. Besides, you like to discuss your answers with others to confirm them because you lack a certain degree of confidence in yourself. You need to stay focused. Devise ways of studying that can help you avoid procrastinating and daydreaming. Highlight your book and reread the material to memorize it. Do not stay quiet when you should defend yourself, and do not compromise when your rights are being neglected.

Test 2 Questions

Math Test 2 – 50 Questions

1. Subtract 420 from 600 and express the answer in Roman numerals.

    a. LXXX.

    b. MXXX.

    c. CXXX.

    d. CLXXX.

2. Multiply 25 by 3 and express the answer in Roman numerals.

    a. LXV.

    b. LXVV.

    c. LXXV.

    d. LXVX.

3. Subtract XXXV from C and write the answer in Arabic numerals.

    a. 75.

    b. 36.

    c. 65.

    d. 88.

4. What is the product of 45 and 2 in Roman numerals?

    a. XVVV.

    b. CXX.

    c. XC.

    d. DDD.

5. How many kilograms are there in 45 pounds?

    a. 22.57 kg.

    b. 20.4117 kg.

    c. 97.209 kg.

    d. 19.45 kg.

6. A baby weighs 10 kilograms at birth. What is the baby's weight in pounds?

    a. 22.05 lb.

    b. 24.7 lb.

    c. 24.5 lb.

    d. 25.6 lb.

7. When mixing some substances, a painter is expected to add 5 cups of water. He can't find a cup but can measure in liters. How many liters of water must he add?

    a. 1.2 liters.

    b. 3.4 liters.

    c. 1.1 liters.

    d. 1.12 liters.

8. While taking a patient's temperature, a nurse measured 38 degrees Celsius. Convert the temperature to degrees Fahrenheit.

    a. 67 °F.

    b. 89 °F.

    c. 100 °F.

    d. 99 °F.

9. Which conversion requires the subtraction of 32 from an original reading before the conversion can calculated?

    a. Celsius to Kelvin.

    b. Fahrenheit to Kelvin.

    c. Kelvin to Celsius.

    d. Fahrenheit to Celsius.

10. Multiplication of a temperature by 1.8 or 9/5 is a part of the conversion process from ...

    a. Celsius to Kelvin.

    b. Fahrenheit to Celsius.

    c. Celsius to Fahrenheit.

    d. Kelvin to Celsius.

11. A sales representative sold 500 units of a product in four months. What is her average monthly sale?

    a. 150 units.

    b. 200 units.

    c. 125 units.

    d. 175 units.

12. In order to meet her quarterly sales target of 1,200 units of a product, a sales representative should sell an average of ... monthly.

    a. 500 units.

    b. 450 units.

    c. 350 units.

    d. 400 units.

13. In an entrance examination, a student scored 250 out of 300. What is her percentage score?

    a. 78.63%.

    b. 83.33%.

    c. 54.87%.

    d. 29.97%.

14. An employee was absent from work for 5 out of the 20 working days in a month. What percentage of the time was she absent from work?

    a. 25%.

    b. 75%.

    c. 80%.

    d. 55%.

15. A shopper bought some goods worth $500 and paid $200 in cash and the balance through her credit card. What percentage of the money was paid with a credit card?

    a. 67%.

    b. 56%.

    c. 45%.

    d. 60%.

16. If a pair of shoes costs $20, how many pairs can you purchase with $175?

    a. 8 pairs.

    b. 12 pairs.

    c. 25 pairs.

    d. 30 pairs.

17. How many days will it take a student to complete reading a 200-page book if he reads an average of 5 pages daily?

    a. 35 days.

    b. 40 days.

    c. 33 days.

    d. 11 days.

18. How many cell phones are in a carton containing two dozen cell phones?

    a. 36.

    b. 24.

    c. 50.

    d. 45.

19. While recording the weight of a parcel, the store attendant mistakenly measured it in pounds instead of in kilograms. What is the actual weight of the 450-pound parcel in kilograms, rounded to the nearest kilogram?

    a. 900 kg.

    b. 220 kg.

    c. 204 kg.

    d. 200 kg.

20. A cat consumed 75% of its food and left the rest. What fraction of the food is left?

    a. 1/3.

    b. 2/5.

    c. 1/4.

    d. 4/7.

21. After paying $250 out of her $400 school fees, Sharon promised to pay the balance within the next three weeks. What fraction of her fees must she still pay?

    a. 3/7.

    b. 3/8.

    c. 2/3.

    d. 2/5.

22. Express the difference between 77 and 38 in Roman numerals.

    a. XXIV.

    b. XXXIX.

    c. XXXVIX.

    d. XXIVX.

23. What percentage of his income does Richard save if he saves $100 out of every $250 he makes?

    a. 45%.

    b. 40%.

    c. 50%.

    d. 90%.

24. If only 45 members of staff of an organization of 78 employees deserve a promotion, which of the following formulas can be used to find the number of employees who will not be promoted?

    a. Number of employees – number of absent employees.

    b. Number of older employees – number of female employees.

    c. Number of employees – number of promoted employees.

    d. Number of employees – number of male employees.

25. In a nursing school of 300 students, only 125 are male nurses. What percentage of the students are male students?

    a. 41.67%.

    b. 43.65%.

    c. 76%.

    d. 45.89%.

26. What percentage of the students in the nursing school are female nurses if there are 300 students and only 125 male nurses?

    a. 76.45%.

    b. 58.22%.

    c. 87.76%.

    d. 58.33%.

27. Each unit in a hospital has three doctors and 15 nurses. How many doctors are in the hospital if it has 10 units?

    a. 25.

    b. 30.

    c. 27.

    d. 150.

28. Each unit in a hospital has three doctors and 15 nurses. What fraction of the entire staff are nurses if the hospital has 10 units?

    a. 5/6.

    b. 5/7.

    c. 8/9.

    d. 3/7.

29. 8 boys must share 400 apples equally. How many apples does each boy get?

    a. 40.

    b. 50.

    c. 60.

    d. 75.

30. 8 boys must share 400 apples equally. If 5 boys have already been given their apples, how many apples are left?

    a. 100.

    b. 150.

    c. 120.

    d. 110.

31. 8 boys must share 400 apples equally. What percentage of the apples is shared among 7 boys?

    a. 87.5%.

    b. 67.9%.

    c. 98.5%.

    d. 34.8%.

32. If a cyclist covers 30 km in 1 hour, how long will it take him to travel 120 kilometers?

    a. 4 hours.

    b. 6 hours.

    c. 5 hours.

    d. 3 hours.

33. A boy has 20 oranges stored in a box. How many oranges in total did he store in 12 boxes of the same size?

    a. 40.

    b. 240.

    c. 120.

    d. 260.

34. When planning a field trip, a school plans to use 18-passenger buses. How many buses can transport 360 students?

    a. 30.

    b. 20.

    c. 25.

    d. 33.

35. 60% of the students in the school above are female. How many buses are needed to transport the female students?

    a. 12.

    b. 11.

    c. 25.

    d. 8.

36. If each student, in the school above, pays $12 for the trip, how much did the students pay altogether?

    a. $4,350.

    b. $4,320.

    c. $4,500.

    d. $3,500.

37. If each book in a box costs $20, what's the total price of 23 books in the box?

    a. $340.

    b. $450.

    c. $460.

    d. $40.

38. In an entrance examination, 3,579 students passed the exam while 12,345 failed. How many students took the test?

    a. 14,567.

    b. 18,790.

    c. 15,924.

    d. 19,876.

39. If a hospital has three wards, and there are 45 patients in a maternity ward, 2,453 in a children's ward and 876 in the male ward, how many patients are in a hospital?

    a. 3,374.

    b. 3,453.

    c. 6,543.

    d. 2,387.

40. A library has 350 books in French, 45 in Latin and 590 in English. What is the percentage of the books in French?

    a. 35.55%.

    b. 35.53%.

    c. 35.64%.

    d. 34.76%.

41. A company manufactured 36 test tubes in the first week of the month, 58 in the second week, 29 in the third week and 37 in the fourth week. What is the average number of test tubes produced per week?

    a. 45.

    b. 40.

    c. 65.

    d. 42.

42. A woman saves $200 weekly. How much will she save in a year?

    a. $10,450.

    b. $10,400.

    c. $9,600.

    d. $10,800.

43. An artisan could only complete 1/3 of his work in 6 days. How long will it take him to complete the job?

    a. 20 days.

    b. 24 days.

    c. 26 days.

    d. 18 days.

44. If I cut a 30-cm-long ribbon into four equal lengths, how long is each part?

    a. 7.7 cm.

    b. 8.0 cm.

    c. 7.5 cm.

    d. 6.7 cm.

45. 48 balloons are shared among 12 students. How many balloons does each student receive?

    a. 5.

    b. 6.

    c. 4.

    d. 3.

46. If 5 books cost $100, and these all cost the same, what is the cost of three books?

    a. $20.

    b. $60.

    c. $50.

    d. $40.

47. In a class of 45 students, 20% of the students are absent on a particular day. How many students are present on the same day?

    a. 32.

    b. 33.

    c. 47.

    d. 36.

48. The school fees of a nursing school increased from $2,500 to $3,000 per semester. What is the percentage increase in the fees?

    a. 20%.

    b. 5%.

    c. 10%.

    d. 8%.

49. 325 of 400 seats in a hall were occupied. Express the proportion of attendees as a fraction of the whole hall of seats.

    a. 13/16.

    b. 12/15.

    c. 14/15.

    d. 12/17.

50. A retail store slashed the prices of its commodities by 20%. Express the discount as a fraction.

    a. 1/5.

    b. 2/7.

    c. 3/8.

    d. 2/3.

Reading Test 2 – 47 Questions

Read the following passages and answer the questions that follow.

Passage 5 – Are Video Games Good for Kids?

Kids' increasing crave for video games has become a concern for parents across the globe. They are genuinely concerned about the potential impact of such games on their kids. This raises the question: "Are video games good for kids?" Let's consider the pros and cons of video games on kids to decide whether they are good for them or not.

The result of a study conducted by Oxford University shows that children benefit from playing video games for about an hour daily. According to the research, such children are more socially active, less hyperactive, and happier than their mates who don't engage in such activity.

Thus, according to the study published in Pediatrics, your kids stand to benefit immensely from playing video games an hour daily, as found in their research that involved kids of both sexes, aged between 10 and 15 years old.

Video games also enhance kids' decision-making and problem-solving skills. Some video games that involve solving puzzles or mentally-challenging problems will boost a kid's ability to solve problems and make crucial decisions. Angry Birds, The Incredible Machine, and Cut the Rope are some games in this category. These games task a player's creativity and logic skills. Thus, parents can use these games and related ones to train their kids to improve their decision-making skills.

Video games can also improve a player's spatial and fine motor skills. This is in addition to their ability to improve hand-eye coordination. Several adventure games require a player to keep the position of players in mind and predict the opponent's movements while coordinating their eyes and hands to make the right move. A kid's ability to do this effortlessly will impact their spatial skills and hand-eye coordination massively. Introducing them to such games early in life may have a profound effect on them as adults when they are faced with situations that put their motor and spatial skills to the test.

Kids who play video games also learn to become better resource managers. They outperform their counterparts who don't play such games in planning and logistics. In many games, players must manage the limited resources at their disposal to complete a task or achieve a goal. Thus, they learn how to maximize the resource in preparation for adulthood where they will, more often than not, have to make the best use of limited resources. Some strategy games like Age of Empires, SimCity and Railroad Tycoon are those that can assist a player to develop these skills.

However, video games for kids aren't all about positivity. The worry of some parents, about the impact of video games on kids, is based on some side effects of devoting too much time to the game.

Granted, video games may become addictive if not put in their place. Thus, parents are scared of their kids becoming too dependent on such games at the expense of their academic life.

Consequently, although playing video games can be beneficial for children, parents should be aware of its potential danger too. Hence, each parent must answer the question of whether video games are good for their kids or not.

1. Why are many parents interested in knowing the impact of video games on their kids?

    a. Out of curiosity.

    b. To quench their thirst for knowledge.

    c. Kids' increasing interest in video games.

    d. All of the above.

2. What is the recommended time limit for kids to play video games daily?

    a. 2 hours.

    b. 45 minutes.

    c. 3 hours.

    d. 1 hour.

3. Which of the following is not a benefit of playing video games regularly?

    a. It makes players less hyperactive.

    b. It increases player's social activeness.

    c. It makes players happier.

    d. It makes players more reserved.

4. The study conducted by Oxford University involved which group of people?

    a. Pre-teens.

    b. Teens.

    c. Pre-teens and teens.

    d. Adults in their mid-20s.

5. What is the effect of mentally-challenging video games on kids?

    a. They overwork kids.

    b. They are too demanding and energy-sapping.

    c. They help kids develop their decision-making skills.

    d. They help kids develop their motor skills.

6. What is a key feature of adventure games?

    a. The ability to complete tasks easily.

    b. The ability to monitor both your players and opponents.

    c. The ability to win bonuses and other incentives.

    d. None of the above.

7. Which of these sets of games can help kids develop their resource management skills?

    a. Age of Empires and Railroad Tycoon.

    b. SimCity and Angry Birds.

    c. Cut the Rope and The Incredible Machine.

    d. Crossword puzzles and Checkers.

8. What does "effortlessly" mean as used in the passage?

    a. It means without learning it.

    b. It means at your convenience.

    c. It means with ease.

    d. All of the above.

9. What does "put in its place" mean?

      a. It means "properly arranged."

      b. It means "well organized."

      c. It means "put under control."

      d. It means "done at the right time."

10. What is one danger of playing video games?

      a. They are too expensive.

      b. They are designed for adults.

      c. They are addictive.

      d. They are readily available.

11. How do video games help to enhance players' resource management skills?

      a. They help players live within their means.

      b. They help players use scarce resources judiciously.

      c. They help players become more success-oriented.

      d. They help players learn communication skills.

12. Which of the following words can replace "profound" as used in the passage?

      a. Practical.

      b. Positive.

      c. Immense.

      d. Drastic.

Passage 6 – The Effect of Globalization on the Economy

The Internet and technology brought globalization with them. Through them, countries across the globe can engage in businesses with relative ease and without physical boundaries. Thus, African and Asian countries can conduct trades with their counterparts in Europe and America and vice versa. While this is laudable, what effect does globalization have on the global economy?

One of the most pronounced impacts of globalization is the competitive advantage it offers businesses. For instance, business owners can promote their goods or services to potential clients or customers in any part of the world. By giving businesses such wide exposure, globalization has contributed immensely to many businesses' growth.

Thanks to globalization, manufacturing companies can source materials where they are more affordable. This decreases the cost of production and makes many products readily available at affordable prices. For instance, cocoa is relatively more available and cheaper in Africa than in Europe. Through globalization, cocoa-dependent manufacturing companies can get their raw materials cheaper than if they have to source them locally.

Outsourcing is another important effect of globalization on the economy. A company can outsource its entire production to another country where labor or raw materials are cheaper. It is not uncommon for some production companies to outsource different sections of their production to different countries based on several factors such as availability of raw materials, labor cost and the availability of experts. This wouldn't have been possible without globalization.

Globalization has also led to job creation in many countries. As companies outsource their jobs to other countries, locals and professionals in those countries can seize the opportunity to get gainfully employed as more jobs are created by foreign companies.

On the downside, globalization has some cons too. For instance, while outsourcing may create employment opportunities for the host countries, locals in the companies' country of origin are denied job opportunities that are taken abroad. This may increase unemployment rates among the locals.

Income disparity is another drawback of globalization. According to some studies, globalization may trigger income inequality between trained professionals and unskilled workers. While the more-educated professionals can work in any part of the world with attractive offers, their unskilled counterparts are always at the mercy of their employers and more often than not, have to contend with poor wages and salaries.

Globalization has created an environment that is conducive to money laundering. Unscrupulous people can capitalize on it to launder money through shady international business trades and transactions with international companies.

The increasing demand for the production of goods may affect domestic industries adversely too. If a company can get better working environments in other countries, domestic companies will bear the brunt as they make way for foreign companies and employees to take over jobs that can be handled domestically. This is aside from the tendency to abuse natural resources when companies are hell-bent on meeting increasing demands for their goods.

Thus, globalization, although beneficial, has its downside. While the global economy benefits from it, this is usually at the expense of domestic companies and resources.

1. According to the passage, what is globalization?
    a. Globalization is the process through which businesses are allowed to operate internationally.
    b. Globalization refers to the global changes that make it easier for businesses to be conducted internationally.
    c. Globalization refers to the coming together of the global community to achieve a common goal.
    d. Globalization is the amalgamation of the global community.

2. Define "laudable" as used in the passage.
    a. It means surprising.
    b. It means encouraging.
    c. It means commendable.
    d. It means achievable.

3. What does "competitive advantage" mean?
    a. It means being in a favorable condition.
    b. It means being more expensive than others.
    c. It means financially better than others.
    d. None of the above.

4. What is the benefit of outsourcing to consumers?

    a. Cheaper products.

    b. Higher purchasing ability.

    c. Availability of products and services.

    d. A variety of options to choose from.

5. Which of the following is not a factor behind outsourcing?

    a. Availability of experts.

    b. Availability of raw materials.

    c. Labor cost.

    d. Availability of super-rich customers or clients.

6. How does globalization contribute to increasing unemployment rates in some countries?

    a. It enables companies to outsource their production to other countries, rendering their local employees jobless.

    b. There is no connection between the two.

    c. It enables companies to deny their employees the right job.

    d. It supports commercialism.

7. How does globalization support money laundering?

    a. It enables money launderers to be more courageous.

    b. It enables money launderers to use foreign companies for laundering.

    c. It reduces the complexities of money laundering.

    d. All of the above.

8. What impact does globalization have on unskilled workers?

    a. It makes them become more skillful.

    b. It takes away their right to work.

    c. It encourages income disparity.

    d. It offers them better job opportunities.

9. What impact can increasing demands have on natural resources?
    a. It helps to boost natural resources.
    b. It leads to the abuse of natural resources.
    c. It leads to deforestation.
    d. It promotes better natural resources management.

10. What does "bear the brunt" mean?
    a. It means to experience the worst part of a problematic situation.
    b. It means to be at the forefront of globalization.
    c. It means to benefit immensely from globalization.
    d. It means to promote unity among local workers.

11. What does "capitalize on" mean?
    a. It means to raise capital from.
    b. It means to take advantage of.
    c. It means to contribute immensely to.
    d. None of the above.

12. Which of the following words can replace "shady" as used in the passage?
    a. Illegal.
    b. Unprofitable.
    c. Profitable.
    d. Resourceful.

Passage 7 – Principles of Medical Errors Prevention in Hospitals

The result of a search conducted by Johns Hopkins shows that medical errors make up the top 3 common causes of medical-related death in the United States. As reported by The MJ, the research shows that some 250,000 people lose their lives to preventable medical errors annually. What preventive measures can hospitals and medical personnel take to curb this menace and prevent this sudden death?

The strategies discussed below will help health workers and medical facilities reduce medical errors drastically:

Diagnostic errors should be avoided at all costs. Ranging from the wrong diagnosis to over-diagnosing, diagnostic error is one of the leading causes of medical errors. Wrong diagnoses may lead to wrong treatment. Wrong medications can trigger a wide range of medical conditions that may ultimately terminate the victim's life.

Thus, medical workers must ensure that diagnoses are expertly and meticulously done to prevent unfortunate errors that may affect the victim adversely. To start with, the diagnosis should be done by professionals only. It is also recommended that the entire care team, including radiologists and physicians, should be involved in the diagnosis. By bringing their expertise into it, errors in diagnosis can easily be spotted and rectified before it is too late.

Sometimes, complications may arise from hospital-acquired infections. Hospitals have the responsibility of making their facilities as infection-free as possible through regular disinfection of medical equipment such as surgical tools, patient rooms, and others. The medical facility should also have policies that are geared toward making the environment infection-free. Members of staff should be encouraged to comply strictly with such policies.

Medical facilities should work at increasing their patients' safety by increasing the safety measures in some areas such as easily confused drug names, high-risk processes, high-risk populations, and high-alert medications. Some safety tips that they should implement in such areas include medication preparation and administration with barcode technology, using portless epidural tubing, and smart infusion pumps.

Medication errors are prevalent too. Medical facilities and personnel should work at reducing these errors if their pharmacy takes medication arrangement and storage seriously. This will minimize the tendency to select the wrong medication for a patient. When appropriate, alerts and labeling should be used to differentiate one medication from another, another preventive measure against wrong medication administration.

A further contributor to medical errors is miscommunication during shift changes. If the team handing over to another one fails to properly communicate the condition of their patients to the team taking over, the miscommunication can lead to wrong diagnosis, wrong medication, and other related mistakes that may eventually trigger a medical error. Conversely, when the team that is taking over is fully briefed on the patients' conditions, errors can be averted.

Thus, when handing over duties, medical workers are required to include the following in their handover notes:

The severity of a patient's illness. The treatments or interventions required must be fully communicated as well. Aside from the illness, the information should also include the patient's general condition to enable the new team to treat the patient accordingly.

1. How dangerous are medical errors?
    a. Medical errors account for a third of all deaths in the US.
    b. Medical errors are insignificant in comparison to other medical problems.
    c. Death resulting from medical errors is listed among the top 3 causes of deaths in the US.
    d. Medical errors have been on the decline since a couple of years ago.

2. What constitutes diagnostic errors?
    a. Improper record keeping.
    b. Wrong diagnosis.
    c. Multiple diagnoses.
    d. Diagnosis conducted early in the morning.

3. What is the danger of wrong medication?
    a. It is very expensive.
    b. It jeopardizes the patient's health.
    c. It is difficult to identify.
    d. It is complicated.

4. What other word can replace "imperative" as used in the passage?
    a. Special.
    b. Urgent.
    c. Crucial.
    d. Wonderful.

5. Replace "meticulously" with any of the adverbs below.

    a. Carefully.

    b. Conscientiously.

    c. Urgently.

    d. Immediately.

6. Which of the following experts should be involved in diagnosis?

    a. Dentists.

    b. Radiologists.

    c. Record keepers.

    d. Chief Medical Officers.

7. What can trigger hospital-acquired infection?

    a. Contaminated medical equipment.

    b. Contaminated drugs.

    c. Contaminated roads.

    d. All of the above.

8. What conditions can compromise the patients' safety?

    a. High-risk processes and confused drug names.

    b. Insensitive medical personnel.

    c. Patient's attitude to treatment.

    d. None of the above.

9. Which of the following factors can trigger medication errors?

    a. Improper medication storage.

    b. Drug abuse.

    c. Drug substitution.

    d. All of the above.

10. What is an effective antidote to medical errors arising from miscommunication?
    a. The medical facility should install loudspeakers.
    b. Medical personnel should always use the microphone when communicating.
    c. Giving detailed information about a patient when handing over to the next team.
    d. All of the above.

11. Which of the following words can aptly replace "prevalent" in the passage?
    a. Rife.
    b. Important.
    c. Scarce.
    d. Necessary.

12. Which of the following piece of information should not be included when handing over to another team?
    a. The severity of the patient's illness.
    b. The treatments required.
    c. The patient's general condition.
    d. None of the above.

Passage 8 – Clinical Trials: The Pros and Cons

The National Institute of Aging defines a clinical trial as "research studies performed in people that are aimed at evaluating a medical, surgical, or behavioral intervention." According to the source, researchers use clinical trials to find out if a new medication is safe for human use and effective as well. Why are people engaging in clinical trials? What are the pros and cons of such trials?

The need for a better and more effective treatment for some medical conditions may call for clinical trials to experiment with possible alternatives. Hence, individuals may volunteer themselves for such trials with a view to ascertaining the effectiveness, or otherwise, of the potential replacement for existing treatment options.

Clinical trials have their benefits and downsides. Some common pros and cons of such trials are highlighted below:

During clinical trials, researchers have the opportunity to put their years of research to the test. They can test their products and see whether they meet the desired outcome or not.

Clinical trials also give people the opportunity to get a shot at a more effective treatment option, especially if their current treatment is seemingly less effective. Thus, they can try something else and hopefully, get a better result.

Sometimes, effective treatment or medication may have less than desirable side effects. This may trigger a request for better alternatives with more tolerable or zero side effects. Only through clinical trials can researchers be guaranteed of getting a platform to see if their new products tick the boxes.

Individuals who participate in clinical trials also enjoy the benefit of being attended to by highly-qualified medical professionals as a part of the trial process. This increases their chances of getting the best treatment for their ailment.

However, it is noteworthy that participating in clinical trials will expose participants to the cons of such trials.

While researchers' expectations may be very high, clinical trials are not always successful because their treatments may sometimes be ineffective. Since participants always have high expectations about the trials, this may lead to disappointment.

The problem of side effects may also arise during clinical trials. Patients who want to participate in clinical trials as a form of immunity against the side effects of their current medications or treatments may not find the perfect solution after all.

Participating in clinical trials can be time-consuming. As a participant, you may spend a significant amount of time visiting the study site and staying in hospitals. If you are not prepared for this, you may be surprised at what participating in the trial may cost you in terms of your time.

Clinical trials have been around for years. They have proven to be instrumental in the development of many medical treatments and medications. The benefits, as highlighted above, are reasons why the trials have achieved some measures of success. However, before you participate in a clinical trial, be aware of the potential side effects of the trial, and thus determine whether you are comfortable with the trial or not.

1. What is the primary objective of clinical trials?
   a. To determine the efficiency and safety of a new treatment or drug.
   b. To give wide coverage to a new line of treatment.
   c. To increase the researchers' popularity.
   d. To give maximum promotion to new medications or treatment.

2. Why do some people volunteer for clinical trials?
   a. To replace their current treatment options or medications.
   b. To show their bravery.
   c. It is a part of their medical training.
   d. It helps them gain an insight into the medical profession.

3. Which of the following is not a benefit of participating in clinical trials?
   a. Access to professionals.
   b. Opportunity to get better treatments and medications.
   c. Less expensive treatment options.
   d. Potential to get medications with little or no side effects.

4. Replace "desirable" with any of the words listed below.
   a. Appealing.
   b. Surprising.
   c. Iconic.
   d. Scintillating.

5. What is the probability that a clinical trial will give the desired result?

    a. 100% assurance.

    b. Nothing is guaranteed.

    c. 10% assurance.

    d. 20% assurance.

6. Are clinical trials devoid of side effects?

    a. Yes, they are.

    b. No, they are not.

    c. This can't be determined.

    d. It depends on the participants.

7. Which of the following is one of the cons of participating in clinical trials?

    a. It is done by amateurs.

    b. It is time-consuming.

    c. It is restricted to some medical conditions.

    d. None of the above.

8. What does "instrumental to" mean when used in the context of this passage?

    a. Contributory to.

    b. Dependent on.

    c. Dependent with.

    d. Irrespective of.

9. What does "may not find the perfect solution after all" imply?

    a. It implies that there are no effective solutions.

    b. It implies that there are no effective solutions without side effects.

    c. It means clinical trials are flawed from the beginning.

    d. It means researchers are imperfect.

10. What can you deduce from the passage?
    a. Clinical trials are dangerous.
    b. Clinical trials are a necessity.
    c. Clinical trials are the panacea to all problems.
    d. Clinical trials should be performed under ideal conditions.

11. What is the opposite of "downsides" according to the passage?
    a. Benefits.
    b. Dangers.
    c. Side effects.
    d. Important points.

Vocabulary Test 2 – 50 Questions

1. What does HPS stand for?

    a. Hantavirus Pulmonary Syndrome.

    b. Hypertensive Pulsating Syndrome.

    c. Hyperventilating Pulmonary Syndrome.

    d. High Pension Syndrome.

2. A young lady was diagnosed with Type-2 diabetes or ...

    a. Insulin-Dependent Diabetes Mellitus.

    b. Insulin-Daring Diabetes Medical Problem.

    c. Insulating-Daring Diabetes Mellin.

    d. Insulating-Dependent Diabetes Mellitus.

3. An emergency health procedure that involves the use of artificial ventilation and chest compression to maintain brain function is ...

    a. Cardiopulmonary resurrection.

    b. Cardiopulmonary resuscitation.

    c. Cardiopensive resuscitation.

    d. Cardiopensive resurrection.

4. ANED is a medical condition that is characterized by ...

    a. Heavy bleeding.

    b. High blood pressure.

    c. No evidence of disease.

    d. Not needing a doctor's appointment.

5. A patient allowed to move around freely within the hospital environment is medically said to be …

    a. At freedom.

    b. At liberty.

    c. Ad lib.

    d. At unrestricted.

6. Respiratory failure with a wide range of symptoms such as shortness of breath or rapid breathing is known as …

    a. ARDS.

    b. SDRS.

    c. ARSD.

    d. DSAR.

7. ARDS stands for …

    a. Acute Respiratory Disease Syndrome.

    b. Acute Respiratory Distress Symptoms.

    c. Acute Respiratory Disease Symptoms.

    d. Acute Respiratory Distress Syndrome.

8. A form of heart disease that is trigged by the buildup of plaque in the arterial walls is called …

    a. Acute Cardiovascular Disease.

    b. Acute Cardiovascular Distress.

    c. Atherosclerotic Cardiovascular Disease.

    d. Atherosclerotic Cardiovascular Distress.

9. All of the following are examples of ASCVD except …

    a. Descending thoracic aneurysm.

    b. Abdominal aortic aneurysm.

    c. Carotid artery stenosis.

    d. None of the above.

10. A bilateral Salpingo-Oophorectomy is a medical procedure that refers to ...

    a. The removal of the fallopian tubes.

    b. The removal of the two ovaries.

    c. The removal of the two ovaries and the fallopian tubes.

    d. The removal of the fallopian tube and the readjustment of the two ovaries.

11. A health condition that affects the gastrointestinal tract is referred to medically as ...

    a. Inflammatory Bowel Distress.

    b. Inflammatory Bowel Disease.

    c. Infectious Bowel Distress.

    d. Infectious Bowel Disease.

12. A patient with a blood clot in a large vein is suffering from ...

    a. Deep Venous Thrombosis.

    b. Deep Venous Tract Disorder.

    c. Deep Venous Tissue Disorder.

    d. Deep Venous Thrombosis Disorder.

13. The economic condition of the country has been labile in recent years. This means it is ...

    a. Changing at an alarming rate.

    b. Deteriorating beyond control.

    c. Remaining constantly bad despite all attempts to make it better.

    d. Changing the fate of business people.

14. The ... will determine the next action to be taken.

    a. Prognosticm.

    b. Prognosis.

    c. Predisposition.

    d. Disintention.

15. A fluid's ... should be considered when determining the right storage for it.
    a. Consistency.
    b. Volume and density.
    c. Freezing and melting points.
    d. Intensity.

16. The vehicle stopped ... as the driver applied the brakes unexpectedly.
    a. Suddenly.
    b. Professionally.
    c. A little after the demarcation.
    d. Behind the trailer.

17. While the story was heartbreaking, it was actually ... to gain more sympathy.
    a. Exaggerated.
    b. Rationalized.
    c. Superimposed.
    d. Flabbergasted.

18. The ... of the ailment are yet to be fully identified despite running a series of tests.
    a. Syndromes.
    b. Symptoms.
    c. Signs.
    d. Health challenges.

19. When the patient's health started ..., she was referred to a specialist for more comprehensive treatment.
    a. Deteriorating.
    b. Recuperating.
    c. Appreciating.
    d. Improving.

20. The ... is a special section of a medical facility for people with critical health problems.

    a. Intensive Treatment Unit.

    b. Specialized Treatment Unit.

    c. Intensive Care Unit.

    d. Intensive Caretaking Unit.

21. Special care should be exercised while treating some ailments as a preventive measure against ...

    a. Complications.

    b. Excessive drug usage.

    c. Attacks by the patient's friends and family.

    d. None of the above.

22. Nursing students must ... to the rules and regulations laid down by the various medical and academic bodies.

    a. Ignore.

    b. Adhere.

    c. Consider.

    d. Revolt.

23. You can ... your reading efforts by listening to professionals in your field and attending workshops and seminars, as well as engaging in meaningful conversations with your colleagues.

    a. Supplement.

    b. Compliment.

    c. Detract from.

    d. Understand.

24. Many people don't understand the ... behind the government's new policies.

    a. Statistics.

    b. Rationale.

    c. Evidence.

    d. Proof.

25. Self-medication is usually discouraged because of its ... danger for consumers.

    a. Latent.

    b. Unknown.

    c. Expensive.

    d. Paramount.

26. What does "plasty" mean?

    a. It means a medical procedure that involves the reconstruction of a specific part of the body.

    b. It means a medical procedure that involves the removal of a specific part of the body.

    c. It means a medical procedure that involves the obstruction of a specific part of the body.

    d. It means a medical procedure that involves the replacement of a specific part of the body.

27. Which of the following conditions can cause indigestion?

    a. Gallbladder disease.

    b. Gastroesophageal reflux.

    c. Dyspepsia.

    d. All of the above.

28. Differentiate between appendectomy and lumpectomy.

    a. The removal of the appendix is known as appendectomy while that of the lump is medically referred to as lumpectomy.

    b. The replacement of the appendix is known as appendectomy while that of the lump is medically referred to as lumpectomy.

    c. The correction of the appendix is known as appendectomy while that of the lump is medically referred to as lumpectomy.

    d. The suspension of the appendix is known as appendectomy while that of the lump is medically referred to as lumpectomy.

29. What is the human heart beat range?

    a. Between 50 and 80 beats per minute.

    b. Between 50 and 75 beats per minute.

    c. Between 60 and 100 beats per minute.

    d. Between 80 and 150 beats per minute.

30. The branch of medicine that focuses on bacterial and viral infections is known as what?

    a. Biochemistry.

    b. Microbiology.

    c. Virology.

    d. Bacteriaology.

31. People with mental issues are usually treated by who?

    a. Mental health experts.

    b. Psychiatrists.

    c. Psychoanalyst.

    d. Pendiantrists.

32. Newborns with special care are better taken for what medical treatment?
    a. Prenatal treatment.
    b. Postnatal treatment.
    c. Neonatal treatment.
    d. Pronatal treatment.

33. Experts that treat problems with kidneys are called what?
    a. Kidney experts.
    b. Urologists.
    c. Kidneylogists.
    d. Urealogists.

34. What is the normal blood pressure?
    a. 90/80.
    b. 120/80.
    c. 120/100.
    d. 80/120.

35. Which of the following words is associated with milk?
    a. Lactose.
    b. Bifurcation.
    c. Myocrismus.
    d. Amenorrhea.

36. Cell-related terminologies are suffixed with which of the following?
    a. Ismus.
    b. Centesis.
    c. Cyte.
    d. Aemia.

37. Differentiate between "ferri" and "hist".

    a. "Ferri" is a prefix that denotes "iron" while "Hist" is a prefix for tissue-related terms.

    b. "Hist" is a prefix that denotes "iron" while "Ferri" is a prefix for tissue-related terms.

    c. "Ferri" is a prefix that denotes "milk" while "Hist" is a prefix for blood-related terms.

    d. "Hist" is a prefix that denotes "blood" while "Ferri" is a prefix for bone-related terms.

38. An excessive volume of blood in the body is known as what?

    a. It is known as psellismus.

    b. It is known as hypervolemia.

    c. It is known as anemia.

    d. It is known as lymphadenitis.

39. Differentiate between hypotension and hypertension.

    a. "Hypertension" means low blood pressure while "hypotension" means high blood pressure.

    b. "Hypotension" means low blood sugar while "hypertension" means high blood sugar.

    c. "Hypotension" means low blood pressure while "hypertension" means high blood pressure.

    d. "Hypertension" means low blood sugar while "hypotension" means high blood sugar.

40. Mr. A has an 80 beats per minute pulse rate while Mr. B has a 90 beats per minute pulse rate, which of them has the ideal pulse rate?

    a. Mr. A.

    b. Mr. B.

    c. Both of them.

    d. None of them.

41. Which of the following refers to the dilation or expansion of the lung's bronchi?
    a. Bronchiectasis.
    b. Bronchiectanomy.
    c. Bronchiectanosis.
    d. Bronchiepepsia.

42. What does the "ante" prefix mean?
    a. It means before.
    b. It means after.
    c. It means in between.
    d. It means in the future.

43. What does the "micro" in microorganism stand for?
    a. It stands for small.
    b. It stands for big.
    c. It stands for before.
    d. It stands for within.

44. Which of the following is not an example of ASCVD?
    a. Aortic atherosclerotic diseases.
    b. Coronary heart disease.
    c. Cerebrovascular disease.
    d. Central nervous system disease.

45. Define Pulmonary Embolism.
    a. It is a medical condition that affects the lower abdomen.
    b. It is a medical condition that affects the kidney.
    c. It is a medical condition that affects the lungs.
    d. It is a medical condition that affects both intestines.

46. What is activity-triggered shortness of breath called?

    a. It is called dyspnea on exertion.

    b. It is called dyspnea on activity.

    c. It is called temporary dyspnea.

    d. It is called temporary bibasilar.

47. Define diagnosis?

    a. It is a test conducted on pregnant women.

    b. It is a test conducted on people with special medical condition.

    c. It is a test conducted by physicians on their patients to identify the nature of an ailment.

    d. It is a test conducted to verify the accuracy of an experiment.

48. What triggers atrophy?

    a. A decrease in the size of a body part or tissue.

    b. An increase in the size of a body part or tissue.

    c. All of the above.

    d. None of the above.

49. What are the symptoms of MTBI?

    a. Impaired cognitive function and high blood pressure.

    b. Depression and fatigue.

    c. Low blood pressure and depression.

    d. Suicidal thoughts and irritation.

50. Which class of people is more prone to bradycardia?

    a. People aged 10 to 15.

    b. People aged 20 to 30.

    c. People aged 60 and above.

    d. Teenagers.

Grammar Test 2 – 50 Questions

1. The modification of an adjective, an adverb, a group of words or a verb can be done with ...

    a. Pronouns.

    b. Adverbs.

    c. Adjectives.

    d. Interjections.

2. A word used within a sentence to connect phrases, locations or the time of a sentence is described as a/an ...

    a. Adverb.

    b. Interjection.

    c. Preposition.

    d. None of the above.

3. Adverbs are classified into ... groups.

    a. Three.

    b. Eight.

    c. Six.

    d. Five.

4. Most of the adverbs identified with the "-ly" suffix are ...

    a. Adverbs of place.

    b. Adverbs of time.

    c. Adverbs of manner.

    d. Adverbs of frequency.

5. The intensity of the level of an adjective or adverb can be described with ...

    a. Adverbs of place.

    b. Adverbs of time.

    c. Adverbs of manner.

    d. Adverbs of degree.

6. The type of preposition used when expressing different devices, instruments and machines is the ...

    a. Preposition of instrument.

    b. Preposition of time.

    c. Preposition of devices.

    d. Preposition of machines.

7. Two or more words and clauses are connected with ...

    a. Interjections.

    b. Conjunctions.

    c. Connectors.

    d. Adverbs of connection.

8. Adjectives that ask questions and include which and what are ...

    a. Interrogative adjectives.

    b. Questionnaire adjectives.

    c. Informative adjectives.

    d. Supportive adjectives.

9. You can compare or contrast words or ideas by connecting pairs through ...

    a. Interrogative conjunctions.

    b. Informative conjunctions.

    c. Correlative conjunctions.

    d. Predicative conjunctions.

10. You can show strong feelings and sudden emotions with ...
    a. Interjections.
    b. Connections.
    c. Prepositions.
    d. Adverbials.

11. Adverbial conjunctions are otherwise known as ...
    a. Predictive adverbs.
    b. Conjunction adverbs.
    c. Conjunctive adverbs.
    d. Adjectival adverbs.

12. Some of the most common examples of adverbial conjunctions include all of the follow except ...
    a. Indeed.
    b. Accordingly.
    c. However.
    d. Whoever.

13. Words and ideas can be compared and contrasted with ...
    a. Comparative conjunctions.
    b. Contrasting conjunctions.
    c. Correlative conjunctions.
    d. Descriptive conjunctions.

14. Interjections are usually identified by ...
    a. Exclamation marks.
    b. Interjection marks.
    c. Question marks.
    d. Interrogative marks.

15. In the sentence, "The footballer kicked the ball," what is the object?

    a. The footballer.

    b. Kicked.

    c. The ball.

    d. None of the above.

16. Differentiate between a suffix and a prefix.

    a. A prefix is added to the end of a word to change its meaning while a suffix is added to the beginning of a word for the same purpose.

    b. A prefix is added to the beginning of a word to change its meaning while a suffix is added to the end of a word for the same purpose.

    c. A suffix is a member of the adverb group while a prefix is a member of the adjective group.

    d. A suffix can be used interchangeably with an adverb while a prefix can be used interchangeably with an adjective.

17. What is a phrase?

    a. A phrase is a group of words without the appropriate adjective.

    b. A phrase is a group of words without a predicate and a subject.

    c. A phrase is a collection of similar words.

    d. A phrase is a part of speech specifically restricted to academic writing.

18. A clause that can stand on its own and is meaningful is termed a/an ...

    a. Standing clause.

    b. Independent clause.

    c. Dependent clause.

    d. Meaningful clause.

19. A verb converted to a nominal with the "-ing" suffix is a ...

    a. Gerund.

    b. Converted noun.

    c. Intransitive verb.

    d. Adjectival verb.

20. *Sun* and *son* are common examples of ...

    a. Antonyms.

    b. Synonyms.

    c. Homophones.

    d. Soundphones.

21. An introductory word, phrase or clause must be followed immediately with a ...

    a. Comma.

    b. Exclamation mark.

    c. Interjectional mark.

    d. Apostrophe.

22. "She plays with her daughter because she is happy" is an example of a/an ...

    a. Vague pronoun reference.

    b. Indirect pronoun reference.

    c. Vague noun usage.

    d. Indirect noun usage.

23. You have a run-on sentence when ...

    a. Two independent clauses are connected together without the appropriate punctuation.

    b. Verbs are wrongly used in a sentence.

    c. An independent and a dependent clause are wrongly interchanged in a sentence.

    d. A sentence is devoid of the appropriate parts of speech.

24. What is the difference between *further* and *farther*?

    a. *Further* refers to metaphorical distance while *farther* refers to physical distance.

    b. *Farther* is a measure of metaphorical distance while *further* refers to physical distance.

    c. *Further* is a special form of pronoun while *farther* is a unique adjective.

    d. *Further* uses a single verb while *farther* uses a plural verb.

25. Differentiate between *imminent* and *eminent*.

    a. *Imminent* means approaching or close by while *eminent* means revered or popular.

    b. *Imminent* means revered or popular while *eminent* means close by or approaching.

    c. *Imminent* is an adjectival verb while *eminent* is a descriptive pronoun.

    d. *Imminent* is a correlative pronoun while *eminent* is an interrogative adjective.

26. What are considered irregular verbs?

    a. Verbs that are used for special types of writing.

    b. Verbs that deviate from the principles of verb formation.

    c. Verbs that are not frequently used.

    d. None of the above.

27. Identify the grammatical error in this sentence: "This is the boys' house. His mother is in the garden."

   a. Subject-verb agreement error.

   b. Wrong use of apostrophe.

   c. Wrong word usage.

   d. Vague pronounce reference.

28. Correct this sentence: "I can sing, and I can dance."

   a. I can sing and I can dance.

   b. It is error-free.

   c. I can sing and dance.

   d. I can sing and I can also dance.

29. What grammatical error can you identify in "He yelled at his son because he is drunk"?

   a. Subject-verb agreement error.

   b. Noun-pronoun agreement error.

   c. Vague pronoun reference.

   d. None of the above.

30. Differentiate between "it's" and "its".

   a. "Its" is a reflective pronoun while "it's" is a shortened form of "it is" or "it has."

   b. "Its" is a possessive pronoun, indicating possession. On the other hand, "it's" is a shortened form of "it is" or "it has."

   c. "Its" is a possessive adjective while "it's" is a shortened form of "it is" or "it has."

   d. "It's" is a possessive adjective while "its" is a shortened form of "it is" or "it has."

31. What's the difference between "effect" and "affect"?

   a. "Affect" means to have an impact on something or someone while "effect" means the impact that something or someone has on another thing or person.

   b. "Effect" means to have in impact on something or someone while "affect" means the impact that something or someone has on another thing or person.

   c. "Affect" and "effect" are synonyms.

   d. "Affect" and "effect" are antonyms.

32. Which of the following sentences is correct?

   a. He was told to share the money among the two brothers.

   b. He was told to share the money between the two brothers.

   c. Neither a. nor b.

   d. Both a. and b.

33. Words such as "illusion" and "allusion" are referred to as what?

 a. Homophones.

 b. Antonyms.

 c. Synonyms.

 d. Anecdotes.

34. Differentiate between "lose" and "loose."

 a. "Lose" is a verb while "loose" is an adjective.

 b. "Loose" is a verb while "lose" is an adjective.

 c. "Lose" is a verb while "loose" is an adverb.

 d. "Lose" is an adverb while "loose" is a verb.

35. The woman went to the store to purchase what?

 a. Stationary.

 b. Stationery.

 c. Library.

 d. None of the above.

36. Which of the following is not an example of common noun?

 a. Newspaper.

 b. Animals.

 c. People.

 d. None of the above.

37. Differentiate between proper nouns and common nouns.

    a. Common nouns are usually started with capital letters while proper nouns are written in small letters unless they start a sentence.

    b. Proper nouns are usually started with capital letters while common nouns are written in small letters unless they start a sentence.

    c. Proper nouns are usually started with capital letters while common nouns are written in small letters irrespective of where they appear in a sentence.

    d. Common nouns and proper nouns are written in small letters.

38. What are two attributes of uncountable nouns?

    a. They can't be counted and are very few.

    b. They can't be counted but can be pluralized.

    c. They can't be counted and can't be pluralized.

    d. They can't be counted and are the commonest type of nouns.

39. Differentiate between "mother's" and "mothers'."

    a. The latter refers to a single mother while the former refers to at least two mothers.

    b. The former is acceptable in American English while the latter is preferred in British English.

    c. The former refers to a single mother while the latter refers to at least two mothers.

    d. The former is preferred in British English while the latter is acceptable in American English.

40. Which of the following sentences contains some personal pronouns?

    a. I wish to see him before the week runs out.

    b. The red car is speeding.

    c. Schools will resume next week.

    d. None of the above.

41. Which of these sentences contains an auxiliary verb?

    a. He is preparing for his entrance examination.

    b. We all need him here.

    c. She vows everyone with her angelic voice.

    d. The twins dance beautifully.

42. What type of adjective does "The boy is 10 years old" contain?

    a. It contains a descriptive adjective.

    b. It contains a possessive adjective.

    c. It contains an attributive adjective.

    d. It contains a demonstrative adjective.

43. "She is currently at home" contains what type of preposition?

    a. It contains a preposition for place.

    b. It contains a preposition for position.

    c. It contains a preposition for instrument.

    d. It contains a preposition for direction.

44. One of the sentences below contains a subordinating conjunction, identify it.

   a. Unless she comes around, we can't help her.

   b. We are all fully aware of the current situation.

   c. The two friends are currently on their way home.

   d. Life is full of adventure.

45. What is the appropriate conjunction for connecting sentences of elements of the same grammatical type?

   a. Adverbial conjunction.

   b. Subordinating conjunction.

   c. Coordinating conjunction.

   d. None of the above.

46. Define the object of a sentence.

   a. The object of a sentence is the primary focus of the sentence.

   b. The object of a sentence defines the action performed by the subject of the sentence.

   c. The object of a sentence provides more information about the subject.

   d. The object of a sentence is the main point of the sentence.

47. Differentiate between "less" and "fewer".

    a. "Less" is used for countable things while "Fewer" is used to describe singular mass nouns.

    b. "Fewer" is used for uncountable things while "less" is used to describe plural mass nouns.

    c. "Fewer" is used for countable things while "less" is used to describe plural mass nouns.

    d. "Fewer" is used for countable things while "less" is used to describe singular mass nouns.

48. Which of the following sentences is not correct?

    a. That is the boy's mother.

    b. There are 40 students in the class.

    c. Their are 40 students in the class.

    d. Her father's workshop is around the corner.

49. What is the difference between "infer" and "imply"?

    a. "Infer" is an indirect reference to something while "imply" refers to stating what hasn't been specifically stated.

    b. "Imply" is a direct reference to something while "infer" refers to an indirect reference.

    c. "Imply" is an indirect reference to something while "infer" refers to stating what hasn't been specifically stated.

    d. "Imply" and "infer" are synonyms.

50. Explain the difference between "all together" and "altogether".

    a. "All together" means "entirely" while "Altogether" means "in a group."

    b. "Altogether" means "entirely" while "All together" means "in a group."

    c. "Altogether" means "entirely" while "All together" means "everything

    d. "Altogether" means "everywhere" while "All together" means "in a group."

Biology Test 2 – 25 Questions

1. Substances produced by either cells or living organisms are known as ...
    a. Biological molecules.
    b. Organism molecules.
    c. Biosynthetic molecules.
    d. Evolutionary molecules.

2. Biological molecules are classified into ... groups.
    a. Four.
    b. Five.
    c. Eight.
    d. Ten.

3. Arguably the most abundant molecules in nature are ...
    a. Proteins.
    b. Minerals.
    c. Carbohydrates.
    d. Minerals and water.

4. A complex carbohydrate is otherwise known as ...
    a. Sugar.
    b. Fructose.
    c. Starch.
    d. Amino acids.

5. Which of the following are examples of sugar?
    a. Fructose from fruit.
    b. Table sugar.
    c. Milk-laced lactose.
    d. All of the above.

6. A member of the complex carbohydrate class that can't be digested is ...

    a. Starch.

    b. Sugar.

    c. Fiber.

    d. Water-soluble carbohydrates.

7. Complex carbohydrates are identified by their ...

    a. Long chains only.

    b. Sugar molecules only.

    c. Sugar molecules and long chains.

    d. None of the above.

8. Carbohydrates perform all of the following functions in the body apart from ...

    a. Increasing blood sugar.

    b. Aiding digestion.

    c. Producing energy.

    d. Correcting sight.

9. Children are fed with more protein than other classes of food due to its ...

    a. Delicious taste.

    b. Use as a substitute for breast milk.

    c. Function as building blocks for body tissues.

    d. Function as an inexpensive substitute for other foods.

10. Some enzymes in proteins that can cause biochemical reactions are ...

    a. Glucose and lactase.

    b. Sucrose and glucose.

    c. Lactase and fructose.

    d. Sucrose and lactase.

11. Some proteins that act as chemical messengers in the body are ...
    a. Hormones.
    b. Enzymes.
    c. Amino acids.
    d. Some special types of proteins.

12. The protein synthesis process is directed by ... in the body.
    a. Nucleic complexes.
    b. Nucleic acids.
    c. Nucleic process boosters.
    d. Nucleic production accelerators.

13. Guanine, thymine, cytosine and adenine are four nitrogenous bases found in ...
    a. DNA.
    b. RNA.
    c. Genes.
    d. Cells.

14. The genetic materials in all living organisms and in most viruses are made up of ...
    a. DNA.
    b. Genetic materials.
    c. RNA.
    d. Cells.

15. What happens when a cell divides?
    a. It copies its DNA and passes it to the next generation of cells.
    b. It duplicates its DNA.
    c. Nothing extraordinary.
    d. It undergoes a complete metamorphosis.

16. Humans pass "programmatic instructions" down to their offspring through …

    a. DNA.

    b. Programmatic information conveyors.

    c. Internal message transporters.

    d. Essential tissues in the body.

17. The major components of lipids are …

    a. Fats and oil.

    b. Essential minerals and amino acids.

    c. Carbon, hydrogen and oxygen.

    d. None of the above.

18. Esters with fatty acids and alcohol are commonly known as ….

    a. Complex carbohydrates.

    b. Complex starches.

    c. Complex fibers.

    d. Complex lipids.

19. Carbs that contain one or two sugar molecules are …

    a. Complex carbs.

    b. Complex fibers.

    c. Simple carbs.

    d. Simple fibers.

20. The group of carbohydrates with the "-ose" suffix are …

    a. Amino acids.

    b. Complex.

    c. Sugars.

    d. Fructose and glucose.

21. The three classes of carbohydrates are ...

    a. Starch, sugar and fiber.

    b. Sugar, fructose and sucrose.

    c. Starch, sucrose and sugar.

    d. Sucrose, fructose and fiber.

22. This class of carbohydrate is referred to as complex carbohydrates.

    a. Sugar.

    b. Fiber.

    c. Starch.

    d. Sucrose and fructose.

23. What does RNA stand for?

    a. Ri-DNA Acid.

    b. Ribonucleic acid.

    c. Rest nucleic acid.

    d. None of the above.

24. What does DNA stand for?

    a. Decreasing neural awareness.

    b. Dichomic neuropathic advancement.

    c. Deoxyribonucleic acid.

    d. Dicotyledonous ribonucleic acid.

25. Differentiate between DNA and RNA.

    a. DNA replicates genetic information and stores it while RNA works on the genetic information and converts it to a format that is used for protein building.

    b. DNA is a major topic in genetic engineering while RNA is extensively used in molecular engineering.

    c. DNA supports a wide range of chemical processes while RNA does not.

    d. DNA determines the X chromosomes while RNA determines the Y chromosomes.

Chemistry Test 2 – 25 Questions

1. The reaction between an acid and a base is commonly known as an ...
   a. Acid-base/neutralization reaction.
   b. Amalgamation reaction.
   c. Acid-base fusion reaction.
   d. None of the above.

2. ... are substances that turn litmus paper blue and neutralize acids in aqueous solutions.
   a. Salts.
   b. Bases.
   c. Concentrated acids.
   d. All of the above.

3. Common examples of bases include all of the following except ...
   a. Cleaning agents.
   b. Bleach.
   c. Toothpaste.
   d. Sodium chloride.

4. A reaction that involves the replacement of an element with another in a compound is a/an ...
   a. Single replacement reaction.
   b. Multiple replacement reaction.
   c. Substitution replacement reaction.
   d. Elimination replacement reaction.

5. The reaction between ... and ... is an example of a double replacement reaction.

    a. Sodium chloride and silver fluoride.

    b. Silver fluoride and magnesium oxide.

    c. Sodium chloride and table salt.

    d. None of the above.

6. The relationship between radiation and radioactive elements was discovered by ...

    a. Frederick Soddy.

    b. Isaac Newton.

    c. Marie Curie.

    d. Albert Einstein.

7. Nuclear changes and radiation are classified into ...

    a. Alpha radiation, beta radiation and gamma radiation.

    b. Gamma radiation, theta radiation and beta radiation.

    c. Beta radiation, alpha radiation and theta radiation.

    d. Alpha radiation, theta radiation and gamma radiation.

8. Which of the following types of radiation can't penetrate human skin?

    a. Alpha radiation.

    b. Theta radiation.

    c. Gamma radiation.

    d. Beta radiation.

9. Carbon-14 decay is an example of ...

    a. Gamma radiation.

    b. Beta radiation.

    c. Alpha radiation.

    d. Theta radiation.

10. Radiation that doesn't involve particle emission is ...
    a. Gamma radiation.
    b. Theta radiation.
    c. Beta radiation.
    d. Alpha radiation.

11. Penetrating radiation is another name for ....
    a. Alpha radiation.
    b. Theta radiation.
    c. Gamma radiation.
    d. Beta radiation.

12. The two classes of nuclear reactions are ...
    a. Nuclear fission and nuclear fusion.
    b. Permanent and temporary reactions.
    c. Positive and negative reactions.
    d. Simple and complex reactions.

13. Smaller atoms combine together to form a larger atom during ...
    a. Nuclear fission.
    b. Nuclear reaction.
    c. Nuclear fusion.
    d. Nuclear combination.

14. Highly radioactive particles are produced during ...
    a. Nuclear fission.
    b. Nuclear reaction.
    c. Nuclear fusion.
    d. Nuclear combination.

15. An electron is transferred from one atom to another in ...

    a. Covalent bonding.

    b. Hydrogen bonding.

    c. Dative bonding.

    d. Ionic bonding.

16. In ..., bonds are formed through the sharing of valence electrons.

    a. Coordinate bonding.

    b. Covalent bonding.

    c. Ionic bonding.

    d. Hydrogen bonding.

17. Covalent bonds are classified into ...

    a. Nonpolar covalent bonding, polar covalent bonding and coordinate covalent bonding.

    b. Dative covalent bonding, ionic covalent bonding and hydrogen covalent bonding.

    c. Hydrogen covalent bonding, dative covalent bonding and coordinate covalent bonding.

    d. Polar covalent bonding, nonpolar covalent bonding and ionic covalent bonding.

18. A common bonding type between metal ions and ligands is ...

    a. Coordinate covalent bonding.

    b. Hydrogen bonding.

    c. Ionic chemical bonding.

    d. None of the above.

19. The polarization of two adjacent molecules triggers ...
    a. Ionic bonding.
    b. Chemical bonding.
    c. Coordinate covalent bonding.
    d. Hydrogen bonding.

20. $CaCl_2$, K_2O, MgO and $NaBr$ are some examples of ...
    a. Ionic bonding.
    b. Hydrogen bonding.
    c. Coordinate covalent bonding.
    d. Polar covalent bonding.

21. The energy produced during fission is used for ...
    a. Carbon-free electricity production.
    b. Producing radioactive materials.
    c. Chemical reactions such as gamma and beta radiation.
    d. Manufacturing different forms of electrolytes.

22. All of the following are notable gamma radiation emitters except ...
    a. Technetium-99m.
    b. Cobalt-60.
    c. Cobalt-80.
    d. Iodine-131.

23. Clothing is a preventive measure against the harmful impact of ...
    a. Gamma radiation.
    b. Alpha radiation.
    c. Theta radiation.
    d. Beta radiation.

24. Alpha radiation is emitted by all of the following except …

    a. Radon.

    b. Radium.

    c. Uranium.

    d. Iodine.

25. What happens to an atom when it emits a beta particle?

    a. It breaks down into smaller unrecognizable parts.

    b. It experiences a huge change in mass.

    c. The change of mass is negligible.

    d. It reacts with the environment to form another atom entirely.

Anatomy and Physiology Test 2 – 25 Questions

1. All the bones and joints in the body are major components of the ...
    a. Respiratory system.
    b. Circulatory system.
    c. Muscular system.
    d. Skeletal system.

2. The human skeletal system contains ... bones.
    a. 206.
    b. 500.
    c. 126.
    d. 176.

3. The appendicular skeleton includes all of the following bones except ...
    a. Upper limbs.
    b. Pelvic girdle.
    c. Shoulder girdle.
    d. Chin bones.

4. The lungs would be nothing except tissue without the ... to hold them in place.
    a. Rib cage, coastal cartilages and intercostal muscles.
    b. Intercostal muscles, rib cage and protective cartilages.
    c. Rib cage, coastal cartilages and protective cartilages.
    d. Intercostal muscles, rib cage and preventive cartilages.

5. The bone marrow produces red blood cells through a process known as ...
    a. Cytosis.
    b. Ematopherences.
    c. Hematopoiesis.
    d. None of the above.

6. The brain is protected from damage from external forces by the ...

    a. Skull.

    b. Skeletal system.

    c. Protective tissues in the head.

    d. Flexible bones and protective tissues in the head.

7. Some body processes require the assistance of some important minerals such as ... and ... to function properly.

    a. Nickel and chlorine.

    b. Calcium and sodium.

    c. Calcium and phosphorus.

    d. Iodine and chlorine.

8. The respiratory system is divided into the ... and ...

    a. Upper respiratory tract and lower respiratory tract.

    b. Primary respiratory tract and lower respiratory tract.

    c. Flexible and rigid respiratory tract.

    d. Auxiliary and dependent respiratory tract.

9. A patient was diagnosed with a genetic lung disorder. This condition could very possibly be ...

    a. Cystic fibrosis.

    b. Cystic deficiency.

    c. Lung disease.

    d. Lung cancer.

10. Which of the following is not a health problem that can be triggered by a damaged respiratory system?

    a. Asthma.

    b. Bronchiectasis.

    c. Idiopathic pulmonary fibrosis.

    d. Zika virus.

11. A component of the immune system that keeps a record of invaders and destroys potential enemies is ...

    a. The lymphocytes.

    b. The brycomphytes.

    c. The immune sentry.

    d. The attack squad.

12. Harmful bacteria in the body are usually attacked by a special type of phagocyte called ...

    a. The phagocytus.

    b. The neutrophils.

    c. The bacterium nemesis.

    d. The defensive phagocyte.

13. A child's immunity at birth is known as ...

    a. Primary immunity.

    b. Innate immunity.

    c. Natural immunity.

    d. Childhood immunity.

14. Another name for adaptive immunity is ...

    a. Childhood immunity.

    b. Natural immunity.

    c. Active immunity.

    d. Flexible immunity.

15. Breast milk is a form of ... immunity.

    a. Childhood.

    b. Innate.

    c. Passive.

    d. Secondary.

16. The ... prevent(s) many pathogens from entering the body.

    a. Bronchi.

    b. Defensive cytosis.

    c. Defensive duodenum.

    d. Protective mechanism.

17. What role does hydrochloric acid play in the body's defense system?

    a. It prevents the pathogens we accidentally consume from harming us.

    b. It lays the foundation for other defensive mechanisms to operate.

    c. It serves as the medium between the pathogens and useful bacteria in the body.

    d. It supports the protection of important body organs.

18. How do saliva and the airways boost the body's immune system?

    a. They support the hydrochloric acid in protecting important body organs.

    b. They absorb harmful pathogens.

    c. They contain an enzyme that renders bacteria inactive by destroying their cell walls.

    d. They provide essential nutrients needed by the body to fortify its defenses.

19. All of the following immunodeficiency disorders may weaken the immune system except ...

    a. Overeating.

    b. Some types of cancer.

    c. HIV.

    d. None of the above.

20. A weak immune system can play host to all of the following health problems except …
    a. Meningitis.
    b. Inflammation.
    c. Pneumonia.
    d. None of the above.

21. Some of the natural killer cells that provide innate immunity are …
    a. White blood cells.
    b. Red blood cells.
    c. Green blood cells.
    d. Platelets.

22. Lymphocytes are classified into … classes.
    a. Three.
    b. Five.
    c. Four.
    d. Two.

23. What is the difference between oxygenated and deoxygenated blood?
    a. Oxygenated blood doesn't have oxygen while deoxygenated blood does.
    b. Oxygenated blood contains oxygen while deoxygenated blood does not.
    c. Humans use deoxygenated blood while animals use oxygenated blood.
    d. Humans use oxygenated blood while animals use deoxygenated blood.

24. Another name for air sacs is …
    a. Pulmonary alveoli.
    b. Pulmonary sac.
    c. Alveoli sac.
    d. Alveoli pulmonary.

25. A muscular tube in the body about 8 inches long is the ...

    a. Esophagus.

    b. Muscular pipe.

    c. Capillary tube.

    d. None of the above.

Physics Test 2 – 25 Questions

1. Petroleum, coal and nuclear energy are some examples of ...
    a. Nonrenewable sources of energy.
    b. Combustible sources of energy.
    c. Fundamental energy.
    d. Irreversible energy.

2. Which of the following nonrenewable sources of energy produces enormous heat that can be used for operating ships and aircraft?
    a. Petroleum.
    b. Combustible gas.
    c. Coal.
    d. Wood.

3. Calculate the work done by a weightlifter who holds 100 kg of heavy metal on his head while standing in one spot.
    a. 10 N.
    b. 100 N.
    c. 0 N.
    d. 50 N.

4. Define a joule.
    a. The work done by a force of one Newton through a distance of one meter.
    b. The work done by a force of one Newton in a stationary position.
    c. The work done in lifting an object.
    d. The product of one Newton and a distance of one meter.

5. Under what condition is work done?

    a. The force applied to an object must act on it vertically.

    b. The force applied to an object must act on it horizontally.

    c. The force applied to an object must cause a displacement in the direction of the force.

    d. The force applied to an object must cause a reduction in its overall weight.

6. Calculate the work done by a man who pulls an object up an inclined 50-meter plane at a 60-degree angle while applying a force of 20 N.

    a. 250 joules.

    b. 160 joules.

    c. 100 joules.

    d. 500 joules.

7. A 100-kg weightlifter carries a 50-kg weight up a 10-meter ladder. Calculate the work done by the weightlifter, taking $g = 10$ ms^{-2}.

    a. 7 kJ.

    b. 5.5 kJ.

    c. 6 kJ.

    d. 15 kJ.

8. During road construction, a bulldozer dropped a 100-kg stone from a height of 25 m. Calculate the work done on the stone, taking $g = 10$ ms^{-2}.

    a. 55 kJ.

    b. 25 kJ.

    c. 50 kJ.

    d. 60 kJ.

9. The energy an object has due to its position is ...

    a. Potential energy.

    b. Kinetic energy.

    c. Rotational energy.

    d. All of the above.

10. The law of conservation of energy states that ...
    a. Energy can be created and destroyed.
    b. During a change of energy, its value can be drastically reduced.
    c. Energy can change from one form to another, but it can't be destroyed.
    d. Energy can be safely stored for future use.

11. Which of the following are examples of objects that have kinetic energy?
    a. A moving object.
    b. An object falling under gravitational force.
    c. A flying plane.
    d. All of the above.

12. Calculate the kinetic energy of a 100-kg body moving at a speed of 20 meters per second.
    a. 20 kJ.
    b. 45 kJ.
    c. 50 kJ.
    d. 15 kJ.

13. A soldier shot a 50-g bullet. Calculate the kinetic energy of the bullet if it moves at a speed of 100 km per hour.
    a. 2.6 kJ.
    b. 0.019 kJ.
    c. 3.2 kJ.
    d. 2.3 kJ.

14. 1 horsepower is equivalent to ...
    a. 746 watts or .75 kW.
    b. 500 watts or .5 kW.
    c. 800 watts or .8 kW.
    d. 1,500 watts or 1.5 kW.

15. Calculate the power of a water pump that lifts 500 kg of water to a height of 8 meters in 10 seconds. Use $g = 10 \ ms^{-2}$.

    a. 6 kW.
    b. 5 kW.
    c. 4 kW.
    d. 10 kW.

16. Convert 2 horsepower into kilowatts.

    a. 1.5 kW.
    b. 2.5 kW.
    c. 3.0 kW.
    d. 5.0 kW.

17. What is another way to describe the thickness of a fluid?

    a. Its melting point.
    b. Its frictional force.
    c. Its consistency.
    d. Its freezing point.

18. How does friction support walking?

    a. Friction prevents you from slipping.
    b. Friction offers you stability.
    c. Friction helps you to walk faster.
    d. Friction makes the ground soft.

19. Which of the following is not a law of friction?

    a. Sliding friction is independent of speed.
    b. Friction is directly proportional to the force pressing the surfaces together.
    c. Sliding friction is less than static friction.
    d. Friction depends on the temperature of the environment.

20. The type of friction that exists between two objects in relative motion to each other is ...

    a. Sliding friction.

    b. Slippery friction.

    c. Translational friction.

    d. Supportive friction.

21. Which type of friction makes climbing rock walls possible?

    a. Static friction.

    b. Adhesive friction.

    c. Supportive friction.

    d. Climbing friction.

22. Define wavelength.

    a. Wavelength is the distance between the points of two successive waves.

    b. Wavelength is the destructive power of a wave.

    c. Wavelength refers to the highest point a wave can reach.

    d. None of the above.

23. Find the wavelength of a sound with frequency 30 cycles per second if the speed of sound is 340 meters per second.

    a. 11.55 m.

    b. 20.0 m.

    c. 310 m.

    d. 11.33 m.

24. A motorboat's wave travels across a lake at a velocity of 2.5 m/s. The distance between successive wave crests is 3.5 m. Calculate the frequency of the waves.

    a. 0.71 Hz.

    b. 1.4 Hz.

    c. 7.0 Hz.

    d. 1.0 Hz.

25. Convert 5 horsepower to kilowatts.

    a. 3.73 kW.

    b. 4.2 kW.

    c. 5.25 kW.

    d. 3.3 kW.

Learning Style Test 2 – 14 Questions

1. What type of books do you like to read the most?

a. Books with orderly chapters

b. Colorful books

c. Books with pictorial descriptions

d. Books with a lot of text

2. Your friends are calling you to get together, but you have a test the next day. What will you do?

a. Go out with friends

b. Prepare for the test and skip hanging out

c. Take your books with you to see your friends

d. Call your friends at your home

3. On the first day of your nursing job, what will you ask the doctor?

a. What your job description is

b. What the doctor expects you to do

c. Nothing.

d. What the doctor's name is.

4. You made a mistake, and the doctor catches you and scolds you. What will your reaction be?

a. Gracefully accept your mistake even if you feel hurt

b. Argue with him

c. Blame someone else

d. Silently start looking for a new job

5. What type of assignments do you prefer?

a. Problem-solving activities

b. Essays

c. Oral tests

d. MCQs

6. If you are given a task, what is your immediate response to the person assigning the task?

a. "Yes, I will do it."

b. "How should I do this task?"

c. "Why should I do this task?"

d. "When should this task be completed?"

7. You are being taught how to draw blood. Which of the following questions will you instantly ask the teacher?

a. "Why should the blood be drawn?"

b. "Where should we draw the blood?"

c. "How much blood should be drawn at one time?"

d. "What are the types of blood cells?"

8. You are determined to do a specific task but everyone around disapproves of it. What will you do?

a. Get confused

b. Not do the task

c. Do the task

d. Draw straws to decide

9. A teacher gives a continuous lecture of four hours and the other breaks the lecture into four one-hour sessions. Which one is better for you?

a. A four-hour lecture

b. A divided lecture

c. Either of the two

d. None of the two

10. A patient describes his condition in great detail, talking about each and every aspect. How will you respond?

a. Ignore half of it

b. Pay attention to each detail

c. Ask him to narrate it to the doctor

d. Ask him to shut up

11. An injured patient is brought to the emergency room. What will you do to make sure he is alive?

a. Panic and forget the first aid rules

b. Follow everything in an orderly manner

c. Call the doctor

d. Check if the patient is alive

12. A doctor asked you to inform the parents about a difficult and dangerous diagnosis of a disease in the patient, but they start crying halfway through. What will you do?

a. Continue telling them about the diagnosis but also help them calm down

b. Inform the doctor

c. Stop in the middle and wait until they calm themselves down

d. Ask some other nurse to tell them the facts

13. Which of the following best helps you remember lectures?

a. Notes

b. Tests

c. Practical demonstrations

d. Experiments

14. If you have scored good grades in one test. Will you get good grades in the next test?

a. Yes

b. No

c. Maybe

d. Definitely

Personality Style Test 2 – 15 Questions

1. After your education is completed and you are not getting a job, which of the following things would you prefer to do in your free time?

a. Read books

b. Take part in community service programs

c. Go out with friends

d. Plan a trip

2. If you are in an environment with no friends and acquaintances, how will you deal with it?

a. Instantly make friends

b. Stay silent until asked something

c. Try to find a job at a place where you know people

d. Leave that place immediately

3. If you were not a nurse, which of the following occupations do you think you would have done the best?

a. Engineer

b. Designer

c. Teacher

d. Baker

4. If people around you are sad, how will you behave?

a. Crack jokes to ease the tension

b. Stay quiet

c. Leave the place

d. Be in your own space

5. If you are left on duty with a patient of your age in the hospital, how will you keep up with her?

a. Be in your own space

b. Respond when asked for something

c. Make friends with her and tell her stories

d. Sleep

6. How will you respond if you receive a genuine compliment for your work or your nature?

a. Feel awkward

b. Appreciate it and compliment the person back

c. Thank the person and move on

d. Smile at the person

7. If the doctor asks you to work in the children's ward, how will you treat the children who can also disturb you a lot?

a. Get annoyed with them

b. After some time, ask another nurse to replace you

c. Control them easily by telling them stories

d. Scold them if they make any noise

8. How will you deal with having too much work?

a. Get tired and leave it for another day

b. Make an excuse and leave

c. Enjoy doing it and complete it during the given time

d. Take help from a fellow nurse

9. A friend comes to visit you at the hospital, but you have a lot of work piled up. What will you do?

a. Get busy with the friend and forget about the work

b. Ask the friend to come later

c. Assign the work to someone who is free

d. Talk to the friend and do the work simultaneously

10. A junior nurse is promoted, but you are not. How will you react?

a. Stay quiet and continue the work

b. Complain to the head doctor and resign

c. Cut off contact with the nurse

d. Start looking for a new job

11. A document is brought to you when you are extremely busy and the person asks for your signature. What will you do?

a. Read, discuss, and then sign

b. Immediately sign without reading it

c. Ask the person to bring the document some other time

d. Keep the document for when you have time

12. You ask an assistant nurse to make a blood report and bring it to you. The report is fine but has some minor errors that you could ignore. What will your reaction be?

a. Ask her to fix the minor errors

b. Take the report if it were correctly done

c. Fix the minor errors yourself

d. Ask another nurse to review the report for you

13. You are offered a job, but the employer says that it pays the same as your current job. They also say that in the future they will increase your salary. How will you respond to the offer?

a. Accept it

b. Reject it

c. Discuss it with your parents/friends/seniors

d. Recommend someone else

14. A doctor asked you to keep quiet about a certain detail of a patient's condition, but the patient's family members keep insisting and trying to persuade you to give them information. What will you do?

a. Get angry and scold them

b. Spill the details

c. Tell them to ask the doctor

d. Ignore them

15. You have worked throughout the day, but a nurse friend of yours asks you to take her shift. How will you respond to her?

a. Say no

b. Say yes

c. Complain to the department

d. Ask some other nurse in the department

Test 2 Answers

Math Test 2 Answers

1) d: CLXXX.

The first step is to subtract the Arabic numbers. Thus, 620 − 420 = 180. Find the different components that add to make 180. You have 100, 50 and 30. These are C, L and XXX respectively. Thus, 180 = 100 + 50 + 30 = CLXXX.

2) c: LXXV.

25 times 3 = 75. That is 50 + 20 + 5. That gives you LXXV. When you have such questions, perform the first operation in Arabic numbers and break down the result into smaller numbers. Then, find the corresponding Roman numerals.

3) c: 65.

This is the reverse of the operation above. Convert to Arabic numbers to subtract XXV from C. 100 − 35 = 65.

4) c: XC.

The product of 45 and 2 is 90. Since 90 is 10 less than 100, the result will be formed with C and X. To show that it is subtract, the smaller value is placed first.

5) b: 20.4117 kg.

This is a conversion problem involving kilograms and pounds. 1 kilogram is 2.2046 pounds. Therefore, 45 pounds = 45/2.2046. The result is 20.4117 kg. It is advisable to have the conversion memorized.

6) a: 22.05 lb.

This question is similar to the one above. They are both conversions between kilograms and pounds. Hence, by using the formula, 1 kilogram is 2.2046 pounds, multiply 10 kg by 2.2046. the answer is 22.046 or approximately 22.05 pounds.

7) a: 1.2 liters.

This is volume conversion. One cup of any liquid is the same as 0.23658 liters of the same liquid. Thus, 5 cups of water is the same as $5 \cdot 0.23658$ liters. Thus, 5 cups of water is equal to 1.182 or 1.2 liters of water.

8) c: 100 °F.

Check the conversion section for the appropriate formula and convert the temperature. It is approximately 100 degrees Fahrenheit.

9) d: Fahrenheit to Celsius.

When converting from Fahrenheit to Celsius, the temperature will decrease in numerical value. Hence, it is necessary to subtract 32 from the given figure before you multiply the result by 0.5555 to get the Celsius equivalent of Fahrenheit.

10) c: Celsius to Fahrenheit.

You can also make temperature conversions from Celsius to Fahrenheit. The first step is to multiply the given temperature by 1.8 or 9/5. Then, add 32 to the result to give you the Fahrenheit equivalent of Celsius.

11) c: 125 units.

If 500 units is the total sale for four months, you can get the average monthly sale by dividing the total units sold by the number of months. Thus, 500/4 = 125. That's her average monthly unit sale.

12) d: 400 units.

This is another division problem. The quarter of a year is 3 months. Thus, to sell 1,200 items in 3 months, the sales representative must sell an average of 1,200/3 items monthly. That translates to an average of 400 units every month.

13) b: 83.33%.

This is a percentage question. You can find the percentage by representing the grade attained with respect to the attainable grades in fraction or decimal form. Then, multiply the result by 100. The calculation is $(250/300) \cdot 100$ and the result is 83.33%.

14) a: 25%.

The employee was absent for 5 out of 20 working days. Represent this value as a decimal or fraction and multiply by 100. The employee was absent 25% of the total working days for the month.

15) d: 60%.

First, calculate the amount paid by credit card. Subtract the amount paid in cash from the total cost, i.e., $500 − $200 = $300. Then, represent $300 as a fraction of $500 ($300/$500). Simplify the fraction and multiply by 100 to get 60%.

16) a: 8 pairs.

If a pair of shoes costs $20, $175/$20 = 8.75 pairs of shoes. Disregard the fractional part and you have 8 pairs.

17) b: 40 days.

If a student reads an average of 5 pages daily, he or she will complete a 200-page book in (200/5) days. Provided the reading pace remains constant, the student will complete the book in 40 days.

18) b: 24.

A dozen is 12. Thus, each carton contains 12 cell phones. To find the number of phones in 2 cartons, multiply 12 by 2. Hence, there are 24 cell phones in the two cartons.

19) c: 204 kg.

Convert the weight from pounds to kilograms by dividing it by 2.2046. The result is 204 kg.

20) c: 1/4.

Start by finding the percentage of the uneaten food. In this case, the uneaten food can be calculated by subtracting 75 from 100 since the whole food represents 100%. Thus, the uneaten portion is 25% of the food. Then, express 25% as a fraction of 100% (25/100) and simplify it.

21) b: 3/8.

Start your calculation by subtracting the paid fee from the total fee. That leaves $150 unpaid. Then, express the unpaid as a fraction of the total fee and you have 150/400. A further simplification of the expression gives 3/8. Hence, 3/8ths of her fee are unpaid.

22) b: XXXIX.

77 − 38 = 39. Then express 39 as a Roman numeral. 39 is 10 + 10 + 10 − 1 + 10 which is represented by XXXIX.

23) b: 40%.

For each $250 Richard makes, he saves $100. The fraction of his income he saves is 100/250. Thus, he saves 2/5th of his income. Multiply the fraction or its decimal equivalent by 100. Thus, Richard saves 40% of his income.

24) c: Number of employees − number of promoted employees.

In the organization of 78 employees, only 45 deserve a promotion. Subtract the number of the promoted employees from the total employees to know the number of unpromoted employees.

25) a: 41.67%.

The number of male nurses is 125. Express this figure as a fraction of the total number of students. That gives 125/300. By multiplying the result by 100, you will get the percentage of male students. Thus, 0.4167 · 100 or 41.67%.

26) d: 58.33%.

The number of female nurses is the total students − the number of male students, 300 − 125. Express the result as a fraction or decimal of the total number of students, 175/300. For the percentage, multiply the result by 100. That is 0.5833 · 100 or 58.33%.

27) b: 30.

Each unit of the hospital has three doctors. Hence, ten units will have 3 · 10 doctors. The hospital has 30 doctors in total.

28) a: 5/6.

Find the number of nurses first. If each unit has 15 nurses, the 10 units have $10 \cdot 15$ or 150 nurses. The total number of staff is 150 nurses + 30 doctors, making 180 staff members. Represent the number of nurses with respect to the total number of employees. This gives 150/180 which simplifies to 5/6.

29) b: 50.

If 8 boys share 400 apples equally, divide the number of apples by the number of boys that share them. Each boy will get 400/8 apples. Thus, each of the boys gets 50 apples.

30) b: 150.

From the calculation above, each boy gets 50 apples. Therefore, 5 boys will get $50 \cdot 5$ or 250 apples, leaving $400 - 250$ or 150 apples for the remaining three boys. 150 apples are left after the five boys have received theirs.

31) a: 87.5%.

7 boys will share $7 \cdot 50$ or 350 apples from the 400 apples. Hence, they have shared 350 out of 400 or 350/400 apples. That is 0.875 of the apples. Thus, 7 boys have shared $0.875 \cdot 100$ or 87.5% of the total apples.

32) a: 4 hours.

In 1 hour, the cyclist covers 30 kilometers. To find the time to cover 120 kilometers traveling at the same speed, divide the total distance by the cyclist's average distance per hour. It will take him 120/30 hours to cover 120 kilometers. Thus, the cyclist will cover the distance in 4 hours.

33) b: 240.

Each of the boxes contains 20 oranges. To know the number of oranges the boy can keep in 12 boxes, multiply the number of oranges in a box by the total number of boxes. Therefore, the boy has $20 \cdot 12$ or 240 oranges in total.

34) b: 20.

There are 360 students in the school. Each of the buses can accommodate 18 passengers. Therefore, divide the number of students by the number of passengers per bus. Hence, the school needs 360/18 or 20 buses to transport all the students.

35) a: 12.

If 60% of the students are female, that implies that (60/100) · 360 students are female. Hence, 216 female students are in the school while the rest are male students. With 18 passengers per bus, the school needs 216/18 or 12 buses for the female students.

36) b: $4,320.

Each of the students pays $12 for the trip. To know the total amount paid, multiply the total number of students by the amount paid per student. Thus, the students pay 360 · $12 or $4,320 altogether for the trip.

37) c: $460.

There are 23 books in the box. If each book costs $20. Multiply the number of books by the price of each book to get the total price of the books in the box. Thus, the total is 23 · $20 = $460.

38) c: 15,924.

3,579 students passed the examination while 12,345 failed it. The total number of students that took the test is the addition of the number of students that passed the exam and the number that failed it. Thus, 12,345 + 3,579 or 15,924 students took the test.

39) a: 3,374.

There are 2,453 patients in the children's ward and the maternity ward has 45 patients. In the male ward, there are 876 patients. Add these figures together to get the number of patients in the hospital. Thus, 2,453 + 45 + 876 = 3,374 patients in the hospital.

40) b: 35.53%.

In the library, there are 350 books in French, 590 in English and 45 in Latin. First find the total number of books in the library. Next, find the number of French books as a fraction or decimal of the total number of books: 350/985. Multiply your result by 100.

41) b: 40.

Before you find the average number of test tubes produced over the given time frame, first calculate the number of test tubes produced altogether. Thus, within the month, 36 + 58 + 29 + 37 = 160 test tubes were produced. Divide this figure by the number of weeks in a month to obtain the average production per week.

42) b: $10,400.

If she saves $200 weekly, you can find out how much she will save in a year by multiplying her weekly savings by the number of weeks in a year. Since there are 52 weeks in a year, she will save $200 · 52 or $10,400 in a year.

43) d: 18 days.

If the artisan could only complete 1/3 of his work in 6 days, multiply the figure by 3 to determine how long it will take him to complete all the work. 6 days · 3 = 18 days to complete it.

44) c: 7.5 cm.

If the length of the ribbon is 30 cm and you cut it into four equal lengths, each part is 30 cm/4 long. This translates to 7.5 cm long.

45) c: 4.

To share 48 balloons equally among 12 students, divide the number of balloons by the number of students. 48/12 = 4 balloons per student.

46) b: $60.

If 5 books cost $100, each book will cost $100/5 or $20. Thus, three books will cost $20 · 3 = $60. Note that you can't find the cost of three books without first knowing the cost per book.

47) d: 36.

If 20% of 45 students in a school are absent on a particular day, find the number of absentees. Convert 20% to a fraction and multiply by 45. Thus, you have (20/100) · 45 = 9 students. Hence, 45 − 9 = 36 students were present on that day.

48) a: 20%.

The increase in school fees can be calculated with the formula: new school fees / old school fees. $3,000 / $2,500 = 1.2. The percent increase is .2 which converts to 20%. Thus, the school fees increased by 20%.

49) a: 13/16.

If 325 of 400 seats in a hall are filled, that can be expressed as a fraction: 325/400. Both numbers are multiples of 5, making it easier to simplify. The final result is 13/16.

50) a: 1/5.

If a retail store slashed the prices of its commodities by 20%, it offers 20/100 of its price as a discount. You can express this as a fraction by simplifying 20/100. Since both the numerator and denominator are multiples of 5 and 10, you can break them down to 1/5.

Reading Test 2 Answers

Passage 5 Answers and Explanations

(1)   c: Kid's increasing interest in video games.

Kids are increasingly interested in video games. Thus, parents are duly concerned about the potential impact of such games on their children.

(2)   d: 1 hour.

The result of a study conducted by Oxford University shows that children benefit from playing video games for about an hour daily.

(3)   d: It makes players more reserved.

Some of the numerous benefits of playing video games regularly include making players less hyperactive, increasing their social activeness, and making them happier. It doesn't increase their reserved nature.

(4)   c: Pre-teens and teens.

The research conducted by Oxford University involved kids of both sexes, aged between 10 and 15 years old. Thus, pre-teens and teens were involved.

(5)   c: They help kids develop their decision-making skills.

Some video games that involve solving puzzles or mentally-challenging problems will boost a kid's ability to solve problems and make crucial decisions.

(6)   b: The ability to monitor both your players and opponents.

Several adventure games require a player to keep the position of players in mind and predict the opponent's movements while coordinating their eyes and hands to make the right move.

(7)   a: Age of Empires and Railroad Tycoon.

Some strategy games like Age of Empires, SimCity, and Railroad Tycoon are those that can assist a player in developing their resource management skills.

(8)   c: It means with ease.

"Effortlessly" means "Needing little or no effort, so that it seems easy." Simply put, it means "with ease".

(9) c: It means "put under control."

"Put in place" is an idiomatic expression that means "Restore to normal or upright position." Hence, contextually, it means to put their passion for video games under control.

(10) c: They are addictive.

Video games, like all other forms of entertainment, can become addictive if not properly checked. This is one of the reasons why parents are concerned about their children's increasing passion for such games.

(11) b: They help players use scarce resources judiciously.

In many games, players must manage the limited resources at their disposal to complete a task or achieve a goal.

(12) c: Immense.

In the context, "immense" can aptly replace "profound." It gives an idea into the potential impact of some games on children when they become adults.

Passage 6 Answers and Explanations

(1)   b: Globalization refers to the global changes that make it easier for businesses to be conducted internationally.

According to the passage, globalization has made it easier for businesses to be conducted internationally. Irrespective of your physical location, you can make business transactions with anyone in any part of the world.

(2)   c: It means commendable.

Contextually, "laudable" means "commendable." It refers to the positive impact of globalization on business.

(3)   a: It means being in a favorable condition.

"Competitive advantage" is used to indicate that someone or something is in a favorable condition with respect to another person or thing. Thus, businesses who are taking advantage of globalization are at an advantaged position than their counterparts that allow such an opportunity to pass them by.

(4)   a: Cheaper products.

One of the numerous benefits of outsourcing is that it enables manufacturing companies to cut their production cost down. This will result in cheaper products for consumers.

(5)   d: Availability of super-rich customers or clients.

Companies outsource their production for several reasons. This may include availability of experts, cheaper raw materials, and a more affordable labor cost. Super-rich customers or clients are not a factor.

(6)   a: It enables companies to outsource their production to other countries, rendering their local employees jobless.

In some countries, employees are laid off when companies outsource their production to other countries. This increases the unemployment rates in their countries.

(7)   b: It enables money launderers to use foreign companies for laundering.

Globalization supports money laundering because it makes it easier for launderers to launder money through foreign companies under the pretext of business transactions.

(8)   c: It encourages income disparity.

According to some studies, globalization may trigger income inequality between trained professionals and unskilled workers. Skilled workers can get better offers from elsewhere while unskilled workers are stuck.

(9)   b: It leads to the abuse of natural resources.

Companies have the tendency to abuse natural resources when they are hell-bent on meeting the increasing demands for their goods.

(10) a: It means to experience the worst part of a problematic situation.

To bear the brunt means to experience the worst part of a situation. During outsourcing, local companies in the country which the company outsources to will feel the impact more.

(11) b: It means to take advantage of.

When you capitalize on something, you take advantage of the thing or situation. It is a way of turning something for your own benefit.

(12) a: Illegal.

According to the passage, "shady" means "illegal." Hence, the latter can replace the former accurately in the passage.

Passage 7 Answers and Explanations

(1)   a: Medical errors account for a third of all deaths in the US.

The result of a search conducted by Johns Hopkins shows that medical errors make up the top 3 common causes of medical-related death in the United States.

(2)   b: Wrong diagnosis.

Wrong diagnosis is a part of diagnostic errors. Another constituent is over-diagnosing. These errors can have a significant impact on a patient if they are misdiagnosed and given wrong treatment.

(3)   b: It jeopardizes the patient's health.

Wrong medication can trigger a wide range of medical conditions that may ultimately terminate the victim's life.

(4)   c: Crucial.

In the context of the passage, "imperative" is synonymous with "crucial." It highlights the significance of ensuring that diagnoses are perfectly done to prevent medical errors that may have dire consequences.

(5)   b: Conscientiously.

To do something meticulously means to give it the best attention in order to leave no room for error. Thus, "conscientiously" can replace it in the passage.

(6)   b: Radiologists.

To start with, diagnoses should be done by professionals only. It is recommended that the entire care team, including radiologists and physicians, should be involved in the diagnosis.

(7)   a: Contaminated medical equipment.

Contaminated medical equipment, such as surgical tools, can transmit infection to patients and thus compromise their safety. The same goes for contaminated patient rooms and others.

(8)   a: High-risk processes and confused drug names.

The patients' safety can be compromised by some factors such as confused drug names, high-risk processes, high-risk populations, and high-alert medications.

(9)   a: Improper medication storage.

Improper medication arrangement and storage can trigger medication error. Hence, it is advisable that pharmacies take these two issues seriously as a preventive measure against such a costly error.

(10) c: Giving detailed information about a patient when handing over to the next team.

When handing over to the next team, workers on duty should provide detailed and accurate information about a patient to the team that is taking over. This is another preventive measure against medical errors.

(11) a: Rife.

Rife is a synonym of prevalent.

(12) d: None of the above.

When handing over to another team, the outgoing team should provide some pieces of information about their patients. The provided information should include the severity of each patient's illness, treatments required, and their general condition.

Passage 8 Answers and Explanations

(1)   a: To determine the efficiency and safety of a new treatment or drug.

Clinical trials have been around for years. They have proven to be instrumental to the development of many medical treatments and medications.

(2)   a: To replace their current treatment options or medications.

Clinical trials also give people the opportunity of getting a shot at a more effective treatment option, especially if their current treatment is seemingly less effective. Thus, they can try something new.

(3)   c: Less expensive treatment options.

Clinical trials offer many benefits. This include access to professional physicians, opportunities to get better treatments and medications as well as the potential to get medication with little or no side effects. The benefits don't include less expensive treatment options.

(4)   a: Appealing.

Something desirable is equally appealing because "desirable" and "appealing" are synonyms. Hence, the latter can replace the former in the passage.

(5)   b: Nothing is guaranteed.

While researchers' expectations may be very high, clinical trials are not always successful because their treatments may sometimes be ineffective. So, nothing is guaranteed.

(6)   b: No, they are not.

The problem of side effects may arise during clinical trials. Patients who want to participate in clinical trials as a form of immunity against the side effects of their current medications or treatments may not find the perfect solution after all.

(7)   b: It is time-consuming.

Clinical trials are not conducted by amateurs. In fact, they are done by professionals. They are not restricted to some medical conditions because the medical community is always ready to improve on existing drugs and treatment. However, it is time-consuming.

(8)   a: Contributory to.

"Instrumental to" means "contributory to" according to the passage. Thus, clinical trials have made significant contributions to the growth of the medical field.

(9)   b: It implies that there are no effective solutions without side effects.

The clause means that patients who are looking for effective solutions with zero side effects may not see their dreams come true because there are no effective solutions without a downside.

(10) b: Clinical trials are a necessity.

Although clinical trials have some cons, their benefits to the medical community make them a necessity. Hence, they have come to stay.

(11) a: Benefits.

Within the context, "downsides" means "side effects." Hence, the opposite is "benefits."

Vocabulary Test 2 Answers

1) a: Hantavirus Pulmonary Syndrome.

HPS stands for Hantavirus Pulmonary Syndrome. This is a contagious and infectious disease that can be contracted through rats.

2) a: Insulin-Dependent Diabetes Mellitus.

There are two types of diabetes: Type-1 diabetes and Type-2 diabetes. The latter is also known medically as Insulin-Dependent Diabetes Mellitus. It is caused by excess sugar in the blood.

3) b: Cardiopulmonary resuscitation.

An emergency health procedure that involves the use of artificial ventilation and chest compressions to maintain brain function is cardiopulmonary resuscitation. This is to keep the patient alive until better health care is available.

4) c: No evidence of disease.

Sometimes, a patient may be taken to the hospital while the medical team sees no signs of ailment. That condition is known as ANED, meaning "alive, no evidence of disease."

5) c: Ad lib.

Ad lib is the medical term for a condition where a patient is allowed to move freely within the health facility. It is coined from the Latin words *Ad libitum*, meaning "as you desire" or "at one's pleasure."

6) a: ARDS.

Respiratory failure with a wide range of symptoms such as shortness of breath or rapid breathing is known as ARDS. ARDS stands for Acute Respiratory Distress Syndrome in reference to the impact of the ailment on the victim's respiratory abilities.

7) d: Acute Respiratory Distress Syndrome.

ARDS stands for Acute Respiratory Distress Syndrome in reference to how the disease impacts the respiratory system.

8) c: Atherosclerotic Cardiovascular Disease.

A form of heart disease that is triggered when plaque builds up in the arterial walls is known as Atherosclerotic Cardiovascular Disease. Just like every other cardiovascular disease, the condition requires urgent attention.

9) d: None of the above.

Atherosclerotic Cardiovascular Disease (ASCVD) includes a wide range of diseases such as descending thoracic aneurysm, carotid artery stenosis and abdominal aortic aneurysms. Other examples are coronary heart disease, peripheral artery disease and ischemic stroke.

10) c: The removal of the two ovaries and the fallopian tubes.

A Bilateral Salpingo-Oophorectomy is a surgical procedure that involves the removal of both the fallopian tubes and the two ovaries during a hysterectomy.

11) b: Inflammatory Bowel Disease.

Inflammatory Bowel Disease is a health condition that affects the gastrointestinal tract. This is an umbrella term which includes some disorders that specifically trigger the digestive tract's inflammation. Some examples include ulcerative colitis, chronic inflammation and ulcers.

12) a: Deep Venous Thrombosis.

Deep Venous Thrombosis is a health problem that is characterized by blood clotting in the patient's large vein. It targets the lower legs, the thighs and some other areas of the body where it can do much damage.

13) a: Changing at an alarming rate.

The word "labile" means "changing often at a rapid rate." Hence, the economy is changing at a rapid or alarming rate.

14) b: Prognosis.

The *prognosis* will determine the next course of action to be taken. Prognosis means the outcome of an event, the likely course of a medical condition or the predicted outcome of a situation.

15) a: Consistency.

The consistency of a fluid should be considered when determining the most appropriate safe storage for it.

16) a: Suddenly.

The vehicle stopped *suddenly* as the driver applied the brakes unexpectedly. Suddenly, in this context, means unexpectedly and quickly. Thus, "some distance after the demarcation", "behind the trailer" and "professionally" are irrelevant.

17) a: Exaggerated.

While the story was heartbreaking, it was actually *exaggerated* to gain more sympathy. Exaggerated means blown out of proportion, indicating that the story wasn't as heartbreaking as it was portrayed.

18) b: Symptoms.

The *symptoms* of the ailment are yet to be fully identified despite running a series of tests. Symptoms help physicians determine what a specific ailment is and how it should be treated.

19) a: Deteriorating.

When the patient's health started *deteriorating*, she was referred to a specialist for more comprehensive treatment. To deteriorate means to go from bad to worse.

20) c: Intensive Care Unit.

The Intensive Care Unit is a special section of a medical facility for people with critical health problems. The ICU, also known as an intensive therapy unit or critical care unit, is designed to offer patients intensive treatment if the regular treatment isn't effective enough to solve the health problem.

21) a: Complications.

Special care should be exercised while treating some ailments as a preventive measure against *complications*. A complication is a secondary condition that aggravates the existing medical condition.

22) b: Adhere.

Nursing students must *adhere* to the rules and regulations as laid down by the various academic and medical bodies. To adhere means to abide by or obey the rules and regulations set by the nursing school.

23) a: Supplement.

You can *supplement* your reading by listening to professionals in your field and attending workshops and seminars, as well as engaging in meaningful conversations with your colleagues. Supplement means to support your existing efforts in order to enhance them.

24) b: Rationale.

Many people don't understand the *rationale* behind the government's new policies. The rationale behind something refers to the underlying reason for the action. In this case, it refers to the reason why the government implements certain policies.

25) a: Latent.

Self-medication is usually discouraged because of its *latent* danger for consumers. Latent, in this context, means hidden or unknown. Hence, the danger of self-medication is usually unknown until a problem occurs.

26) a: It means a medical procedure that involves the reconstruction of a specific part of the body.

This suffix means reconstruction or repair and is used extensively to form compound words such as galvanoplasty, angioplasty, heteroplasty, etc.

27) d: All of the above.

Indigestion may be triggered by a wide range of other medical conditions such as ulcers, gastroesophageal reflux, or gallbladder disease.

28) a: The removal of the appendix is known as appendectomy while that of the lump is medically referred to as lumpectomy.

Appendectomy refers to the removal of the appendix while lumpectomy refers to lump removal.

29) c: Between 60 and 100 beats per minute.

The normal heart rate isn't the same from person to person but differs. However, for an adult, a normal range is between 60 and 100 beats per minute.

30) b: Microbiology.

Microbiology is a branch of science that focuses on viral infections and bacterial infections. Microbiologists study infections with a view to proffering solutions to them.

31) b: Psychiatrists.

Psychiatry is a special medical field for medical professionals who are interested in helping people with mental problems to overcome them. Thus, psychiatrists treat patients with mental disorders.

32) c: Neonatal treatment.

Neonatal treatment is special care for newborn babies who have special needs. It is the first line of medical assistance to ensure that such a child overcomes the health challenges without having a huge or permanent impact on them.

33) b: Urologists.

Urology refers to problems associated with the kidneys and bladder. Most kidney and bladder-related health problems are corrected by urologists with medications, and in some cases, with surgical operations.

34) b: 120/80.

The normal blood pressure reading is 120/80. Any figure outside that may lead to low or high blood pressure, depending on whether the figure is below or above the normal reading respectively.

35) a: Lactose.

"Lacto" is a prefix associated with milk-related terms. Hence, lactose is the only milk-related option.

36) c: Cyte.

Cyte is a suffix that denotes cell. Some examples are chondrocyte, granulocyte, gangliocyte, electrocyte, thrombocyte, and spongiocyte.

37) a: "Ferri" is a prefix that denotes "iron" while "Hist" is a prefix for tissue-related terms.

"Ferri" as a prefix is associated with iron while tissue-related terms have the "hist" prefix. Examples are histocompatible, histology, ferric acid, ferric chloride, etc.

38) b: It is known as hypervolemia.

Excess volume of blood in the body is known as hypervolemia. On the other hand, anemia refers to blood shortage.

39) c: "Hypotension" means low blood pressure while "hypertension" means high blood pressure.

Hypotension means low blood pressure. This occurs when the blood pressure reads below 90/60. Hypertension or high blood pressure gives a reading of 140/90 and above.

40) c: Both of them.

Both of them have regular heart beat rates. The normal heart rate varies from person to person. However, for an adult, a normal range is between 60 and 100 beats per minute.

41) a: Bronchiectasis.

"Ectasis" refers to a medical condition that is characterized by the dilation or expansion of a hollow organ in the body. When this problem occurs in the lung's bronchi, it is referred to as bronchiectasis.

42) a: It means before.

"Ante" is a prefix that means before. Examples include anteroom and antedate.

43) a: It stands for small.

"Micro" is a prefix that means small. Aside from microorganism, it is also used in microscopic, microscope, microprocessor, etc. It represents the small version of whatever it prefixes.

44) d: Central nervous system disease.

ASCVD refers to some health conditions such as coronary heart disease, peripheral artery disease, and cerebrovascular disease such as carotid artery stenosis and ischemic stroke. Aortic atherosclerotic diseases such as descending thoracic aneurysm and abdominal aortic aneurysm are also examples of ASCVD.

45) c: It is a medical condition that affects the lungs.

This is a blood clot condition that affects the lungs. When this problem occurs, one or a couple of the lungs' arteries are blocked.

46) a: It is called dyspnea on exertion.

Dyspnea on exertion refers to activity-triggered shortness of breath. People experience dyspnea on exertion when they engage in physical exercise. With rest, the condition will improve.

47) c: It is a test conducted by physicians on their patients to identify the nature of an ailment.

To identify the cause of a medical condition, physicians diagnose their patients. Without the diagnosis, they won't identify the medical condition and treatment will be difficult, if not outrightly impossible.

48) a: A decrease in the size of a body part or tissue.

Atrophy is a medical condition that is characterized by the wasting away or the decrease in size of a body tissue or part. The ailment is usually caused by the degeneration of the patient's cells.

49) b: Depression and fatigue.

MTBI means "Mild Traumatic Brain Injury" or "concussion" in simpler term. This may be caused by a violent shaking of the body or head. A blow to the head may cause it as well. Its signs and symptoms include fatigue, headaches, anxiety, impaired cognitive function, depression, and irritability.

50) c: People aged 60 and above.

Bradycardia refers to an extremely slow or abnormal heartbeat. This condition is determined by the patient's physical condition and age. Elderly people are more prone to the ailment than other people. Thus, people aged 60 and above are more vulnerable to the medical condition than other classes of people.

Grammar Test 2 Answers

1) b: Adverbs.

Adverbs are used for modifying adjectives, adverbs, a group of words or verbs. Adverbs provide more information about the object's manner, time, circumstance, place and degree. They also express frequency, level of certainty, place and to what extent something happens.

2) c: Preposition.

A preposition is a word used within a sentence to connect phrases, locations or time. They are usually found before a noun or in some special cases, they prefix gerund verbs. Some examples of prepositions are over, belong, on and under.

3) d: Five.

Adverbs are classified into five groups: adverbs of time, adverbs of place, adverbs of manner, adverbs of degree and adverbs of frequency. As the names imply, these adverbs are used to modify the corresponding type of words or expressions suggested by the names.

4) c: Adverbs of manner.

Adverbs of manner are arguably the most common adverbs and are easily identifiable. Most of these adverbs are identified with the "-ly" suffix. Some examples are *slowly, kindly, quickly* and *loudly*.

5) d: Adverbs of degree.

The intensity of the level of an adjective or another adverb can be described with adverbs of degree. They are mostly placed before the adverb, adjective or verb they intend to modify. *Almost, enough, quite* and *so* are examples of this type of adverb.

6) a: Preposition of instrument.

Prepositions of instruments are mostly used for expressing different devices, instruments and machines. These prepositions are used for connecting these nouns with some other words in a sentence. Examples are *with, by* and *on*.

7) b: Conjunctions.

Conjunctions are words that are used to connect two or more words, clauses or phrases together.

8) a: Interrogative adjectives.

Adjectives that ask questions and include *what* and *which* are typical examples of interrogative adjectives. Thus, they modify nouns by indicating the type or the number of a noun.

9) c: Correlative conjunctions.

Correlative conjunctions are used for comparing or contrasting ideas. Some examples include *both/and, either/or* and *not only/but also.*

10) a: Interjections.

Interjections are parts of speech that are used specifically for expressing strong feelings and sudden emotions. They are more often included at the start of a sentence to express strong sentiments such as disgust, surprise, enthusiasm and excitement.

11) c: Conjunctive adverbs.

Another name for adverbial conjunctions is conjunctive adverbs. These are adverbs that are used for modifying two independent clauses and connecting them together. Thus, they share some functional similarities with coordinating conjunctions.

12) d: Whoever.

There are several examples of adverbial conjunctions. Some notable examples are *however, accordingly* and *indeed. Whoever* is not an adverbial conjunction. Other examples are *otherwise, meanwhile, moreover, instead, otherwise, meanwhile, nevertheless* and *therefore.*

13) c: Correlative conjunctions.

Correlative conjunctions are used for comparing and contrasting words and ideas. This helps to establish the relationship between the ideas or words in sentences. Most common correlative conjunctions are *neither/nor, either/or* and *both/and.*

14) a: Exclamation marks.

Interjections are identified in sentences by their exclamation marks (!). When expressing surprise or sudden emotion, your feelings can easily be identified when you add an exclamation mark to a sentence.

15) c: The ball.

The object in the given sentence is "the ball." An object of a sentence is the part of the subject that receives the action performed by the subject. In the sentence, "the footballer" is the subject, and "kicked" is the action applied to the object: "the ball."

16) b: A prefix is added to the beginning of a word to change its meaning while a suffix is added to the end of a word for the same purpose.

Prefixes and suffixes are added to words to change their meanings. While prefixes are added to the beginning of words, suffixes are added to the end of words.

17) b: A phrase is a group of words without a predicate and a subject.

A phrase is a group of words without a subject and a predicate or a verb. Thus, a phrase, unlike a clause, doesn't give a complete meaning. This explains why a phrase can't stand alone as a complete sentence.

18) b: Independent clause.

A clause that can stand on its own because it has a subject and a predicate and is meaningful is called an independent clause. On the other hand, dependent clauses can't stand on their own.

19) a: Gerund.

A gerund is a verb converted to a nominal with the "-ing" suffix. Such verbs perform the functions of nouns regardless of their verb-like formation.

20) c: Homophones.

Sun and *son* are common examples of homophones. Homophones are words with similar sounds, different spellings and different meanings. Some other examples are *our and hour, cell and sell, here and hear* and *compliment and complement.*

21) a: Comma.

An introductory word, phrase or clause must be followed immediately with a comma. Commas are used to separate or divide parts of a sentence. The goal is to make the sentence clearer to read. A comma in a sentence requires the reader to pause a little.

22) a: Vague pronoun reference.

"She plays with her daughter because she is happy" is an example of a vague pronoun reference. In the sentence, it is not immediately clear who is happy. Is it the mother or the daughter? The pronoun does not clarify that.

23) a: Two independent clauses are connected together without the appropriate punctuation.

When two main clauses are connected together without the appropriate punctuation, you have what is grammatically called a run-on sentence. Although the two clauses are independent and can stand on their own, joining them together without using the appropriate punctuation is a grammatical error.

24) a: *Further* refers to metaphorical distance while *farther* refers to physical distance.

Although many people mistake one of these words for the other, they have different meanings. While *further* is used to refer to metaphorical distance, *farther* is used when making reference to a physical distance.

25) a: *Imminent* means approaching or close by while *eminent* means revered or popular.

These are two commonly mixed-up words. While *imminent* means something fast approaching, *eminent* refers to someone of great personality or influence.

26) b: Verbs that deviate from the principles of verb formation.

These are some verbs that take exceptions to the general rules of verb formation. Verbs without the −ed suffix in their past forms are parts of irregular verbs.

27) b: Wrong use of apostrophe.

The apostrophe is wrongly used in the sentence. According to the sentence, the subject is singular, a boy. Hence, to show possession in this case, the sentence should have been "This is the boy's house. His mother is in the garden."

28) c: I can sing and dance.

The correct expression is "I can sing and dance." This eliminates the unnecessary comma error in the original expression.

29) c: Vague pronoun reference.

In vague pronounce reference, the reference is ambiguous, leaving readers confused about what you are actually referring to. Who is drunk? The son? The father? The pronoun used in the sentence is ambiguous.

30) b: "Its" is a possessive pronoun, indicating possession. On the other hand, "it's" is a shortened form of "it is" or "it has."

Although "it's" and "its" are often mistaken for each other, "Its" is a possessive pronoun, indicating possession while "it's" is a shortened form of "it is" or "it has."

31) a: "Affect" means to have an impact on something or someone while "effect" means the impact that something or someone has on another thing or person.

These are homophones. "Affect" means to have an impact on something or someone while "effect" means the impact that something or someone has on another thing or person.

32) b: He was told to share the money between the two brothers.

"Between" is used to express the relationship between two people or things. On the other hand, for more than two people, "among" is the correct word.

33) a: Homophones.

Homophones are two words with similar sounds but different spellings and meanings. *Allusion and illusion* and *son and sun* are some examples.

34) a: "Lose" is a verb while "loose" is an adjective.

This is another pair of homophones. Lose is a verb that means not to win or to misplace. Conversely, loose is an adjective. It means not tight.

35) b: Stationery.

Stationary means in a standing position or standing still while *stationery* means a writing paper or other writing material. So, the woman went to the store to purchase some writing materials or stationery.

36) d: None of the above.

A common noun is a word that is used for naming a general item or a group of similar objects or items. Common examples are people, furniture, cars, ideas, animals, and so on.

37) b: Proper nouns are usually started with capital letters while common nouns are written in small letters unless they start a sentence.

While proper nouns are the types of nouns that are usually started with capital letters, common nouns are not initialized with capital letters unless the noun starts a sentence.

38) c: They can't be counted and can't be pluralized.

As the name implies, uncountable nouns are the type of nouns that can't be counted. More so, you can't pluralize such nouns. Examples are water, sand, salt, sugar, and so on.

39) c: The former refers to a single mother while the latter refers to at least two mothers.

This example highlights the importance of understanding the apostrophe. While "mother's" refers to possession involving one mother, "mothers'" refers to possession involving more than one mother.

40) a: I wish to see him before the week runs out.

The sentence above contains some personal pronouns, specifically, "I" and "Him." Other examples of personal pronouns include you, her, we, them, us, and others.

41) a: He is preparing for his entrance examination.

The above sentence contains the auxiliary verb "is." Some auxiliary verbs include has, have, had, do, and the different forms of the "be" verb such as are, am, were, been, was, and being. Others are need, may, should, can, and will.

42) c: It contains an attributive adjective.

Attributive adjectives are used to modify shapes, size, age, color, material, and quality. Thus, in the sentence, it modifies the subject's age.

43) a: It contains a preposition for place.

The sentence contains "at," and indicator of a preposition for place. The preposition is used in the sentence to address the place, in this case, the subject's home.

44) a: Unless she comes around, we can't help her.

The sentence contains a subordinating conjunction "unless." Other examples of subordinating conjunctions are because, whether, since, while, so that, and so on.

45) c: Coordinating conjunction.

Coordinating conjunctions are connecting words that are used to connect sentence elements of the same grammatical type. Thus, they are used for connecting phrases with phrases, words with words, sentences with sentences, and clauses with clauses.

46) b: The object of a sentence defines the action performed by the subject of the sentence.

An object of a sentence is the person or thing that receives the action performed by the subject in the sentence.

47) d: "Fewer" is used for countable things while "less" is used to describe singular mass nouns.

"Fewer" is the ideal word when the subject is a countable thing. On the other hand, "less" is used when discussing singular mass nouns. For example, people, houses, cars, and others attract fewer while love, money, salt, and others attract less.

48) c: Their are 40 students in the class.

"Their are 40 students in the class" is incorrect because it replaces "there" with "their." "There" means "that place" as an adverb. However, "their" is a possessive pronoun.

49) c: "Imply" is an indirect reference to something while "infer" refers to stating what hasn't been specifically stated.

This is another pair of wrongly-used words. Imply is an indirect reference to something while infer refers to stating what hasn't be specifically stated.

50) b: "Altogether" means "entirely" while "All together" means "in a group."

"Altogether" is an adverb. It means "entirely" or "completely." "All together" is a phrase and means "in a group."

Biology Test 2 Answers

1) a: Biological molecules.

Biological molecules are substances that are produced by either living organisms or cells.

2) a: Four.

Biological molecules are classified into four groups: proteins, lipids, nucleic acids and carbohydrates. The molecules perform different functions in the body.

3) c: Carbohydrates.

Carbohydrates are arguably the most abundant molecules in nature. Carbohydrates are starches, sugars and fibers and are found in grains, fruits, milk products and vegetables.

4) c: Starch.

A complex carbohydrate is also known as starch. Starchy foods provide some key nutrients such as calcium, iron and B complex vitamins. They are found in grains, vegetables, beans and a wide range of other foods.

5) d: All of the above.

Milk-laced lactose, fructose from fruits and table sugar are all examples of sugar. Sugar can also be found in lactose and sucrose.

6) c: Fiber.

Fiber is a member of the complex carbohydrate class that can't be digested. Fiber is not digested and keeps humans satisfied and full after consumption. A healthy carbohydrate, fiber is present in whole grains, fruits, beans and vegetables.

7) c: Sugar molecules and long chains.

A great way to distinguish between complex carbohydrates and other forms of carbohydrates is through their long chains and sugar molecules.

8) d: Correcting sight.

As a class of food, carbohydrates produce energy, aid digestion, prevent ketosis, regulate biological recognition processes and increase blood sugar. However, carbohydrates do not correct sight.

9) c: Function as building blocks for body tissues.

Children are fed more protein than other classes of food during their formative years. This is to enable them to leverage its components as building blocks for their growing bodies.

10) d: Sucrose and lactase.

Sucrose and lactase are two enzymes in proteins that can cause biochemical reactions. For instance, lactase is produced by the body for the digestion of lactose in dairy products.

11) a: Hormones.

Hormones are proteins in the body whose primary responsibility is to act as messengers. They are secreted into the human body and transported to other body tissues and organs to get them to carry out their responsibilities.

12) b: Nucleic acids.

Nucleic acids direct the protein synthesis process in the body. These molecules contain the nucleotides they need for directing cellular activities such as protein synthesis and cell division. DNA and RNA are the two nucleic acids and perform different functions during the protein synthesis process.

13) a: DNA.

The major components of DNA are four nitrogenous bases and a phosphate-deoxyribose sugar. The bases are guanine (G), thymine (T), adenine (A) and cytosine (C). Deoxyribose is the five-carbon sugar with double-stranded structure.

14) a: DNA.

The genetic materials in all living organisms and in most viruses is made up of Deoxyribonucleic acid (DNA). DNA is the custodian of the genetic instructions that humans and other living things need for development. Thus, it is primarily a database of information.

15) a: It copies its DNA and passes it to the next generation of cells.

When a cell divides, it doesn't simply duplicate its DNA and store it. The cell also passes a copy of its DNA to the next generation of cells for use. It doesn't undergo metamorphosis in the process.

16) a: DNA.

It is through DNA that humans pass programmatic instructions and genetic codes to their offspring. This explains why children share some traits with their parents, and sometimes, with their grandparents.

17) c: Carbon, hydrogen and oxygen.

Carbon, hydrogen and oxygen atoms are the major components of lipids. Lipids are nonpolar molecules and are insoluble in water but soluble in nonpolar solvents such as benzene, carbon tetrachloride, hexane, diethyl ether, gasoline and methylene chloride.

18) d: Complex lipids.

Esters with fatty acids and alcohol are commonly known as complex lipids. Complex lipids abound and include sulfolipids, carbohydrates, amino lipids and steroid hormones.

19) c: Simple carbs.

Simple carbs refer to the class of carbs that contain just one or two sugar molecules. They are naturally broken down in the body. The primary sources of simple carbohydrates are foods such as table sugar, milk and milk products, soft drinks and syrups.

20) c: Sugars.

Sugar is a class of carbohydrate that is associated with the "-ose" suffix. This group includes some members of the monosaccharides, disaccharides and polysaccharides, such as cellulose, lactose, sucrose, maltose, fructose, glucose and galactose.

21) a: Starch, sugar and fiber.

Carbohydrates are divided into three groups: starch, sugar and fiber. Starch is a complex carbohydrate and includes iron, calcium and B complex vitamins found in vegetables, grains and beans. Sugar is found in fruits, vegetables and milk while fiber is a healthy carb present in beans, grains, vegetables and fruits.

22) c: Starch.

Another name for complex carbohydrates is starch. Starch is referred to as complex due to the sugar molecule's long chains. Nutrient-rich starch can be found in edibles such as grains, pasta, potatoes, rice and beans. Iron, calcium and B complex vitamins are some of starch's key nutrients.

23) b: Ribonucleic acid.

RNA stands for ribonucleic acid. This is a polymeric molecule that performs various roles in the biological process. It is necessary for coding genes as well as decoding, regulating and expressing them.

24) c: Deoxyribonucleic acid.

DNA specifically duplicates and stores the genetic information present in an organism. Such information can be passed from one generation to another.

25) a: DNA replicates genetic information and stores it while RNA works on the genetic information and converts it to a format that is used for protein building.

This is the basic difference between the two terms. While DNA focuses on replicating and storing genetic information, RNA focuses on converting it for protein building.

Chemistry Test 2 Answers

1) a: Acid-base/neutralization reaction.

The reaction between an acid and a base is commonly known as an acid-base reaction. It is also referred to as a neutralization reaction because the reaction of the base and acid will produce a salt and water as the final product. Hence, the product is neither acidic nor alkaline.

2) b: Bases.

Bases are substances that turn litmus paper blue. In aqueous solutions, bases neutralize acids in what is commonly known as a neutralization reaction. Water and salt are produced by the reaction. Thus, base + acid = salt + water.

3) d: Sodium chloride.

Toothpaste, bleach and cleaning agents are bases. They all possess the characteristics of bases mentioned above. On the other hand, sodium chloride is a salt produced by the reaction between a base and an acid. Thus, it isn't a base.

4) a: Single replacement reaction.

A single replacement is a reaction that involves the replacement of an element with another element in a compound. The general equation for a single replacement reaction is A + BC –> B + AC. In most cases, this reaction occurs if B is less reactive than A.

5) a: Sodium chloride and silver fluoride.

The reaction between sodium chloride and silver fluoride is an example of a double replacement reaction. This is a chemical reaction that involves ions being exchanged between two ionic compounds. The result is usually two new ionic compounds. The general equation is AB + CD –> AD + CB.

6) c: Marie Curie.

Award-wining physicist Marie Curie discovered the relationship between radiation and radioactive elements. This led to another proposition: atoms are the custodians of radiation. This new finding was in opposition to the previous belief that the chemical property of a compound was responsible for radiation.

7) a: Alpha radiation, beta radiation and gamma radiation.

Nuclear changes and radiation are classified into three groups: alpha radiation, beta radiation and gamma radiation. These types of radiation are different in attributes, functions and importance. Generally, though, they all play some important roles in the lives of organisms.

8) a: Alpha radiation.

Unlike highly penetrating gamma radiation, alpha radiation can't penetrate human skin and is thus less harmful to humans than other types of radiation. However, inhaling or swallowing alpha-radiation-emitting substances can be hazardous.

9) b: Beta radiation.

Carbon-14 decay is an example of beta radiation. This type of radiation is caused by the transmutation of a neutron into a proton and an electron. The result is the emission of the electron—otherwise known a beta radiation—from the nucleus of the atom.

10) a: Gamma radiation.

This is represented by γ. In gamma radiation, electromagnetic energy, rather than a particle, is emitted from the nucleus of an atom. This radiation can be emitted during alpha or beta radioactive decay.

11) c: Gamma radiation.

Gamma radiation can penetrate human skin and, unlike alpha and beta radiation, can't be stopped by anything such as cloth or skin.

12) a: Nuclear fission and nuclear fusion.

Nuclear reactions can be classified into two types: nuclear fission and nuclear fusion. While fusion deals with the coming together of atoms to form a bigger atom, fission causes the disintegration of bigger atoms into smaller ones.

13) c: Nuclear fusion.

Nuclear fusion involves smaller atoms coming together to form a larger atom. A typical example of such a reaction is when two hydrogen atoms slam into each other to form a helium atom. A huge amount of nuclear energy is generated during the reaction.

14) a: Nuclear fission.

During nuclear fission, highly radioactive particles are produced. During nuclear fission, the nucleus of an atom splits into two smaller atoms. The fission is the result of the slamming of a neutron into a larger atom. This forces the atom to split into two, each smaller than the original atom.

15) d: Ionic bonding.

Bonds are formed in ionic bonding through electron transfer from one atom to another. As one of the atoms loses an electron, the other gains it. Thus, one of the ions will carry a negative charge while the other one will carry a positive charge.

16) b: Covalent bonding.

Unlike in ionic bonding, where electron transfer forms the foundation for the bond, covalent bonds are formed through the sharing of valence electrons. These atoms arrange themselves in a manner that supports strong stability.

17) a: Nonpolar covalent bonding, polar covalent bonding and coordinate covalent bonding.

Covalent bonds are classified into nonpolar covalent bonding, polar covalent bonding and coordinate covalent bonding. Although the bonds are created through electron sharing, each type of covalent bond has distinct attributes.

18) a: Coordinate covalent bonding.

Ligands and metal ions may bond together through coordinate covalent bonding. Only one atom provides both electrons needed to form the bond. Coordinate covalent bonding is also called a 2-electron, 2-center covalent bond.

19) d: Hydrogen bonding.

The polarization of two adjacent molecules causes hydrogen bonding. For example, two adjacent water (H_2O) molecules are polarized. Thus, they can combine together to form a hydrogen bond. The electronegative hydrogen atom of one of the water molecules becomes attracted electrostatically to the electropositive oxygen atom of the adjacent H_2O molecule.

20) a: Ionic bonding.

Examples of ionic bonding abound around us. You can find it in $CaCl_2$, K_2O, MgO and NaBr. However, the most common example of this type of bonding is between sodium and chlorine ions. Sodium chloride is the product of the bonding.

21) a: Carbon-free electricity production.

During fission, a huge amount of energy is produced. The energy released will turn water into steam. The steam spins a turbine, a process that results in the production of carbon-free electricity.

22) c: Cobalt-80.

Several substances emit gamma radiation. Among these are cobalt-60, technetium-99m and iodine-131. Cesium-137 and radium-226 are other known gamma radiation emitters. Cobalt-80 does not emit gamma radiation.

23) d: Beta radiation.

Beta radiation has a weak penetrative power that makes it easier to prevent it from penetrating the skin with clothing.

24) d: Iodine.

Alpha radiation, the weakest of the three classes of radiation, is usually emitted by a wide range of radioactive substances. Radium, radon and uranium top the list of alpha radiation emitters. Other radionuclides such as members of the actinium and thorium decay series emit it as well. However, iodine is not a member of this family and doesn't emit radiation.

25) c: The change of mass is negligible.

When an atom emits a beta particle, its change in mass is so small it can be considered negligible. This is because the beta particle's mass is a lot smaller than a proton. However, the addition of a neutron increases the atomic number by one.

Anatomy and Physiology Test 2 Answers

1) d: Skeletal system.

The skeletal system is made up of all the joints and over 200 bones in the body. The skeleton provides protection and support for the soft tissues. Without the skeleton, movement is impossible because muscles are attached to it.

2) a: 206 bones.

There are 206 bones in the human skeletal system. They are grouped into the axial skeleton and appendicular skeleton. The former contains 80 bones while there are 126 bones in the latter. The skeletal system supports upright motion and makes locomotion possible.

3) d: Chin bones.

126 bones form the appendicular skeleton. These are the bones in the pelvic girdle, upper limbs and pectoral girdle. The appendicular skeleton is divided into six groups which are the arms and forearms, shoulder girdles, hands, pelvis, feet and ankles, and thighs and legs.

4) a: Rib cage, coastal cartilages and intercostal muscles.

Without some supportive organs such as coastal cartilages, the rib cage and intercostal muscles, nothing would hold the lungs in place.

5) c: Hematopoiesis.

Red blood cell production takes place in the bone marrow through hematopoiesis. It occurs in the cranium, pelvis, sternum and vertebra of adults. In children, it takes place in the tibias and femurs. The bone marrow produces red blood cells, white blood cells and platelets.

6) a: Skull.

The brain is protected from damage from external forces with the help of the skull, a part of the skeletal system.

7) c: Calcium and phosphorus.

Some body processes require the assistance of important minerals such as calcium and phosphorus to function properly. This highlights the importance of these minerals in the body and the danger of mineral deficiencies.

8) a: Upper respiratory tract and lower respiratory tract.

The respiratory system is divided into the upper respiratory tract and lower respiratory tract. While the upper respiratory tract consists of the nose, the nasal cavity and the sinuses, the lower respiratory tract is made up of the air sacs, the airways, the larynx and the trachea.

9) a: Cystic fibrosis.

Cystic fibrosis is a genetic disorder that may gradually trigger stubborn and incurable lung infections. This disease is hereditary and can be terminal.

10) d: Zika virus.

A functional respiratory system keeps individuals free from respiratory-related ailments. On the other hand, a faulty respiratory system may trigger a long list of ailments that include asthma, idiopathic pulmonary fibrosis and bronchiectasis, among others.

11) a: The lymphocytes.

The immune system works with the assistance of different organs playing a wide range of roles. One such organ is the lymphocyte. These keep a record of invaders in the body and destroy potential enemies on sight.

12) b: The neutrophils.

Special phagocytes known as neutrophils fight against harmful bacteria in the body. Neutrophils are usually among the first line of defense summoned to attack invaders. They trap bacteria and thereby prevent it from spreading.

13) b: Innate immunity.

At birth, a child has innate immunity. Two typical examples of innate immunity are the immune system and the human skin.

14) c: Active immunity.

Active immunity is also referred to as adaptive immunity. It is the type of immunity an individual develops throughout his/her life span. When we receive vaccines against diseases, we develop this type of immunity. We also develop active immunity whenever we are exposed to diseases.

15) c: Passive.

Passive immunity is acquired through the transfer of antibodies from one person to another. A typical example is the transfer of antibodies from a mother to her offspring during breastfeeding. Thus, breast milk is an example of passive immunity.

16) a: Bronchi.

The bronchi prevent pathogens from entering the body. The pathogens get stuck in the bronchi's mucus and are eventually removed from the airways by cilia, which are hair-like structures.

17) a: It prevents the pathogens we accidentally consume from harming us.

The defense system contains hydrochloric acid which prevents pathogens we accidentally consume from harming us by causing food poisoning. Thus, the stomach acid is a protection against harmful infections.

18) c: They contain an enzyme that renders bacteria inactive by destroying their cell walls.

Two other important members of the immune system are saliva and the airways. They support the immune system and fortify the body against attacks with the help of enzymes. The enzymes destroy the bacteria's cell walls, rendering the bacteria inactive.

19) d: None of the above.

Some disorders may weaken the immune system and increase the body's susceptibility to attacks. Some immunodeficiency disorders that have a negative impact on the immune system are some types of cancer and HIV/AIDS.

20) d: None of the above.

When the immune system is weak, it becomes more susceptible to attack. This could result in things like inflammation, fever, meningitis and pneumonia.

21) a: White blood cells.

Innate immunity can be provided by natural killer cells such as white blood cells. Also known as leucocytes or leukocytes, white blood cells serve as a protection against both foreign invaders and infectious diseases by destroying cancer cells and infectious agents.

22) d: Two.

There are two types of lymphocytes that serve different functions in the body: the T lymphocytes and the B lymphocytes. Lymphocytes, as part of the immune system, recognize antigens and produce antibodies that destroy cells with the potential to damage the body.

23) b: Oxygenated blood contains oxygen while deoxygenated blood does not.

Blood can be oxygenated or deoxygenated. In the former, blood contains oxygen while in the latter, it doesn't. Oxygenated blood delivers oxygen to body tissues while more carbon dioxide is present in the deoxygenated blood.

24) a: Pulmonary alveoli.

The air sacs are also known as pulmonary alveoli. This important part of the respiratory system exchanges carbon dioxide and oxygen molecules to-and-fro in the bloodstream. Through the air sac, oxygen enters the blood while carbon dioxide leaves it.

25) a: Esophagus.

The esophagus is about eight inches long. It connects the stomach and pharynx together, serving as the passageway for drinks and food to travel from the pharynx to the stomach.

Physics Test 2 Answers

1) a: Nonrenewable sources of energy.

Some sources of energy are considered nonrenewable, such as coal, petroleum and nuclear energy. Petroleum produces electricity in power stations. Kerosene is used for domestic cooking, while diesel is a source of energy for vehicles.

2) c: Coal.

While nonrenewable sources of energy perform different functions, coal is specifically used to power certain engines and as fuel for things such as cooking.

3) c: 0 N.

Work is only done when an applied force causes a displacement. This explains the formula: work done = force * distance. However, in the given scenario, the weightlifter only holds the huge weight on his head and remains in a standing position. Hence, the distance is zero. Thus, no work is done.

4) a: The work done by a force of one Newton through a distance of one meter.

The joule is the SI unit of work. One joule is defined as the work done by a force of one Newton if the applied force causes a displacement of one meter. As mentioned above, no work is done if the applied force doesn't cause a displacement.

5) c: The force applied to an object must cause a displacement in the direction of the force.

The conditions for work to be done include the application of force which causes a displacement in the direction of the force. If the applied force doesn't cause the object to move from one location to another, no work is done.

6) d: 500 joules.

The formula for work done on a plane is:

Work done = $f * s \cos\theta$ where f = force, s = distance, and θ = angle of inclination.

Force = 20 N

Distance = 50 meters

$\theta = 60°$

Thus, work done = 20 * (50 cos 60)

= 500 joules.

7) d: 15 kJ.

Mass of man = 100 kg

Mass of weight = 50 kg

Total mass = 150 kg

Distance covered = 10 m

Work done = mgh

m = mass, g = acceleration due to gravity, and h = height.

Work done = 150 * 10 * 10

= 15,000 joules or 15 kJ.

8) b: 25 kJ.

Work done = mgh

m = mass, g = acceleration due to gravity, and h = height

Mass = 100 kg

Height = 25 m

$g = 10 \text{ m/s}^2$

Work done = 100 * 10 * 25

= 25,000 J or 25 kJ.

9) a: Potential energy.

An object has potential energy based upon its position. A stationary object possesses potential energy while an object in motion also possesses kinetic energy. A raised weight, a stretched rubber band and a coiled spring are some examples of objects that possess potential energy as a result of their position.

10) c: Energy can change from one form to another, but it can't be destroyed.

The law of conservation of energy explains the possibility of energy transformation from one form to another or energy transfer from one system to another. However, energy can't be destroyed or created during the transformation.

11) d: All of the above.

A body in motion possesses kinetic energy. This includes things like a skateboard or bicycle in motion, a flying plane and a falling object.

12) a: 20 kJ.

The kinetic energy of a body is given by the formula kinetic energy = ½(mv²).

m = mass of the body; v = speed of the body

Mass of the body = 100 kg

Speed v = 20 m/s

Kinetic energy = ½(mv²)

= 0.5 (100 * 20 * 20)

= 0.5 (40,000)

= 20,000 joules or 20 kJ.

13) b: 1.6 kJ.

Mass of the body = 50 g.

Speed of the body = 100 km/hr

Convert mass to kg by dividing by 1,000 = 0.05 kg

Convert the speed of the body to meters per second.

= (100 * 1000)/3600 = 27.78 meters per second.

Kinetic energy = ½(mv²)

= 1/2 (0.05 * 27.78 * 27.78)

= 19.29 joules or approximately 0.019 kJ.

14) a: 746 watts or .75 kW.

1 horsepower is equivalent to 746 watts or .75 kW of energy. One horsepower is defined as the work done by a body at the rate of 550 foot-pounds each second. It is officially 745.7 watts and approximated to 746 watts. Watts can be converted to kilowatts by dividing by 1,000.

15) c: 4 kW.

power = work done/time

= (force * distance)/time

Force = mass * acceleration due to gravity

Hence, force = 500 * 10

= 5,000 N or 5 kN.

Power = (5000 * 8)/10

= 4,000 W or 4 kW.

16) a: 1.5 kW.

1 horsepower = .75 kW.

2 horsepower = .75 kW * 2

= 1.5 kW.

Therefore, 2 horsepower is equal to 1.5 kW.

17) c: Its consistency.

The consistency of a fluid determines its thickness. It determines how thick or thin a fluid is or the degree of its viscosity.

18) a: Friction prevents you from slipping.

Although friction is sometimes viewed from a negative perspective, thanks to its ability to cause wear and tear, it also has some usefulness. For instance, it makes walking possible. The friction between your legs and the ground prevents you from slipping. Otherwise, you will fall over.

19) d: Friction depends on the temperature of the environment.

Several laws govern friction. Among them is the fact that static friction is greater than sliding friction, sliding friction is independent of speed, and friction is directly proportional to the force pressing the surfaces together. Friction doesn't depend on the temperature of the environment.

20) a: Sliding friction.

Sliding friction exists between two objects that are in relative motion to each other, for instance, between an object sliding over a surface and the surface itself. Sliding friction is less than static friction and therefore requires less effort to overcome.

21) a: Static friction.

Mountain climbers leverage static friction. It allows them to keep a firm grip on the mountain.

22) a: Wavelength is the distance between the points of two successive waves.

The distance between the points of two successive waves is wavelength. This may be the distance between two successive amplitudes or crests. So, it is neither a destructive attribute of a wave nor the highest peak a wave can reach.

23) d: 11.33 m.

The velocity of a wave is given by the equation: $v = f\lambda$ or $\lambda = v/f$.

v = 340 meters per second.

Frequency f = 30 cycles per second.

Wavelength λ = velocity/frequency.

$$= 340/20$$

$$= 11.33 \text{ m.}$$

24) a: 0.71 Hz.

Velocity of wave (v) = 2.5 m/s

Wavelength (λ) = 3.5 m.

$v = f\lambda$

Therefore, $f = v/\lambda$

$$= 2.5/3.5$$

$$= 0.71 \text{ Hz.}$$

25) a: 3.73 kW

1 horsepower = 745.7 watts.

Therefore, 5 horsepower = 745.7 * 5

$$= 3,728.5 \text{ watts.}$$

$$= 3.73 \text{ kW}$$

Thus, 5 horsepower = 3.73 kW.

Learning Style Test 2 Answers

1. a: Books with orderly chapters.

This is because they progress in a patterned way.

2. b: Prepare for the test and skip the hanging out

You are focused, and you like to do one thing at a time.

3. b: What the doctor expects you to do

You like to know what is expected of you.

4. a: Gracefully accept your mistake even if you feel hurt

You prefer the truth over feelings.

5. a: Problem-solving activities

They allow you to explore more dimensions.

6. c: "Why should I do this task?"

You are very interested in the details and why behind everything.

7. a: "Why should the blood be drawn?"

You are very interested in knowing the reasons for doing a certain task.

8. c: Do the task

You are self-motivated, and if you have decided to do something, you do it irrespective of what others think about it.

9. b: A divided lecture

You like things that are detailed be divided into parts, making it easier for you to understand them.

10. b: Pay attention to each detail

You do not like to miss out on anything that is important and needs attention.

11. b: Follow everything in an orderly manner

You are calm and do not panic, no matter how difficult the situation gets.

12. a: Continue telling them about the diagnosis but also help them calm down

You prefer stating facts over bowing down to sudden emotions.

13. b: Tests

You are very fond of tests because they divide the information into parts that make it easy for you to memorize things.

14. d: Definitely

You are focused and extremely goal-oriented. You are consistent and do not like to break patterns.

If most of your responses to the questions match the answers mentioned above, then your learning style is ANALYTICAL.

You analyze things in great detail but also focus on minor things. You are logical, self-motivated, and superbly goal-oriented. If you decide to do something, you do it even if you do not get the necessary support.

You like to do things in a patterned way, and you like to be prepared. Therefore, you also like to take tests and read books that have ordered chapters because you like information that is broken down into parts. It helps you understand and learn it easily. You are always interested in the why behind any concept, along with the how.

You dive deep into the details and prefer to do one thing at a time. Moreover, you like to know what is expected of you. In this way, you prepare better and can give your 100%. You value facts over feelings, so you are not driven by your emotions. You are sensible and mature enough not to make decisions based on a sudden reaction. You enjoy learning and do it an orderly fashion so that when you go back to any of your notes, you can remember what you did before.

Personality Style Test 2 Answers

1. b: Take part in community service programs

You like to stay busy and love to help people.

2. a: Instantly make friends

You are an extrovert who loves to make new friends.

3. c: Teach

You have a talkative nature, and you like to discuss the knowledge you have gained. Due to this, teaching suits you the best.

4. a: Crack jokes to ease the tension

You have a great sense of humor, and you do not shy away in crowds of people.

5. c: Make friends with her and tell her stories

You love to narrate stories about yourself and people associated with you. You can, therefore, make friends easily with people of all ages.

6. b: Appreciate it and compliment the person back

You genuinely appreciate compliments and always compliment the person back too.

7. c: Control them easily by telling them stories

Your favorite thing in life is to tell stories, and kids love listening to stories.

8. c: Enjoy doing it and complete it during the given time

You are a workaholic and always welcome spontaneous activities.

9. a: Get busy with the friend and forget about the work

You, at times, can prefer talking over working if given the option.

10. b: Complain to the head doctor and resign

You are impulsive and make decisions based on your instant feelings.

11. a: Read, discuss, and then sign

If a piece of information is in front of you, you always first read and discuss it.

12. a: Ask her to fix the minor errors

You go into minor details to attain perfection in everything.

13. b: Reject it

You live in the present and are not much concerned about what will happen in the future.

14. b: Spill the details

Because of your talkative nature, you often fail to keep secrets.

15. b: Say yes

You are fond of working and love to help others, especially your friends.

If most of the responses mentioned above are your answers to the questions, your personality type is PEOPLE.

You love interactions with people and are always willing to make new friends. You are really fond of storytelling. Often because of this, you lose focus and spill secrets you are asked not to tell someone. You have an enthusiastic nature, which means you like to work and indulge in spontaneous activities.

Moreover, you live in the present and are not focused on what will come to you in the future. You make decisions based on your immediate feelings and can be very impulsive at times. You have teaching traits because you like to pass on new information you learn. You just need to focus and balance your communication skills to become better within your personality.

Conclusion

Passing the entrance examination is undoubtedly one of the most important steps toward realizing your dream of becoming a professional nurse. This book will assist you with your preparation and help you ace the examination.

Go through the General Section again to familiarize yourself with what is expected of you in the test. Carefully review the test-taking tips.

The Vocabulary and Grammar sections will assist you in improving your vocabulary and grammar by helping you overcome communication and comprehension challenges.

Thus, you have everything you need to pass the nursing entrance examinations with flying colors. The ball is in your court. How you play it will determine the outcome of your efforts.

Good luck!

Made in the USA
Columbia, SC
07 January 2022

53771562R00233